# Shaping Society through Dance

# Shaping Society

# Through Dance

## MESTIZO RITUAL PERFORMANCE IN THE PERUVIAN ANDES

## Zoila S. Mendoza

THE UNIVERSITY OF CHICAGO PRESS
CHICAGO AND LONDON

ZOILA S. MENDOZA is assistant professor of Native American studies at the University of California, Davis.

The University of Chicago Press, Chicago 60637
The University of Chicago Press, Ltd., London
© 2000 by The University of Chicago
All rights reserved. Published 2000
Printed in the United States of America

09 08 07 06 05 04 03 02 01 00   1 2 3 4 5

ISBN: 0-266-52008-0 (cloth)
ISBN: 0-226-52009-9 (paper)

Library of Congress Cataloging-in-Publication Data

Mendoza, Zoila S., 1960–
    Shaping society through dance : mestizo ritual performance
in the Peruvian Andes / Zoila S. Mendoza.
        p.   cm.—(Chicago studies in ethnomusicology)
    Includes bibliographical references (p.   ) and index.
    ISBN 0-226-52008-0 (cloth : alk. paper).—
    ISBN 0-226-52009-9 (pbk. : alk. paper)
    1. Folk dancing—Peru—Cuzco.   2. Festivals—Peru—Cuzco.
3. Indians of South America—Peru—Ethnic identity.   I. Title.   II. Series.
GV1641.P4M46   2000
306.4'84—dc21                                                        99-40310
                                                                          CIP

*A mis padres, Zoila y Eduardo,*
*and to Chuck, María, and Samuel*

# CONTENTS

*Contents of Compact Disc / ix*
*List of Illustrations / xi*
*Acknowledgments / xiii*

ONE
An Introduction to the Study of Ritual Dance
Performance in the Andes / 3

TWO
Folklore, Authenticity, and Traditions in Cusco
Regional Identity / 48

THREE
The People of San Jerónimo, Their Lives,
and Their Main Ritual in Regional and
Historical Perspectives / 84

FOUR
The Majeños Comparsa
*Power, Prestige, and Masculinity among Mestizos / 109*

FIVE
Genuine but Marginal
*Cultural Belonging, Social Subordination, and the
Carnivalesque in the Qollas Performance / 164*

SIX
Contesting Identities through Altiplano Danzas
*Gender and Generational Conflicts in the Cusco Region / 207*

**SEVEN**
Reflections on the Relationship between
Performance and Society / 233

*Notes / 241*
*References / 265*
*Contents of Video/ 275*
*Index / 277*

# COMPACT DISC CONTENTS

1. A qhaswa performed by members of a peasant community at a regional contest. Coya District, Cusco, February 1989.
2. *Saqras,* mestizo Paucartambo danza. Paucartambo, Cusco, 1989.
3. *Qhapaq Negros,* mestizo Paucartambo danza. Paucartambo, Cusco, 1989.
4. Procession music during San Jerónimo's fiesta. San Jerónimo, Cusco, 1989.
5. Majeños characteristic melody performed during pasacalles. San Jerónimo, Cusco, 1989.
6. Majeños jaleo melody. San Jerónimo, Cusco, 1989.
7. Majeños taqracocha melody. San Jerónimo, Cusco, 1989.
8. Majeños marinera. San Jerónimo, Cusco, 1989.
9. Majeños wayno fuga section of the marinera. San Jerónimo, Cusco, 1989.
10. Qollas yawar mayu section. San Jerónimo, Cusco, 1990.
11. Qollas singing at the cemetery. San Jerónimo, Cusco, 1990.
12. Yaraví performed by the Qollas' music ensemble at the cemetery. San Jerónimo, Cusco, 1990.
13. One of the many melodies played for the Tuntuna, an Altiplano danza. San Jerónimo, Cusco, 1990.
14. One of the many melodies played for the Mollos, an Altiplano danza. San Jerónimo, Cusco, 1990.

# ILLUSTRATIONS

Map of Peru and Cusco   2

## FIGURES

1. Members of a peasant community performing an "indigenous" dance   56
2. Member of Centro Qosqo displaying a "mestiza" Cusco outfit   61
3. *Qhapaq Qollas* dancers of Paucartambo   74
4. *Qhapaq Qollas* dancer of Paucartambo   76
5. Machu or leader of Paucartambo *Contradanza*   78
6. Paucartambo *Contradanza* performer during the patron-saint fiesta   79
7. *Qhapaq Negros*, a "mestizo" danza of Paucartambo   80
8. *Qhapaq Negros*   81
9. San Jerónimo women preparing guinea pigs for a celebration   94
10. Imagen of Saint Jerome during the Corpus Christi procession   98
11. Majeño of Paucartambo on horseback at the entrada   128
12. San Jerónimo Majeño donning his costume   129
13. San Jerónimo Majeños showing equestrian prowess   136
14. Detail of San Jerónimo Majeño's hat and mask profile   137
15. San Jerónimo Machu and the Dama   142
16. San Jerónimo Majeño's mask with wide smile   143
17. San Jerónimo Majeños holding a bottle of beer   144
18. San Jerónimo Maqt'a   146
19. Dama of Paucartambo Majeños danza riding a horse   147
20. San Jerónimo Maqt'a pulling a mule   148
21. San Jerónimo Qollas coming out of the church   176
22. San Jerónimo Rakhu and Qolla performing an "act"   183
23. San Jerónimo Rakhu and Imilla   184
24. San Jerónimo Qollas performing one of their games or skits   188
25. San Jerónimo Qolla wearing walqanchis   199
26. San Jerónimo Qollas performing callejón oscuro   201
27. A young San Jerónimo woman performing the Tuntuna   214

28. Young San Jerónimo men displaying their Tuntuna costumes   215
29. San Jerónimo Tuntuna dancers performing acrobatic and athletic movements   216
30. San Jerónimo Tuntuna dancers swinging their hips   217
31. San Jerónimo Mollos performers dancing along a street   226
32. San Jerónimo Mollos wearing walqanchis   227

# ACKNOWLEDGMENTS

This project has been inspired, encouraged, and supported by so many people that I can hardly do justice here. I should begin by thanking the people of San Jerónimo, Cusco, whose willingness to share their lives with me has made this book possible. I owe a great deal to the members of all the comparsas of the town, but particularly to those of the Majeños, Qollas, Tuntuna, and Mollos, who during the two years that we lived in the same town and in my subsequent visits always welcomed me with smiles. Their cariño, enthusiasm, and their tremendous creative capacity has been a constant source of inspiration. Thanks to anthropologists Ricardo Valderrama and Carmen Escalante, I chose San Jerónimo, Ricardo's home town, as a field site. I want to acknowledge my comadre Julia Ascue and musician Modesto Coli for always taking care of me and making me feel at home. I am also indebted to the people of Paucartambo, and especially to the members of the comparsas, who, while dancing and having fun with me during their fiesta, provided me with valuable insights.

During my years in Chicago, where this project first took form, I was fortunate to receive the guidance and intellectual stimulus of extraordinary scholars who were also sensitive and caring human beings. Some of the most interesting ideas and arguments of this book were conceived and developed in discussions with Jean Comaroff. She has always taken me far beyond my own perceptions and awareness of fieldwork and bibliographical materials. I also appreciated her support about my often questioned role of "native" anthropologist. James Fernandez was instrumental in helping me understand and write about the complexity of how human beings create and perform identity. His smiles and warm welcomes in Spanish made the hard years of graduate school easier. Both Jean and James also read and commented on sections of this book.

Two other scholars at Chicago have also been very influential on the shape that this book and my current projects have taken. Philip Bohlman called my attention to the importance of seriously studying music and dance performance. Thanks to him, I incorporated ethnomusicological theories into this and other interdisciplinary efforts I have undertaken. Bernard Cohn, with his intelligent questions and comments, shed light onto an important part of this book, the institutions that promote folklore in Cusco city.

In Cusco city I received the support and encouragement of many people—I cannot possibly mention them all. Ivan Hinojosa helped me establish myself in Cusco and has been a dear friend and guide ever since. The Bartolomé De las Casas Center, my host institution, deserves special acknowledgment. Guido Delrán, Henrique Urbano, Marisa Remy, Gabriela Ramos, Isabel Hurtado, Pilar Zevallos, Lucho Nieto, Julia Rodriguez, Mari Chino, Guadalupe Espinoza, Claudio Oros, and Janett Vengoa de Oros were among those at the center who supported me in different ways. Janett along with my Quechua teachers Inés Callalli and Gloria Tamayo helped me with transcriptions and translations from Quechua. Leo Casas (Father) was my very first Quechua teacher, and he introduced me to many aspects of Andean musical life. I was lucky to count on the research assistance of Nilo Bellota, Margarita Castro, Fernando Pancorvo, Enrrique Pilco, Cirilo Quispe, and Fritz Villasante. While working in Cusco I also appreciated the friendship and support of Flor Canelo, Carlos Gutierrez, Augusto Casafranca, Thomas Krüggeler, and Myriam Quispe.

In Lima I received encouragement from Manuel Marzal and other scholars at the Pontificia Universidad Católica. At the Católica I worked closely with the members of the then called Archives for Traditional Andean Music (renamed Center for Andean Ethnomusicology in 1999). Raúl Romero, the director, and Gisela Cánepa have always been generous with their time and resources. Raúl has also commented on sections of this book. Ethnomusicologist Chalena Vásquez was of great help in my research on Paucartambo dances.

In Davis I would like to thank the faculty and graduate student members of the Hemispheric Institute of the Americas for reading and commenting on sections of the manuscript and for providing a fruitful intellectual community. Ben Orlove has provided useful suggestions and editorial advice. His friendship as well as that of Carol Smith, Christopher Reynolds, Alessa Johns, Alan Taylor, Emily Albu, Arnold Bauer, Stefano Varese and Marta Macri have made Davis an enjoyable place to live and work.

I have also received useful comments from Peter Gose, Marisol De la Cadena, Bruce Lincoln, and the anonymous readers for the University of Chicago Press. Special thanks to JoAnn Kawell, who provided excellent editorial comments and made valuable suggestions that made the book more readable and enjoyable. She also helped me write the video script. JoAnn's friendship, encouragement, and trust have been crucial in completing this project. Thanks to Jim Sloan, who elaborated the map, Robert Knop, who edited the video, Steve Kidner, who edited the audio material for the CD, Joann Hoy, who copyedited the manuscript, and Christina Acosta, who elaborated the index. At the Press, David Brent, Betsy Solaro, and Jenni Fry offered much assistance.

Funding for fieldwork was provided by the Mellon Foundation and a Fulbright-Hays Fellowship. At the University of California, Davis, I have counted on generous support from the Committee on Research, the Humanities Institute, the office of the Dean of Humanities, Arts, and Cultural Studies and the office of the Vice Chancellor for Research. The Wenner-Gren Foundation also helped the completion of the manuscript.

This book is dedicated to those whose love and trust have made this and many other life projects possible. My parents, Eduardo and Zoila, taught me to love highland culture and stimulated me to learn about mestizo identity in Peru. I have learned from them that caring, hard work, and commitment pay off. Words cannot suffice to thank my husband Charles Walker for his unconditional love and support. He discovered and encouraged the academic in me and has made it possible to have a happy family and demanding careers. The light in María's eyes and her beautiful smiles have given meaning to all the days of hard work invested in writing the book. I thank Samuel for giving me a very real deadline to complete the manuscript and after his birth for making every subsequent day a joy.

# Shaping Society through Dance

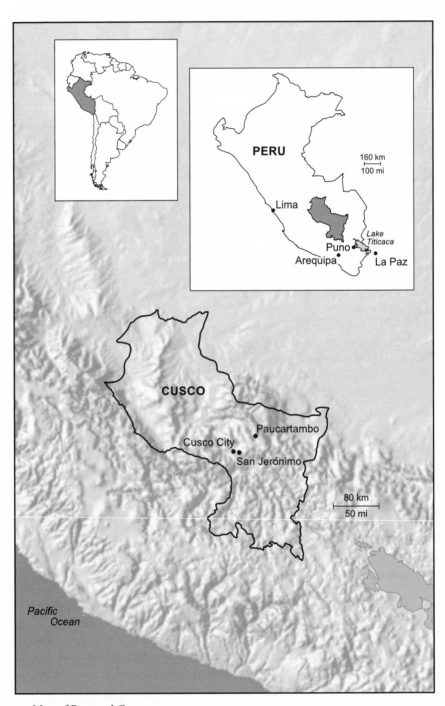

Map of Peru and Cusco

# An Introduction to the Study
# of Ritual Dance Performance in the Andes

*San Jerónimo, Cusco, Peru, September 29, 1990.*

During the afternoon townspeople and visitors have been gathering at the main square of the town, enjoying the food and drinks offered by many vendors. People go in and out of the church, honoring the image of Saint Jerome, the town's patron, with prayers, flowers, and candles. The statue has been placed on the main altar, dressed up, adorned, and lit up with colorful neon lights. All over the town nervous and excited people are running from one house to the other and from the houses to the main square and back, taking care of the final details for the evening's events. As the sun starts to set behind the high mountains that surround San Jerónimo, firecrackers and increasingly louder live music announce that the *entrada* (entrance), the formal beginning of the celebration, is taking place. The crowd's attention focuses on one of the few wide cobbled stone streets of the town, which end at the square. Exhilarated children start screaming, "They are coming! They are coming!" referring to the long-awaited arrival of the key performers and main sponsors of the celebration, the dance troupes.

While only three of the seven dance troupes have brass bands, the music coming from those bands obscures that of the ensembles with accordions, violins, flutes, trumpets, harps, and small portable trap sets. The loudest and largest of those brass bands belong to the two dance groups that feature young unmasked dancers, men and women in equal numbers.

The two groups that close the parade are the ones the crowd has awaited most eagerly. They are San Jerónimo's "traditional" groups, the dancers are masked and costumed, and, except for one female performer, they are all men. In this year's entrada, the

3

Qollas, the troupe led by a dancer pulling a live llama, which represents the llama drivers from higher altitudes, comes first. The dancers trot along the street as they spin a piece of wool in their hands and sing in Quechua, the indigenous language of the area. Right after, to close the parade, come the Majeños, the only group that makes its entrance on horseback and whose members impersonate wealthy merchants and landowners. The dancers hold empty beer bottles in their right hands, they don't sing, and to the music of their brass band they sway side to side as if they are dancing while riding. The audience cheers and claps at their equestrian prowess. While in the remaining three days of the festival all the troupes will compete for the audience's attention, these two "traditional" groups will compete most intensely with each other. As the parade ends in the main square, fireworks, drinking, eating, and dancing fill the rest of the evening, until the eve of San Jerónimo's fiesta comes to an end past midnight.

This book discusses ritual dance associations *(comparsas)* in Cusco, Peru, with the aim of creating an interdisciplinary perspective for the study of public ritual performance and of ethnic/racial identity construction. It focuses particularly on the two comparsas described above, the Majeños and the Qollas, which play a key role in the main *fiesta* (public celebration) of San Jerónimo, a town in the mountainous Cusco region. It also analyzes the two other comparsas mentioned above, those made up of the young people of this town, centering the discussion on issues of gender inequality and generation gaps. The members of comparsas adhere to the cult of a particular Catholic "saint"[1] celebrated in their home town. They sponsor the annual fiesta of this saint, and during the several days of this celebration they perform *danzas* (masked and costumed dance-dramas). My study shows how comparsa members constantly redefine and give form to disputed ethnic/racial, gender, class, and generational distinctions and identities through ritual performance and their associations. I investigate closely how danzas and association members embody key sociocultural categories such as decency, elegance, genuineness, modernity, and folklore, which establish the basis of social distinctions.

Recognizing that identity is fluid (even if people experience it as essential), I show that identity is not merely expressed through the danzas, not merely enacted, but instead that the performance of danzas during the fiesta is a key public context in which identity is defined. Dancers are in view, are in public space, interact with and embody discourses of personhood and social order. These performances, moreover, draw on central dichotomies (i.e., rural/urban, white/Indian, high-land/coastal, center/periphery) within region, nation, and world; the danzas and the discourses about them rest on and comment upon these dichotomies. Comparsas' redefinition of distinctions and identities takes place in the realm of public ritual performance in which different sectors of society have fought against or reinforced the relations of in-equality and subordination that have marked Cusco's history.

Some of those forms of subordination are shared with the inhabitants of other former European colonies worldwide; others are specific to Peru. Cusco, a pre-Hispanic urban center located high in the Andes, was the capital of the Inca empire until the Spanish conquest in 1532. The capital of colonial Spanish Peru was Lima, a few hundred miles away on the Pacific coast. The continued dominance of "white" Catholic colonizers over indigenous Andeans was replicated in political dominance of coast over highlands. At the same time, mixing, cultural and otherwise, between colonizers and "Indians" gave birth to important "ethnic/racial" categories such as "mestizo" and "cholo." In Cusco the "white" and "mestizo" elites dominated subordinates defined as "Indians," especially through ownership of large landed estates called *haciendas*. Many of these trends have continued through the republican period—Peru became an independent republic in 1821—despite nine-teenth- and twentieth-century attempts at social reform. All of these historical conflicts are overlaid, in the present day, by Peru's national position as a poor country viewed as lying at the periphery of a world economy centered on "first world" countries, especially the United States.

Danza performance has been a site of confrontation and negotiation of identities since the beginning of the Andean colonial period in the sixteenth century (Ares Queija 1984; Poole 1990a; Estenssoro 1992). From the time that dance-dramas became part of Andean Catholic celebrations, they entered a dialectic that emerged from ruling elite efforts to curb and control the innovative, sometimes subversive, expressive forms of subordinated groups. This dynamic has rendered these dance-dramas highly meaningful for performers and audiences alike, as it has shaped their individual and group identities.[2] In the twentieth century the process of "folklorization" of Andean music and dance, explained in detail in chapter 2, added a new and powerful dimension to this dialectic for *cusqueños* (inhabitants of Cusco).

Though it is not an everyday event, ritual danza performance deeply affects cusqueños' everyday lives. These performances are a privileged domain where cusqueños explore and make visible the ambiguities and unrealized potentialities of the changing social experience of their everyday lives. Through masks, costumes, dramas, dance styles, and music, performers focus on, intensify, rework, and give new meaning to their changing experience. By privileging the intentionality of the dancers, I prove that their performances and other dance-association activities not only reflect societal changes, but actively transform society. In this study I argue that through comparsa performance the people of San Jerónimo explore their "ethnic/racial" identity and place themselves within the "indigenous" and the "mestizo" past and present, which according to the dominant regional ideology (see below), have both been part of San Jerónimo's reality.

As in many Andean towns, the main public danza performance of San Jerónimo comparsas occurs during the fiesta in honor of the "patron saint" of the town, in this case Saint Jerome.[3] This multiday celebration takes place annually from September 29 through October 2. The significance of this performance for comparsa members and for all *jeronimianos* (inhabitants of San Jerónimo) can be fully understood only if one inquires into the transformative and creative qualities of the highly elaborated symbolic practices that take place during this festivity. Various events during the year, in particular a month and a half before the central day (September 30), frame this festivity as the most important public occasion in which most jeronimianos gather together in what they and outsiders consider San Jerónimo's quintessential community tradition. During this festivity local people and outsiders focus their attention on two main elements, the central personage worshiped in the ritual, the patron saint, and the main form of devotional practice in his honor, comparsa performance. Because the patron-saint fiesta is such a highly socially demarcated time and space in which the symbolic practices organized and performed by the comparsas (such as the danzas) are the focus of attention of the participants, I consider this fiesta a complex "ritual" and the comparsas "ritual" organizations.

The patron-saint fiesta has become a privileged site where jeronimianos, through comparsas, give form to and create relevant local categories that are central in defining distinctions and identities within the town and in relation to the rest of Cusco and Peru. For example, through putting together a series of iconic symbols, themselves already freighted with cultural significance, such as leather jackets, jodhpurs, long noses, brass-band music, slow and swaying body movements, and bottled beer, and by metaphoric associations with muleteers and landowners, the Majeños comparsa has given shape to local concepts of masculinity, elegance, economic power, and prestige. At the same time, the members of this comparsa have become part of an acknowledged local elite that tries to define itself as different from lower-status social groups and from other comparsas that they do not consider as elegant and proper as their own. By contrast, the Qollas, through the use of llamas, knitted ski masks, trotting steps, Quechua songs, whipping battles, and sexual pranks, have embodied concepts such as indigenousness, autochthony, and genuineness. The members of this comparsa have come to be considered by jeronimianos as belonging to a lower social and "ethnic/racial" stratum than the Majeños. Embodying the "high" and the "low" of regional and San Jerónimo society with its multiple expressive forms (see chapter 7) and treating each other during performance as "opposite others," these two comparsas compete intensely for townspeople's recognition as the best "traditional" comparsa of the town.

## CUSCO AND THE HUATANAY VALLEY IN THE EARLY 1990S

Cusco *departamento* is located in the southeastern section of the Republic of Peru.[4] The third largest departamento, it includes a variety of landscapes ranging from tropical jungle to snowcapped peaks. Most of the population—a total of 1,028,763 according to the last national census (INEI 1994a)—lives in the valleys between 3,000 and 4,000 meters above sea level, where agriculture is intensive and where the main urban and trade centers are. The underpopulated areas above 3,800 meters are mostly used for livestock breeding, especially of llamas, alpacas, and sheep, and for cultivation of a few varieties of potatoes and indigenous cereals.[5]

By 1993, when the last national census was held, almost half of the population of this departamento (45.8 percent) lived in urban centers (INEI 1994a).[6] Since at least 1950 the population of this departamento started to concentrate particularly in the areas surrounding the capital city. By 1987, 25 percent of the population of the departamento of Cusco lived in the city of Cusco and its area of urban expansion (Proyecto Ununchis n.d. b), and by 1993 Cusco province had 54.6 percent of all of the urban population of the departamento (INEI 1994a, 37). This persistent tendency should be understood in a national context of massive migration to the cities because of rural pauperization, political violence, and generalized economic underdevelopment of the country.[7] The most dynamic and prosperous economic activities of the departamento are wholesale and retail commerce (supplemented by more stagnant agricultural production), transportation, services, small industry, and tourism.[8] While rural economic activities such as farming are still the most widespread, they are carried out on a small scale and are not particularly profitable.[9]

Cusco city, the capital of the departamento and of the province of the same name, lies at the head of the Huatanay River valley at 3,400 meters above sea level. The former capital of the Inca empire, the ideological implications of which I analyze in chapter 2, it is now also the head of the Región Inka. This new geopolitical division of the republic into *regiones* (regions) aims to decentralize the political-administrative structure of the national government.[10] However, this process of regionalization has not affected national politico-economic structures or the way people identify themselves in terms of a geopolitical unit. Since its installation in 1990, the regional government has primarily been a tool used by some Cusco city authorities and elites to gain power and supremacy over other areas of the southern Andes.

The literature dealing with Cusco has almost always referred to the "region of Cusco" as a synonym for Cusco departamento (Brisseau 1981; Rénique 1991). Because of the process of regionalization referred to above, however, one should now be careful to specify what is actually meant by the word *region*. When I refer in the book to Cusco region, I mean Cusco departamento, unless I indicate otherwise. Because there is also a Cusco province and a Cusco city, all of which will be present in the following discussion, I shall be careful to specify which unit is being referred to at any point.

The guerrilla movement known as Shining Path *(sendero luminoso),* whose activities were most prominent in other parts of the Andes and in Lima during the 1980s and early 1990s, failed to spread its influence or gain strong support in the Cusco region, particularly in the Huatanay valley. During the two years of my research, there were occasional reports of attacks and of proselytizing activities by this movement mainly in the higher provinces of the region (i.e., Espinar, Chumbivilcas, and Paruro) and around some centers of higher education such as the teaching schools at Urubamba and Tinta districts and the main university in the city of Cusco. Yet analysts agree that Shining Path had only a minimal presence in Cusco. Nevertheless, the political crisis of which the bloody guerrilla warfare waged by Shining Path has been the main manifestation for the past two decades has affected the whole country (Poole and Rénique 1992). Fear of guerrilla attacks and of state repression, as well as worsening living conditions due to the severe economic crisis of the country, were clearly part of the reality of most Peruvians during my research. While guerrilla activity lessened after the capture of the main leaders of this movement in the early 1990s, terrorist activities, political violence, and widespread poverty have not ceased in Peru.

Within Cusco departamento is a series of geopolitically and historically unified subregions. One such subregion is the Huatanay valley—

better known by cusqueños as the "Cusco valley" area—which encompasses Cusco city, the district of San Sebastián, and the district of San Jerónimo. The people of the Cusco valley share many common traits that they themselves and people from other subregions within Cusco see as distinctive to this area. For example, middle-aged and older women, specially those who work in the markets, have a distinctive style of dress (see chapter 3). Some special dishes are also typical of this area, such as the famous *chiri uchu,* which is served on festive occasions. Cusqueños also talk about the *danzas del valle* (ritual dances of the valle), which supposedly originate from that subregion or are at least typical of it. As viewed by contemporary cusqueños and outsiders, most of the population and cultural elements of Cusco valley are "mestizo" (see next section).

San Jerónimo district is located twelve kilometers southeast of the capital city Cusco on the main paved commercial road and railroad line connecting Cusco with the other major trade centers of the southern Peruvian Andes. The town of San Jerónimo (site of my intensive field research during 1988–1990), capital of the district and home of about 8,000 people, lies on the banks of the Huatanay River and is 3,240 meters above sea level.[11] At least since the establishment of the Spanish colonial government in the sixteenth century, the character of San Jerónimo and its role within the region of Cusco have been marked by its proximity to the metropolis of Cusco and by its location on the main commercial routes in and out of the city. This has become even more clear since 1979, when this district, together with the district of San Sebastián, was officially declared to be an area of Cusco city's urban expansion. Since the 1970s, facilitated by the 1969 Agrarian Reform Law (see chapter 2), new urban settlements known as *asentamientos humanos* proliferated within the district of San Jerónimo. These asentamientos continue to grow and are increasingly becoming suburbs of the metropolis (see chapter 3). This growth has increased San Jerónimo's proximity to Cusco and has made even clearer the recognition of this town as "mestizo."

## Indios, Cholos, and Mestizos: Issues of Ethnicity, Race, and Class in Cusco and Peru

My choice as a Peruvian anthropologist to conduct research in a place acknowledged by most contemporary students of Andean society, as well as by cusqueños, as a town of "mestizos" or a "mestizo" town was a conscious one. I was interested in learning about the processes of identity creation and redefinition of a sector of the Peruvian highland society (with which I would identify my parents) that, broadly labeled as "mestizo," had often been neglected by anthropologists. In Cusco and Peru "mestizo" is an "ethnic/racial" category, and my own use (as an analytical one) has drawn upon its regional and national "ethnic/racial" meaning. Through this study, however, I seek to move beyond this analytical category and show how the people of San Jerónimo give shape to other categories that are used to define local distinctions and identities and that generally cut across those regional and national "ethnic/racial" ones.

Based upon new perspectives in the study of the subject, I also take ethnicity and race to be historically defined categories. To use the concept of either ethnicity or race alone to analyze the category of "mestizo," as well as categories of "Indian," "cholo" (intermediate category between "Indian" and "mestizo"), and white, would only limit such analysis. Generally the concept of race privileges somatic indexes of status distinction while that of ethnicity emphasizes indexes of style of life such as language, dress, and occupation (Alonso 1994). Race is ostensibly more "naturalized." While it is true that Indian, white, mestizo, and cholo were categories that formed part of the legally established racial hierarchies during colonial times, and that were extralegally reinforced during the republic, it is equally true that, at least since the eighteenth century, phenotype has had less to do with these categories than, for example, occupation and clothing have (Abercrombie 1992). Therefore, because of the importance of both kinds of referents for establishing social distinctions, the biological or somatic and those derived from the style of life of the individual, I have decided to use the compound concept ethnic/racial to refer to the categories above.

In the construction of ethnic/racial identities in the Andes, both the ideology and the practical embodiment of these identities are equally important realities that transform each other historically. Ideology can be defined as a "worldview" of any social grouping, one that "may be more or less internally systematic, more or less assertively coherent in its outward form; . . . [a] regnant ideology of any period or place will be that of the dominant group" (Comaroff and Comaroff 1991, 24). Hegemony is that part of the dominant ideology or worldview, which having been "naturalized" or "hidden itself in orthodoxy, no more appears as ideology at all," in other words, it is the "taken-for-granted" portion of this dominant ideology (23–25).[12] The hegemonic, however, as Comaroff and Comaroff explain, will never be total and "is constantly being made—and by the same token, may be unmade" (25).

In chapter 2 I show how, for the purpose of contests and staged presentations, the members of "folkloric institutions" separate "indigenous" dances from "mestizo" dances. This can be understood in relation to the regional hegemonic ideology, according to which the status of "Indian" and "mestizo" are fixed "and the barriers that separate them are insurmountable" (De la Cadena 1991, 9). However, through everyday practice and, as I argue in this study, through comparsa performance, the status of "Indian" or "mestizo" is acquired or lost by people in a very dynamic albeit conflictual way. Previous studies of ethnic relations in the Peruvian Andes have shown that a person who is the "Indian" of one relation could be the "mestizo" of another (Mayer 1970; Poole 1988; De la Cadena 1991).

Through this study I attempt to understand a key element in the dialectic between the ideology about ethnicity and race, and the everyday practice through which the ethnic/racial relations take place: the important role that ritual performances, in particular comparsa performances, play in this dialectic. In other words I consider that danza performance plays a central role in the construction of ethnic/racial identities precisely because, in this performance, the dancers explore and rework the relationship between the practical embodiment and the ideological aspects of those identities. Through performance, comparsa members give specific form to these identities, allowing all fiesta participants to explore (under the frame of ritual and danzas) the paradoxes and ambiguities of such ethnic/racial reality and giving new meaning to it. It has been in the conflictual arena of danza (ritual or staged) performance and fiestas where cusqueños have identified their ethnic/racial differences and have tended to resist, reinforce, or reshape the relations of inequality and subordination to which these ethnic/racial differences are bound.

In this study I concentrate on the analysis of the categories used by comparsa members of San Jerónimo to define themselves and others, categories such as "decent," "elegant," and "genuine," that cut across regional and national ethnic/racial categories and that have many implicit meanings and signs associated with them. It is necessary nevertheless to discuss some of the meanings associated with the ethnic/racial categories used at the regional and national levels. White, Indian, mestizo, and cholo continue to be part of cusqueño and Peruvian ethnic/racial hierarchies, and the meanings of the categories used by comparsa members are associated with these hierarchies. In fact, one important category used by comparsas, that of cholo, is also central in the national system of ethnic/racial classification. Despite the dangers that accompany the use of this already classical taxonomy (so profusely used by social scientists in the 1960s), and aware that these analytical categories are by themselves not enough to explain relations of inequality in Peru, I shall briefly discuss some meanings associated with these categories, mainly with those of mestizo and cholo.[13] In the process, the relations of "power" that are intertwined with ethnic/racial (and, as discussed below, with class) identity in Peru and Cusco will become more clear. Following definitions of contemporary scholars of performance who have been influenced by the works of Michel Foucault and Pierre Bourdieu, I take power to be a quality inherent in all social relationships, "including those enabling and created through performance," and not something that is exclusively possessed or exercised by particular individuals or groups (Waterman 1990, 8; Cowan 1990, 15).[14]

Although I do not intend to explore the historical evolution of Peruvian ethnic/racial categories, it is necessary to refer briefly to the period in which these categories started to take shape based on ostensible "racial" differentiation, the period of Spanish colonialism. I am interested in showing that the process of classifying people according to these categories was, since early colonial times, a very contested one in that everyday interaction, fiscal interests, and social change gave different meanings to these categories, allowing people to constantly manipulate them.

However, I do not want to suggest that for this reason the hierarchies imposed by the colonial state were less successful at establishing an effective system of inequality and subordination. Throughout this period, and with different strategies, the government tried to keep these hierarchies effective because they constituted the very base of colonial rule. What historians and ethnohistorians have shown, nevertheless, is that even though "race" continued to be the referent, certainly by the end of the colonial period categories such as white, Indian, mestizo, and cholo accounted more for the economic, fiscal, and political position of an individual in the social division of labor than for any specific biological or phenotypic characteristic of that individual (Gootemberg 1991).

The *casta* system that was established throughout colonial Spanish America divided the population into a number of racial groups having three main parent "stocks": blacks, Spaniards or whites, and Indians or *naturales*.[15] A distinction was also made within both groups of Spaniards and Indians. Different legal and fiscal status was granted to Spaniards born in Spain, called *peninsulares,* and those born in the colonies, the *criollos.*[16] Also, a difference was acknowledged between "noble" Indians, called *señores naturales* or *indios nobles* (those who could prove descent of Inca nobility), and common indios.[17]

Mestizo literally meant "mixed blood," Spanish and Indian.[18] Cholo was another "mixed blood" category that was directly linked to that of mestizo. Cholo, however, in contrast to mestizo, would later become a pejorative term associated with low social and ethnic/racial status. José Varellanos (1962) and Linda Seligman (1989), who have studied the cholo/a category in Peru, cite in their works a document that defines this status for the colonial period: "From the male Spaniard and female Indian results a royal mestizo; from the royal mestizo and a female Indian, a cholo is born; from a cholo and female Indian, a common mestizo" (Cangas 1941, 331, cited in Varellanos 1962, 29, and Seligman 1989, 696). As Seligman goes on to explain, "The offspring of marriages between peninsular Spaniards and Indians were alternatively called mestizo or *cholo,* depending upon how much non-Indian blood they could claim. Biological distinctions between Indian and non-Indian over time became impossible to maintain, and *cholos,* who belonged neither to a pure-Indian nor to a pure-Spanish caste, constituted a thorny problem for colonial bureaucrats. Cases were fought to determine when persons of mixed blood were legally exempt from tribute."

In the beginning of the colonial period the state condoned and even encouraged the formation of a "mixed blood" elite that they could control.[19] As for the nonelite populations, according to policies mostly promulgated during Viceroy Toledo's rule in the 1570s, Indians should live separate from Spaniards in different neighborhoods or parishes. Only priests were allowed to live with the Indians. Despite these rules, the unregulated interaction resulting from demographic developments and Indian migration led to the enlargement of the "mixed blood" group that colonial authorities deplored (Wightman 1990, 95).[20] Obviously, these authorities were interested in keeping as much of the population as possible classified under the Indian casta because they could collect taxes from them and have access to their labor.[21] On the other hand, throughout the colony an increasing number of purported Indians tried to escape "into the legal sanctuary of mestizo status, whether through genetic heritage, phenotypic attributes, or deliberate adoption of clothing and occupations reserved for persons of mixed blood" (Wightman 1990, 95).

By the eighteenth century the Spanish Crown, once again threatened by fluid "passing" between legal statuses and by social climbing, gave Spanish elites "an additional tool for preserving their privileges." At that point it became evident that the best indicators of "ethnicity" were occupation and clothing (Abercrombie 1992, 293). These indicators continue to be important in current ethnic/racial distinction.

Because of the hybrid nature of the categories of mestizo and cholo it is not difficult to argue that they became ill-defined terms whose meanings have continued to be redefined into the present. However, it should be clear that Indian and white have been by no means transparent categories. The different meanings of "Indianness" and "whiteness" through time also need deconstruction.[22] For the case of the concept of Indian, as Gootemberg (1991, 141) has argued, "historians [and, I would add, anthropologists] must sort out the multiplicity of social, economic, and political factors that bolstered or weakened the integrity of Indian identity and institutions." As an example of the changing roles of institutions in defining ethnic identity, Gootemberg reminds us of the less important role that the republican state played, beginning with independence, in defining Indianness, at least, in comparison to that of the Spanish colonial state, which had constantly tried to define the concept through judicial, social, and fiscal imperatives.

During the republican period, migration, nativist movements, expansion of public education, tourism, and so forth, started to play a more important role than direct state regulation of ethnic/racial categories. In chapter 2 I show how, since the beginning of this century, through a nativist movement called *indigenismo* and subsequently through the creation of private institutions, Cusco city artists and intellectuals gave new meanings to the concept of Indian. The redefinition of this Indian identity was used by this urban sector, self-defined as mestizo, in an attempt to redefine their regional and national identity while keeping themselves different from the peasant majority that they defined as Indian (Poole 1990b). Nevertheless, the consequences of Spanish colonialism and domination have continued to mark ethnic/racial difference and inequality.

Because of the long history of subordination and violence to which the population defined as Indian has been subject, this category has taken on pejorative meanings indicating inferiority in regional and national hierarchies. In the 1970s the degrading implications of the term Indian were so clear that the military government of General Juan Velasco Alvarado (attempting to reform symbolic aspects of social injustice in highland society) legally promoted the replacement of that ethnic/racial term by the class-related term *campesino* (peasant). Inhabitants of Cusco today continue the struggle to "de-Indianize" themselves through different individual and collective strategies in order to leave behind the violence that the condition of Indian implies in that region (De la Cadena 1991, 21–22).

Since the colonial period cholo has also evolved into a category that commonly carries pejorative connotations.[23] At the national level and largely linked to the massive migration of highlanders to cities (mainly to the coastal capital of the nation) since the 1940s, the term has come to imply a more or less incomplete transition from rural to urban culture and a marginal position within the economic structure. While the material indicators of "choloness" have varied through time, and vary also according to the context in which the term is used, these indicators tend to cluster around preferences in language, clothing, economic activity, and music and dance style.[24] In the national context, a city street vendor who is bilingual (Quechua and Spanish) or has a Quechua accent and who wears cheap clothes is likely to be called disrespectfully a cholo/a.[25] People of San Jerónimo also call cholo a person they consider lower in status than themselves. In the analysis of comparsa characters I explore the particular connotations that this category has for the members of an Andean town and how, in one comparsa, the Majeños, the members have collapsed the categories of Indian and cholo into one character, the Maqt'a.

The category of mestizo at the national level, on the other hand, has become associated with a higher social status than that of cholo. It usually indicates a fuller identification with national/urban culture and a more privileged position in the economic structure than that of cholo. In the highlands the category of mestizo, or *misti* in its Quechua form, has been associated with those who hold an advantageous economic and political position over the peasant population. Before the 1969 national agrarian reform, the widening of the national educational system, and the nationalist discourse that favored class-related terminology over ethnic/racial categories (i.e., the replacement of the term Indian by that of campesino in the 1970s), the term misti was commonly used to refer to landowners, urban dwellers, and Spanish-speaking people.

The contemporary meanings of mestizo are yet to be explored, and it is the purpose of this study to unravel some of its connotations in the context of San Jerónimo and Cusco, especially as these are expressed in performance. As a general statement it can be said that the contemporary meanings of mestizo continue to be associated with ownership of the means of production (i.e., a factory, store, or motor vehicle), advantageous position in labor relations (i.e., boss as opposed to servant or worker), and/or identification with national/urban culture (i.e., through fluent Spanish and formal education).

What has been discussed so far about the meanings of the ethnic/racial categories in Cusco and Peru has made evident two important issues. First, to understand ethnic/racial relations one needs also to understand class relations. Second, both class and ethnic/racial relations in Peru, separate only in abstraction, are today very clearly marked by the differences between city and countryside or rural and urban culture.

In line with my discussion of ethnic/racial identities I use the definition of *class* proposed by Bourdieu (1987), who argues that classes are relational and shaped by various forms of power relations. Classes are not groups that are ready-made in reality; they are defined historically by their members' possession of not only similar economic capital but also similar cultural ("or informational") capital, social capital ("which consists of resources based on connections and group membership"), and symbolic capital ("which is the form the different types of capital take once they are perceived and recognized as legitimate," 4). For Bourdieu (1987, 6) "theoretical classes" may be characterized "as sets of agents who, by virtue of the fact that they occupy similar positions in social space (that is, the distribution of powers), are subject to similar conditions of existence and conditioning factors and, as a result, are endowed with similar dispositions which prompt them to develop similar practices."

However, Bourdieu warns us that these "theoretical classes," "classes on paper," should not be confused with "classes in reality" or "practical classes" because in reality theoretical classes have to compete with ethnic, racial, or national principles "and more concretely still, with principles imposed by the ordinary experience of occupational, communal and local divisions and rivalries" (7).

This concept of class elaborated by Bourdieu is particularly useful for my analysis of comparsas because it permits one to observe the different levels involved in the struggle in which the members of society engage themselves in order to constitute a distinct and/or a dominant class fraction. Comparsa performance has become an important medium through which different social sectors of San Jerónimo have constituted themselves as distinct from other sectors of the town. Mainly through comparsa performance, some jeronimianos (the members of the Majeños comparsa) have become part of an acknowledged prestigious class within the town, creating and using economic, cultural, social, and symbolic resources to establish a superior position in local power relations. This comparsa has itself become a local symbol of economic power and prestige. Also, through comparsas, young jeronimianas are struggling to impose new aesthetics and renovated views of women's roles, based on cosmopolitan international urban culture shared with other Andean young people.

Finally, understanding of class and ethnic/racial relations in Cusco requires analysis of the differences established by the rural/urban dichotomy in this regional society and inspection of the "chain" of power relations that connects the two realms (De la Cadena 1991, 17). From the 1940s on, and more clearly after the reconstruction of Cusco following a devastating earthquake in 1950, the whole Cusco departamento underwent a series of socioeconomic, cultural, and political transformations that led to the destruction of the hacienda system. These culminated with the national agrarian reform during the 1960s and 1970s (see chapters 3 and 4). The city has gradually become pivotal in the regional economy, eclipsing the countryside. In this process the relationship of the hacienda owner and his workers upon which the regional definitions of ethnic/racial relations drew was transformed (De la Cadena 1991, 16). This led to a redefinition of interethnic relations, the former axis of identity differentiation—ownership of land—being replaced "by the city and the culture which according to regional discourse derives from it [i.e., the city]" (18).

As part of the redefinition of ethnic/racial and class relations in the region, new elements have emerged as markers of difference and status. To become part of the urban world through formal education, occupation, language use, clothing, and music and dance styles has become a strategy used by cusqueños to "de-Indianize" themselves and to become more powerful in local society.[26] For jeronimianos to become more mestizo, which is equivalent to being less cholo or less Indian, has meant at least since the 1940s to leave behind elements associated with rural life and to incorporate those associated with urban life. In this process they have tried to blur the differences between themselves and the higher-status inhabitants of Cusco city and other towns considered mestizo. It is obvious that for jeronimianos it has been easier to acquire a mestizo identity than, for example, cusqueños who live in the mostly rural higher provinces of the departamento. This is because San Jerónimo, since 1979 officially declared an area of Cusco city urban expansion, has benefited more from the capital city's increased economic importance and from the growth of public education and communication systems.

In practice, nevertheless, the manipulation of the mechanisms that mark boundaries between rural and urban culture and between Indian and mestizo identity has been for jeronimianos a very conflictual process. This may be due to the fact that two of the central markers of Indian identity are still an important part of their sociocultural reality: rural economic activities and speaking Quechua (see chapter 3). Agricultural activities and a geography still dominated by plotted land make San Jerónimo people "close to the earth" (at least closer than those who live in Cusco city), which is a marker of Indianness (Orlove 1998).

For jeronimianos, comparsa performance has played an important role in becoming acknowledged as mestizos. Through comparsas, jeronimianos have given meaning to local categories such as *decente* and the folkloric, which has allowed them to redefine their own local hier-archies and place themselves in the regional and national spectrum of ethnic/racial and class differentiation. Since this local process has been part of a regional one, comparsas have participated in this wider pro-cess, giving new meanings in regional ideology to what it means to be Indian, cholo, or mestizo.

Urban society not only has offered the material means of survival for a large pauperized rural population but also has offered some of them the means to become less Indian. For the inhabitants of areas distant from the capital city, migration to Cusco city has become necessary. For jeronimianos this is not the case because of their proximity to Cusco city. Local identity has been constantly redefined in relation to their strategic position between a neither completely urban nor rural life. All these changes in ethnic/racial and regional identity occurred in the context of the transformations over the course of Cusco's history dur-ing the pre-Hispanic, Spanish colonial, and republican eras.

## HISTORICAL ASPECTS

### Cusco, the Capital of the Inca Empire

The Inca empire represents for most Peruvians, and particularly for cusqueños, one of the main points of reference for defining national and regional identity. The reconstruction of the memory of the Incas and the Inca empire has been since early colonial times the basis for a wide range of diverse ideological, political, and economic ends inside and outside Cusco (cf. Espinoza 1990; Flores Galindo 1988; Mannheim 1991). These reconstructions have tended to emphasize the positive as-pects of this empire, especially in relation to the experience of Spanish conquest. As one of the most outstanding Peruvian intellectuals has argued, "Mentioning the Incas is commonplace in any type of dis-course. No one is surprised if their ancient technology or their pre-sumed ethical principles are proposed as answers to current problems. The past weighs on the present and neither the right . . . nor the left . . . frees itself from its webs. . . . The Incas inhabit popular culture" (Flores Galindo 1988, 19–21, my translation).

Throughout colonial and postcolonial history, Cusco thinkers, his-torians, and political leaders have argued that the prominence attained by the Incas would never be reached again and have blamed, depending on the type of argument and the context, the arrival of the Spaniards or the emergence of political and economic centralism around Lima, the coastal capital of the Peruvian republic, for the decadence of the region. In chapter 2 I analyze how the reconstruction of the glorious Inca past by the members of the urban nativist movement called indigenismo has influenced the configuration of contemporary cusqueño regional identity. In particular, I analyze how, since the beginning of the twentieth century, the fetishization of the Inca past by the members of this movement has shaped the "folklorization" of cusqueño expressive forms as well as urban cusqueños' obsession with recovering "authentic" forms.

The Incas made Cusco the capital and center of political control of a large empire that at the time of the Spanish invasion (1532) incorporated the area from what is today the southernmost part of Colombia to northern Chile and Argentina. As Mannheim (1991) and other authors characterize it, this empire was militarily expansive and multiethnic, incorporating neighboring ethnic polities into a redistributive economy controlled largely by indirect rule and a policy of resettlement of populations.

At the time of the Spaniards' arrival, the city and valley of Cusco were both densely populated. In general, what Peruvians call the *sierra sur* or southern highlands (roughly what are today Cusco and Puno departamentos) had the highest concentration of indigenous population (Glave 1983, 14). More than 40,000 families lived in the city and 200,000 in the whole valley. While the city was the residence of Inca families, the areas surrounding the capital were inhabited by various groups of non-Inca origin, known as Incas-by-privilege, with which the Inca nobility had matrimonial and economic relations (Zuidema 1990, 2–3).

Within a period of about a century the Incas had subjugated over forty major linguistic groups, and the empire eventually incorporated an estimated six million people (Rowe 1946, cited by van den Berghe and Primov 1977). The ruling elite had imposed Quechua as the administrative tongue and lingua franca of the empire. However, as Mannheim (1991, 2) explains, before the European invasion Quechua "never became hegemonic, nor was it ever standardized, even in the territory immediately surrounding the Inka capital." The expansion and homogenization of this language took place only under colonial rule.

When the Spanish conquerors landed in coastal Peru in 1532, the Inca empire had been torn apart by a civil war waged between competing heirs to the empire, the brothers Atahuallpa and Huáscar. Atahuallpa, based in Cajamarca, in the northern portion of the Peruvian Andes, had executed Huáscar, who was based in Cusco, not long before the Spaniards arrived. When the Spaniards reached Cusco, most of the city had been plundered and most of the Inca nobility in the region had been put to death by the victorious armies of the northern faction of the empire led by Atahuallpa (Zuidema 1990, 1). The Spanish invaders then executed Atahuallpa.

Since colonial times, this Spanish execution of the last governing Inca of the Tawantinsuyu (Quechua name of the Inca empire) has been a theme of theatrical representation in various Andean locales (Flores Galindo 1988, 50–63). Today, mainly in the towns of the Peruvian central Andes, various versions of the death of this last Inca are enacted as part of patron-saint fiestas. These dramas, like the comparsa performances, have become effective ways for people of that region to redefine local class and ethnic relations (ibid., 44–72). In his analysis of the representation in the town of Chiquian of the death of Atahuallpa, Flores Galindo found that this performance, "leaving aside historical accuracy," has become a confrontation between Lima people who go to the fiesta as audiences and people from this highland town, between poor and rich sectors of local society, and between mestizos and white people as against Indians (69), that is, between the dominant and the subservient.

## The Colonial Heritage of Cusco

With the imposition of Spanish colonialism, the Inca empire became the Viceroyalty of Peru. With the new political and spatial reorganization of the territory and with the subjugation of the population to a ruler across the sea, Cusco and the highlands in general were moved from the center to the periphery of the new coastal political and administrative center, Lima. What happened to the official language of the Inca empire under colonial rule was characteristic of the process of subjugation and standardization of the Andean population since the conquest. As Mannheim (1991, 1) argues, through a process of homogenization in a double sense, Quechua became the "stigmatized language of peasants, herders and rural proletarians." On the one hand, Spanish became the language of the dominant sectors of society and one of the main instruments of maintaining this domination. On the other hand, Quechua was spread, at the expense of other native Andean languages, as the language of the conquered people, the Indians (2).

During colonial times Cusco remained an important politico-economic center, at least until the mid–eighteenth century, because of the relevance of silver mining, whose main center was Potosí in Upper Peru (now Bolivia). Cusco constituted a key trade and productive center in the midst of the commercial circuit that linked Lima and the Potosí mines. Cusco region became integrated into the economic system of Upper Peru, providing Potosí not only with labor but also with coca leaves—a mild stimulant used by the miners—sugar, and textiles (Brisseau et al. 1978; Glave 1983). The excellent pre-Hispanic road complex that extended from Cusco into the four *suyus* (sections) into which the Inca empire was divided, facilitated colonial trade circuits (Glave 1983, 12). The colonial government not only used the infrastructural developments of the Incas but also incorporated some of the systems they developed, such as the *mita*—during Inca times "labor exchange or turn owed by people to one another, to chiefs, or to the Inca state" (Spalding 1984, 26)—for labor extraction to work in the mines and other colonial enterprises, and the *kurakas* (local leaders or lords), who became the main intermediaries between the state and local society.

The indigenous population of the new Viceroyalty of Peru diminished drastically (60 to 65 percent in the whole viceroyalty) between 1530 and 1560. This demographic catastrophe was due to battles provoked by the conquest, to forced work in the mines, and above all to the introduction of diseases by the conquerors (Brisseau et al. 1978, 2). In the 1570s, soon after this dramatic decrease in the local population, Viceroy Toledo reorganized the administration of the colonized territory and led a process of resettlement of the indigenous population. As a way to control this population better, he organized the *reducciones* (settlements) according to the Spanish colonial model. The structure of the now traditional Andean town, in which the church and the municipality (in colonial times, the *cabildo*) form the center of the town, was implemented during this period. In Cusco, however, Toledo's resettlement policies failed to incorporate the entirety of the indigenous population in the scheme of reducciones. As a recent study has shown, these policies stimulated population dispersal and migration (Wightman 1990).

From the middle of the eighteenth century until the latter half of the nineteenth, Cusco's economic and political importance declined. The long-standing trade network linking Cusco with the Potosí mines waned, and the city of Arequipa, closer to the coast and therefore able to take advantage of the rise of maritime transportation, replaced Cusco as the most important southern Andean city. A series of revolts in the late colonial period, including the massive Tupac Amaru rebellion (1780–1781), which spread from Cusco well into Upper Peru, heightened social conflicts and discouraged the colonial state from relying on Cusco as an administrative center. With independence in 1824, the city lost many of the remaining prerogatives it had enjoyed in the colonial period. Various schemes to create a confederation between the recently separated Bolivia (formerly Upper Peru) and Peru failed. From the 1820s until the final decades of the nineteenth century, Cusco's economy stagnated and its population declined. Although peasants held on to more of their land than much older historiography has contended, a new class of landowners increased their holdings and political power, spurred by the rising international demand for wool. The hacienda estates expanded, often at the expense of the indigenous peasantry (cf. Tamayo Herrera 1981; Glave 1983). The hacienda system came to an end only during the 1970s with the radical agrarian reform carried out by president Juan Velasco Alvarado (see chapters 2 and 3).

Throughout its Inca and colonial history, Cusco city was not only an important economic and political center but also a powerful religious center. In fact, in the Cusco region the institutional church and the religious orders were two of the main agents of colonial domination and beneficiaries of a large portion of the profits generated by the exploitation of indigenous production (Ramos n.d.). This is particularly important to keep in mind because, as I will explain in chapter 3, the religious orders, mainly the Dominicans and the Mercedarians, were among the largest landowners and administrative figures in San Jerónimo during most of the colonial period. The religious orders had a certain autonomy from the institutional church, allowing them to obtain a tremendous amount of property that they efficiently administered. Not only did they become large landowners in the countryside and in the urban centers, they also possessed sugar and textile mills and became important moneylenders *(prestamistas)* (Ramos n.d., 1). Because the parish of San Jerónimo was one of the seven parishes of the city of Cusco and was also the center of evangelization for a large area *(cabeza de doctrina),* the Catholic Church and Catholic lay organizations played an important economic and administrative role there. This town's central role in the propagation of Catholic liturgy shaped its ritual calendar and practices. This role was strengthened by the fact that the statue of the "patron saint" of San Jerónimo, Saint Jerome, was, and continues to be, one of the main figures of the greatest Catholic celebration in the city of Cusco, the Corpus Christi (a fiesta in honor of the Eucharist).

## The Re-creation of Saints in the Andes

The cult of saints in the Andes has been analyzed in three ways: (1) as a partial or an overarching syncretic system (cf. Marzal 1983, 1985); (2) in relation to specific cases in which the synthesis or fusion between local Andean gods and Catholic saints took place (cf. Silverblatt 1988); and (3) in light of the role that *cofradías* and "fiesta cargo systems" (explained below) have played in the social, political, and economic organization of local groups (cf. Celestino and Meyers 1981; Fuenzalida 1976). The first two have shown the continuity of some elements of pre-Hispanic Andean cosmology in today's beliefs and practices. None of the three kinds of studies, however, have fully investigated the complexity of the dialogue between evangelizing messages and the local people or the creative potential for innovation that the outcomes of this dialogue may have in relation to the redefinition of local distinctions and identities.

Some social-scientific studies in Mexico have focused on this dialogue, analyzing the complexity of indigenous responses to Christianity as well as the incorporation of Catholic themes and patterns into village culture (Lafayé 1976; Klor de Alva 1982; Ingham 1986). These studies have shown the heterodox character of the Spanish Catholicism (both missionary and lay) brought to the Americas. Elements of local religion that were flourishing in sixteenth-century Spain, such as the cult of saints in local chapels and shrines, were re-created in America. In Europe the anecdotes and legends about the lives and miracles of the saints collected in books of exempla, hagiographies, and prayer books, and retold in sermon stories, had proven to be powerful, enduring encapsulations of moral, theological, and mystical messages (Christian 1981). In Peru hagiographies were used in the preaching of Catholicism because evangelizers considered them "an easy pedagogical tool" (Marzal 1983, 204). In both Europe and America the legends and anecdotes collected in such texts have induced the experience of apparitions, as well as of miracles and punishment by the saints.

People in the Andes consider saints to be not only the martyrs or other salient personages of Christian history canonized by the Catholic Church but also different representations of Jesus Christ and the Virgin Mary (Marzal 1977).[27] The physical embodiments (icons) of these "saints"—that is, crosses, paintings, and statues—first brought from Europe and then produced in America have become associated with local distinctions and identities.

My research in the central and southern Andes shows that the characterization of the saints in hagiographies, sermon stories, and iconography laid the groundwork for the local elaboration of the meanings associated with those saints. In the long term, however, what has determined the configuration of the local meanings that the different social groups have associated with those saints has depended on particular aspects of the cultural, social, and personal experience of the devotees. For example, while for the people of the central Andes the meanings associated with the saints were shaped by life models propagated by missionary preaching, actual identification of local groups such as ritual associations and neighborhoods with the cult of a particular saint was determined by two other elements: the groups' experience of local social and economic differentiation, and the way in which the cult of that particular saint was introduced into their lives (i.e., imposed from above or voluntarily chosen) (Mendoza 1988, 1989).

As is the case in many Andean towns, the patron saint, the main religious protector image of the town of San Jerónimo—Saint Jerome—was assigned to it by the colonial administration in the sixteenth century, thus the name of the town.[28] In chapters 3, 4, and 5 I briefly discuss some meanings that the members of comparsas and other townspeople have associated with their patron saint. For example, the members of the Majeños comparsa associate some of the personal characteristics of their powerful, high-status, white-featured male patron saint with some of their own (i.e., their wealth, their elegant clothing, the white features of their masks) in an effort to capture the signs associated with local power and prestige. The Majeños consider the characteristics of their costumes and paraphernalia to be "decent" and "respectable" like those of their patron saint, and according to them these make the Majeños the most appropriate comparsa to accompany the statue to the main regional ritual of which it is part, the Corpus Christi. The members of the Qollas comparsa, on the other hand, who often refer to the "formal" and stern looks of their patron saint, have associated this icon with the threatening and abusive nature of high-status elites or local authorities. These comparsa members have established an ambiguous relationship of fear and respect with the local embodiment of their patron saint in whose honor they perform every year.

### Colonial Antecedents of Ritual Associations: The Cofradías

Contemporary comparsas have their historical antecedents in the colonial cofradías. The cofradía, a religious lay brotherhood in charge of financing and organizing worship for a particular saint, was one significant local mode of organization throughout the colonial period in Cusco and in other Andean areas. From the sixteenth century until the cofradías ceased to exist—in some places in the nineteenth century and in others in the twentieth—the members of a cofradía were in charge of presenting danzas in honor of the image celebrated in the fiesta (Ares Queija 1984). No detailed study of the sociocultural dimensions of the colonial cofradías, similar to that by Ileto for the Philippines, has been done for the Andes. Yet Ileto (1979) shows the range of ends to which such organizations can be directed. These institutions in the Andes have been studied only from perspectives that have emphasized their politico-administrative and economic roles or in relation to the fiesta cargo system (Celestino and Meyers 1981; Fuenzalida 1976). The Andean cofradía was an innovative reinterpretation of an institution imposed in the process of evangelization as part of an effort to bring the local population under cultural and political control. It offered the possibility of an aggregative group within an otherwise hierarchical order.

The cofradías multiplied in the Peruvian Andes during the colonial and early republican periods, becoming central organizational units of the population. Celestino and Meyers (1981) have argued that in the Andes the groups that were brought together in the new political units created by the colonial government institutionalized their rivalries, establishing cofradías and neighborhood cults. Calixto Ccoanqui (n.d.), a San Jerónimo historian and current mayor of the town, asserted in an interview that he had a document in which a land dispute between two local groups in San Jerónimo concluded in the formation of a new cofradía in the town. Unfortunately this document seems to have been lost. The document was purportedly from 1670.

In order to establish a cofradía the lay members who formed it had to follow a series of regulations established by the church hierarchy. Particularly in the rural areas, a cofradía's land and livestock were administered by its members, who each year elected a *mayordomo* (fiesta sponsor). Because this sponsor was expected to serve as host to the entire community, he was allotted cofradía lands to help defray expenses. He was in charge of organizing work parties of cofradía members to assist with planting and harvesting. The mayordomo also had to spend his own resources and to request the help of his friends and relatives to accomplish his task successfully. The cofradías resources were also used to support the local clergy and for charity carried out by the local parish. By the mid–seventeenth century there were at least twelve cofradías in the parish of San Jerónimo. The celebrations in honor of the Catholic saints and images in whose name the cofradías were established pervaded the ritual calendar of San Jerónimo. Among the images celebrated were the Santísimo Sacramento (blessed sacrament) and other Holy Week icons, Saint John the Baptist, the Virgin of the Immaculate Conception, and of course Saint Jerome (Ramos n.d.).

During the eighteenth century the Andean cofradías multiplied, overlooking the established regulations. This proliferation was opposed by the colonial administration, which during this century established a series of reforms to reinforce centralized power, ordering the church to discourage the formation of new cofradías and to fight those that had been established without following the regulations. During this time the tensions between members of the cofradías and the church as well as between cofradías over the administration of cofradía resources became most evident. These conflicts, however, seem to have been present at least since the seventeenth century (Celestino and Meyers 1981, 113).

Decrees about church administration promulgated by the Peruvian republican government in the 1840s, twenty years after independence, forced cofradías to sell or hide their properties, which were considered the real properties of the church. This situation produced conflicts not only between public administration and the local churches but also between the latter and local communities. In the central Andes much of the property of the cofradías was sold by the church, favoring primarily the wealthy people of the towns and increasing internal differentiation. The conflicts created by this new, unequal redistribution of goods were reflected in long legal suits in which the communities demanded the possession of what they considered to be theirs (Celestino and Meyers 1981). There is no study about Cusco that shows what happened to cofradías and their properties after they were officially abolished. In 1935, however, San Jerónimo parish still kept accounts of the properties of at least twenty cofradías and by 1956 of at least five of them (Parroquia de San Jerónimo 1935, 1956). During my research people of San Jerónimo still talked about how some individuals or communities had taken advantage of cofradía properties.[29]

Though the material base of the colonial cofradía was destroyed during the republican period, its organizational principles remained embedded in the life of the communities and have come to mediate postcolonial sociocultural processes. Since the beginning of this century, migrant dance associations that sponsor the fiesta of a saint or image in their central Andean town of origin have shown that these lay Catholic organizations remain an effective collective response to changing political and economic conditions. These associations proliferated with migration from the countryside to mining centers and later to Lima, prompted by the development of the Peruvian export economy. The members of these associations innovated local danzas and introduced new musical styles to their towns of origin. They also promoted new local festivities that replaced the old local ones (Mendoza 1988, 1989). Clearly those cultural forms were highly relevant, meaningful aspects of modern migrant existence.

### Indigenous Dances in Colonial Catholic Rituals

During the colonial period, the Catholic festivals sponsored by cofradías, in particular the danzas performed during those rituals, became an arena of confrontation and negotiation of symbolic practices and identity. The massive participation of the indigenous population in Catholic rituals through the performance of danzas and the constant preoccupation with—and at times, repression of—these forms have suggested to some scholars that these expressive forms were a privileged medium for channeling the capacity for contestation and accommodation of this population during the colonial period (Ares Queija 1984; Poole 1990a; Estenssoro 1992).

The Spanish encountered a rich tradition of public and private ceremonies, most of which included a variety of music and dance. Among these forms the *taqui*, a song/dance genre, attracted the most attention from chroniclers as well as from civil and church administration. This was due to the fact that the performance of taquies was associated with important public ceremonies in honor of local gods, ancestors, or Inca elite members and authorities (Estenssoro 1992). The attitude of the church in the face of these ubiquitous practices varied during the colonial period depending on the order in charge of evangelizing and on the political situation.[30] Nevertheless, the equivalence with certain European devotional traditions according to which dance could be considered "a way of glorifying God" and the possibility that these forms could become the media for the incorporation of the indigenous population into Catholic rituals allowed negotiation between local symbolic practices and imposed overall structures into which they should be incorporated (Ares Queija 1984).

Masked and costumed dances had been an important part of both local and Inca state rituals in pre-Hispanic Peru.[31] The role that indigenous dances, as well as other ritual practices, was to play followed from an "increasingly accommodationist dialogue between Andean practicants and church ideologists over permissible forms of devotion" (Poole 1990a, 108). In particular, those evangelizers who adopted the technique of persuasion over that of coercion attempted to control what they saw as the "idolatrous" character of indigenous dances, channeling them into Catholic rituals.[32] The medieval European Catholic tradition of dance as a devotional form and the evangelizers' view that these expressive forms could become an easy mechanism for incorporating the indigenous population into Catholic practices facilitated this process. The best example of dialogue and accommodation between local forms and imposed ritual structures was the festivity of Corpus Christi in colonial Cusco.

Viceroy Toledo insisted on the key role that this ritual must play in Cusco, providing guidelines about the parts that the different sectors of the hierarchically organized society should play in it. All the parishes of the city of Cusco had to participate in this urban rite, and Toledo explicitly indicated that each parish of "Indians" had to present two or three dances for this occasion (Huayhuaca 1988, 51). Through the Corpus Christi celebration "the rigidly separated parts of the urban body social were reintegrated as the body of Christ" and they all "danced in procession according to their positions in the overarching social hierarchy as defined by Spanish elites" (Abercrombie 1992, 295). San Jerónimo was one of the parishes that participated in this city ritual. Jeronimianos took the image of their patron saint to Cusco every year for Corpus Christi, and they also presented dancers for this occasion.[33]

Since the early years of the colony, evangelizers and chroniclers had pointed out the similarities between the Inca winter-solstice ritual of Inti Raymi and the Catholic ritual of Corpus Christi, emphasizing not only the coincidence in calendars but also the similarity in devotional style (Ares Queija 1984; Poole 1990a). Moreover, there is enough evidence to point out that the fusion of the two ceremonies was not only tolerated but encouraged by several orders during early colonial times (Estenssoro 1990, 156). The indigenous dance-dramas that were presented for the Inca ritual were seen by these orders, among them the Dominicans and the Jesuits, as having the potential to assume in the Andean Corpus Christi celebration the role of the masked dances and grotesque theatrical display that were part of European Carnival.[34] Indigenous dances, having an ambiguous and potentially subversive nature, as did the grotesque images of medieval Carnival, had to be tailored into the Catholic form of worship under the guidance of the evangelizers. The teaching of European dances and the introduction of the well-known theater of evangelization, the *autos sacramentales* (European religious plays), had a central role in this tailoring, giving shape to various new forms of Andean dance and dance-dramas (Burga 1988, cited in Poole 1990a).

Despite the relative license, prohibitions and restrictive measures relating to the dances were also present throughout colonial times (Ares Queija 1984, 457). These started to be more evident after the third Lima church council in 1583. In this council a series of important dispositions that would guide the evangelization of the indigenous population were elaborated. After this council it was clear, for example, that the Jesuits, who had been among those who encouraged the fusion of the Corpus Christi and the Inti Raymi as well as the incorporation of indigenous dances into Catholic rituals, would take a less assimilationist posture. This order actually led a the fight of the church against the external characteristics of the indigenous dances and musics—that is, costumes, instruments used—considered dangerous and evil in themselves. Therefore replacing those dances and musics with those of Spanish origin became even more urgent (Estenssoro 1992). Furthermore, by the end of the seventeenth century the members of the colonial church and civil administration became particularly preoccupied with what was considered the "sensual" dangers of the indigenous dances.

This led to dispositions against the participation of women in the ritual dances, for example. This taboo about women participating in this kind of public performance continues today, but, as we will see in chapter 6, the female members of the young generation of comparsa performers are fighting against it.

These restrictive measures became particularly strong in Cusco after the Tupac Amaru rebellion of 1780–1781, one of the largest indigenous-based rebellions in Spanish America, when the colonial state developed a particular fear of urban and rural popular sectors *(populacho)* and their public manifestations (Cahill 1986, 53).[35] Already the political expressive potential of dances was recognized by those in power. "Immoral" dances were prohibited in the Corpus Christi processions, and such a measure was "directed as much at indigenous Andean celebrants as at the equally threatening Spanish-speaking, or 'mestizo,' pleb" (Poole 1990a, 112). Nevertheless, though having changed much over time, the dances have continued to be part of Catholic fiestas all over the Andes.

As the strict ecclesiastical and state control of religious festivals and devotional dances vanished with the colony in the nineteenth century, these practices were encompassed by a new institutional framework, starting around the beginning of this century. This was the institution of "folklore," discussed in chapter 2, which was first channeled through private organizations and later expanded through state promotion. The meanings and the forms of the fiestas and the danzas have been re-created within this new frame, but the performative practices at the local level continue to be the result of a conflictual dialogue between the members of the controlling institutions and the members of comparsas, who through their performance shape their local sociocultural reality and express and rework some of the contradictions in the wider social system.

## SOME THEORETICAL CONSIDERATIONS

This book advances the growing concern with the historical study of ritual and symbolic practices and how such practices shape history (cf. Kelly and Kaplan 1990; Comaroff and Comaroff 1993). More specifically it contributes to the recent literature in anthropology, dance studies, and ethnomusicology that has demonstrated that music, dance, and dramas are powerful forms of social action in their own right (Coplan 1987; Seeger 1987; Cowan 1990; Fabian 1990; Novack 1990; Waterman 1990; Ness 1992; Erlmann 1992, 1996). This book also furthers the understanding of ethnicity and race as central realms of social differentiation (cf. Alonso 1994), realms often powerfully asserted and reworked in expressive culture. I push forward this understanding in the Andean context by showing how both somatic and style-of-life indexes of status distinction are explicit in danza performance and are central concerns of association members. My contribution here is to show how in Peru, as abroad, colonial ethnic/racial categories of social distinction are reshaped in postcolonial contexts.

While I stress the comparsas that sponsor and perform at the main ritual of the town of San Jerónimo, my study has regional, national, and transnational perspectives in two main respects. First, I analyze the process by which Cusco music, dance, and ritual practices have become incorporated into the boundaries of "folklore" since the 1920s (chapter 2). In examining this phenomenon I study the implications of transnational processes by which the symbolic "artistic" practices of the people of third-world countries become known as "folkloric" and what consequences flow from this.

Second, I emphasize the regional and national narratives into which the danza forms and their transformations fit. In studying regional economic and sociocultural changes since the 1940s, I show how emerging social sectors of Cusco found in ritual danza performance a powerful and effective way to achieve and mark their new status (chapters 3, 4, and 5). As I explained in previous sections, danza performance had been an arena for the definition and reworking of social identities since colonial times. By the 1940s, however, when Cusco region was clearly undergoing important political, economic, and sociocultural changes— some linked to national processes and some linked to regional ones— cusqueños found in danza performance new ways to reshape their ethnic/racial and class identities. The three most important processes affecting Cusco as of the 1940s were the gradual shift of the axis of the region's economy toward the capital city, the demise of the hacienda system, and the emergence of new socioeconomic sectors linked to the growth of the state and to the improvement of infrastructure (i.e., roads, schools). In the context of these processes and their concomitant changes, I analyze the meaning and marking of "modernity" for two generations of comparsa members (chapters 4 and 6) and changing notions of gender relations for the young generation of dancers (chapter 6) and how these notions relate to processes of urbanization, cross-border developments, and global mass-media influence.

Finally, it should be clear from the start that the main focus of my study is not dance, dancing, or ritual. Instead I concentrate on the field of meaningful activity that comparsas create between the religious festival and the everyday lives of the people of Cusco. When jeronimianos use the term *comparsa,* they do not separate the specific expressive form, the danza, from the social identity of the members of the association or from the role that these members have as ritual sponsors. Therefore methodologically my study has two complementary aspects. On the one hand, I analyze the symbolic, performative practices of the comparsa members during the fiesta. On the other hand, I inquire into the lives of the members and of the associations themselves.

### Of Ritual Performance in the Andes and Elsewhere

This study shares some of the main concerns of anthropological studies that have focused on ritual as a particularly transformative realm of experience in which central concerns of the everyday world are addressed and reworked (cf. Schieffelin 1976; Comaroff 1985), and in which "arguments" are made through metaphor, metonym, and other related tropes (Fernandez 1974, 1977, 1986; Fernandez and Durham 1991). At the same time it attempts to overcome some of the limitations of classical anthropological studies that have treated "ritual" as an essentially unchanging conservative force and as a redressive mechanism of the "order" of society (Turner 1967, 1969; Gluckman 1963).[36] With a focus on performance I do not treat ritual as the "reflection" or "inversion" of a fixed system of meanings or the enactment of a preexisting text. Similar to Seeger's analysis (1987, xvi) of music and ritual among the Suyá of Brazil, I see the performance of the fiesta and the danzas as part of the "very construction and interpretation" of social life. As Fabian (1990, 9–13) has put it, "Performance *is* the text in the moment of its actualization . . . . [It] is in essence 'giving form to.' . . . certainly [it] is action, but not merely enactment of a preexisting script; it is making, fashioning, creating." I demonstrate that through ritual performance comparsa members redefine and give shape to central sociocultural categories in a society that is not characterized by "social order" or by "undisputed values and norms" (Fabian 1990, 13).

The public calendric rites in honor of Catholic saints have often been considered in the literature as the "hand-maidens of stability and subordination" (Abercrombie 1986, 9).[37] Many studies of these festivities in the Andes have focused on the investigation of the so-called fiesta cargo system (Stein 1961; Doughty 1968; Martínez 1959).[38] This concentration on the reproduction of social hierarchies and on the "redressive" and conservative effects of ritual has prevented these scholars from inquiring into the transformative and creative qualities of ritual action through which the human actors address, manipulate, and rework sociocultural categories. They have failed to realize that these qualities of ritual may be used as means for different ends (Comaroff 1985, 119).[39]

Through my study of comparsas I inquire into the transformative and creative qualities of ritual action, focusing on how during the fiesta jeronimianos manipulate and give new shape to categories that are relevant to their everyday lives. In his cultural analysis of the Kaluli of Papua New Guinea, Edward Schieffelin (1976) has shown how in ritual as a central "cultural scenario"[40] crucial cultural themes are focused upon and made most visible. Going a little further than Schieffelin I show how through ritual performance relevant sociocultural categories, paradoxes, and ambiguities are not only focused upon and made visible but also how they are given specific form and reshaped, subsequently affecting people's everyday lives.

It should be clear that in my analysis of comparsas I do not make too radical a distinction between a practical instrumental realm of everyday practice and symbolic or "expressive" ritual action. In ritual a series of "pragmatic" acts takes place, and from an analytical point of view they create meaning rather than just reflect it. On the other hand, instrumental action outside ritual is always simultaneously semantic (Munn 1974; Comaroff 1985). As symbolic/cultural analysts have long argued, even the most taken-for-granted shape of the world—definitions of the body, personhood, productivity, space, and time—are embedded with meaning and are the media through which particular historical relations become inscribed (Foucault 1980a, 1980b, and Bourdieu 1977, cited in Comaroff 1985; Turner 1980). The categories manipulated and reworked by comparsas in ritual are also re-created and maintained in everyday life through the set of relationships established among cusqueños and between them and their surrounding world.

In my analysis the patron-saint fiesta and the danzas performed during this event are not treated as belonging to a realm outside the experience of history. Rather I consider that the fiesta and the danzas are important realms in which central concerns of the changing everyday experience are focused, intensified, reworked, and given new meaning. The fiesta is a ritual and not just everyday action, so in it jeronimianos use the superior formal power of rites to speak authoritatively to contingent social reality. My focus on comparsas has allowed me to concentrate on how the members of these organizations have created a field of meaningful activity that connects the fiesta with their everyday lives. This focus cuts across traditional units of analysis such as a town or a ritual. It also permits the analysis of the fiesta as a domain where meanings are created by drawing on an increasingly broad experience of the participants.

The patron-saint fiesta of San Jerónimo has been singled out socially and historically as the main occasion on which jeronimiano comparsas perform danzas. The "action" that takes place in this fiesta, of which danza performance is a crucial part, has particular qualities that effect changes in the participants and that make ritual efficacious. Analytically, these qualities may be seen as deriving from two main interrelated sources. The first is the signifying capacity of symbols upon which ritual constructions play most directly (Munn 1974; Comaroff 1985)[41] and which ritual participants use as means to make assertions and "arguments" in metaphoric, metonymic, or related tropic forms (Fernandez 1974, 1977, 1986).[42]

The second is the key role of festive performance—in particular, danza performance, in which the human body becomes a central focus—which has pragmatic efficacy, a capacity for creating and giving expression to human and social experience (Cowan 1990; Jackson 1990). The series of celebratory practices and "multisensory" communicative channels that are part of the fiesta (i.e., music on the streets, public eating and drinking, firecrackers) are central in framing the danza performance as a realm where the participants explore the relationship between ideology and practical embodiment. As Erlmann (1996, xxii), commenting on recent ethnographies of performance, has put it, performance may "assume a key role in the dialectic between structure, as the givenness of the world, and agency."

### Of Dancing, Dance Anthropologists, and Danza Performance in Cusco

From the beginning of this study my focus has been the field of meaningful activity that comparsa members create between their danza performance and their everyday lives. This focus privileges the perspective of the actors, their intentions, and their experiences, analyzing them within the wider sociocultural field from which these performances emerge and which they actively shape.

The full significance of the body techniques used by comparsa members, masking, costuming, and dance (individual and group patterned movement accompanied by music), can be understood only by analyzing how the performers see themselves, and are regarded by their audiences, as promoters of "tradition" and "folklore," as embodiments of particular ethnic/racial, class, or gender identities, or as sponsors of the main ritual of their town. Therefore the focus of my study is not on dancing or dance forms as phenomena that can be abstracted from their ritual, on-stage contexts or from the wider sociopolitical contexts of which they form an integral part. Already in the 1970s dance anthropologists (Royce 1977; Hanna 1979; Keakiinohomoku 1976) had warned us that separating the "form" of the "dances" (i.e., choreographies) from their contexts and using this "form" to define what dance is can create various problems for a cross-cultural definition of dance. Royce (1977, 10) proposed that these problems could largely be solved by thinking in terms of "dance events" instead of "dances" and "dancing." This approach would allow the anthropologist to investigate better how these "events" are locally understood or experienced.

In formulating my study I was influenced by Royce's perspective, and thus I studied the performance of danzas during the fiesta as a total, integrated "danza event," an event that was an integral dimension of the "ritual action" that takes place during the fiesta and that had the ability to assert meanings and enact ritual "efficacy." I also studied closely the process by which Cusco danzas and fiestas had come to be considered "folklore" and the effect that this had had on the forms and meanings of the ritual danzas at the local level. While studying these performances as part of the larger regional, national, and transnational processes of which they were part, however, I also closely investigated how very specific local processes were mediated by danza performance. In other words I studied carefully how the identification of comparsa members with a particular danza, and the way in which they manipulated and reworked local and regional categories through the performance of this danza during the local fiesta, was a result of these performers' desire to establish and redefine distinctions and identities at the local level. Each comparsa's particular danza was a major vehicle through which its members could locally explore, create, and/or reshape relevant categories of their everyday lives.

By the early 1990s anthropological studies of dance had come a long way in incorporating into their theoretical analysis the immediate (e.g., ritual or staged performances) or larger sociopolitical contexts (e.g., multinational world system, civic promotional projects) of which dance practices are part and parcel (Cowan 1990; Novack 1990; Ness 1992). Ness (1992), for example, in her sensitive, interpretive ethnography of the *sinulog* practice in the central Philippines, avoids some of the limitations of previous anthropological studies of dance by using concepts such as "cultural predicament" (instead of the static concept of "culture") and "choreographic phenomena" (instead of choreography), capturing the many complex dynamics that converge in the focus of her study.[43] Ness shows how a long history of foreign influence has shaped the meanings and the forms of the three different expressions of the sinulog, the individualistic ritual improvisation, the rehearsed group dance, and the civic celebration. Through the study of these practices she successfully shows how the people of Cebu city have combined internal and external forces in order to define their own identity.

Recent anthropological studies of dance (Novack 1990; Ness 1992) also show that, while it is essential to understand the larger processes and the immediate contexts of which the dance practices are part and parcel, it is also essential not to forget about the particular qualities of these practices as dance. That is, they clearly show that closely analyzing the patterned or elaborated use of the body—central to the performance of dance—is key to unraveling the particular significance of this kind of practice. These two studies warn us about the problems that can emerge if one uses dance as a pretext to study something else, or as a "text" to be mined for general cultural/historical content rather than a specific kind of action with particular capacities. For example, probably one of the most widely read and quoted recent books in the relevant anthropological literature, Cowan's study of Greek dance (1990), suffers partially from some of these problems. While this study is excellent at showing that dance practices are embodied discourses of individual and collective identities, because there is not enough information and description about the dances themselves Cowan fails to demonstrate the dance's distinctive "discursive power" (Foster 1991).

By the end of the 1990s the success of cross-fertilization between dance studies and other disciplines, such as anthropology and cultural studies, had been shown (cf. Desmond 1997). Dance studies has not only profited from theoretical developments in other fields and disciplines but, most important, has provided a fruitful and concrete subject for such developments (cf. Browning 1995; Daniel 1995; Savigliano 1995). Humanists and social scientists are increasingly convinced by the calls from dance scholars to pay attention "to movement as a primary, not a secondary, social text, one of immense importance and tremendous challenge" (Desmond 1997, 49), and to carry out a "more meat-and-bones approach to the body based on an analysis of discourses or practices that *instruct it*" (Foster 1997, 235).

Most of this enlightening interdisciplinary literature on the study of dance practices had not yet been published when I carried out my research on comparsas. Nevertheless I had been made aware of the importance of observing and analyzing body movement and discipline by some of the existing literature, by contact with dance anthropologist/ scholars (among them Anya Royce and Brenda Farnell), and by a short training course for nonspecialists.[44] I worked to analyze the significance of bodily movement and instruction by performing with one comparsa and practicing movements during rehearsals with another (see below), through careful observation and videotaping of all comparsa rehearsals and performance during the fiesta, as well as with exegesis— that is, discussing the videos with the performers. I also was careful to analyze local categories of classification with respect to dance or dance-like behavior.

In Cusco, danzas performed by comparsa members are distinguished from *bailes* and staged presentations of *danzas típicas* (also called *folklóricas* or *tradicionales;* see chapter 2), although all three may be translated in English as "dance," and all three may occur during the fiesta. Baile is patterned movement commonly done in couples, without a particular or distinctive set of costumes and certainly without masks. Baile takes place throughout the year, usually at private parties or celebrations such as weddings and baptisms or in *bailes sociales* (see chapter 3) organized by a particular local group or institution in order to raise funds. Participants in a baile event can go in and out of the group performing baile; it is not an "artistic" performance in a marked sense. Baile does not require any special skill different from those of most of the townspeople. Most of the time the music for baile comes from recordings. However, on special occasions such as the bailes sociales or weddings, the music comes from live bands.

Danzas are group-coordinated patterned movement, performed with distinctive matching costumes and sometimes masks, by an exclusive and bounded group. The distinction between performers and audience is more clearly marked than in the case of baile. This demarcation is directly related to the contexts in which danzas take place: in rituals (usually at public plazas or along the streets with a live band) or in "folkloric" staged presentations (usually in auditoriums or school patios with recorded music). From the perspective of jeronimianos the main difference between an on-stage danza típica and the danzas performed by local comparsas during the fiesta is that the latter are authoritative performances that are seeds to make one's own redefinition of local ethnic/racial and class distinctions and identities, and thus the performance of these danzas have a particular transformational and creative quality for the townspeople.

## Dance Groups in a Comparative Perspective: The Performance of Distinctions and Identities

Although the performance of masked and costume dance-dramas has been a central component of public celebrations in honor of Catholic saints in the Andes since the sixteenth century, this performative aspect of Andean ritual has been insufficiently studied by anthropologists who have worked in the area (Salomon 1981; Kessel 1981; Mendoza 1989; Poole 1990a, 1991). Of the studies that exist none has focused on the dance associations. Although all of them give some indication that ritual dancing in the Andes has been a way to re-create local and regional identities and is a practice that deals with ambiguities and paradoxes in history and in everyday life, only Salomon's work (with the exception my own [1988, 1989]) has touched the central analytical perspective of this book: the role of comparsas in the configuration of local and regional distinctions and identities.[45]

Salomon looks at general aspects of the definition of local and regional identity in a context of social and cultural transformation through a focus on the *Yumbada*. The *Yumbada* is a "festal play" or "ritual drama" that takes place during the Corpus Christi celebration in Quito, Ecuador, creating an antiphony between the "savage" *yumbos* (lowland inhabitants) and religious Catholic themes such as resurrection and the display of the Host. According to this author, yumbo dancing or *Yumbada* in Quito belies the idea that costumed dancing is essentially a rural phenomenon that withers at the intrusion of urban culture and economy. The *Yumbada* flourishes most where the expansion of Quito has brought a dramatic invasion of formerly rural communities. According to Salomon (1981, 163), "most yumbo dancers in daily life are thoroughly urban people, working in surrounding factories, construction hands, or service personnel in business and military institutions."

Salomon argues that the *Yumbada* makes particular sense to people who experience a sharp juxtaposition between their peasant-indigenous and urban-Hispanic existence. This "ritual drama" explores the peculiar position of this unnamed, unrecognized, but nonetheless distinctive group "poised in the space between two cultures which have long been spotlighted by folk consciousness as the polar extremes of primally 'savage' and primally 'civilized' identity" (164). According to Salomon, participation in this "festal play" on the theme of ethnicity may serve this Ecuadorian group on several planes: "Cognitively, it clarifies the complex situation of a community with no openly recognized ethnic standing and many inter-ethnic dependencies. Socially, it concentrates and reinforces the indigenous core of neighborhoods awash in outside population movements. Philosophically, . . . it raises and solves theoretically the question of how a person lives both in and against society" (203).

Salomon's study is particularly enlightening for my analysis because the people of San Jerónimo, through comparsa performance, are also attempting to redefine their ethnic/racial identity between rural/peasant and urban/mestizo polarities. For this town is neither clearly rural nor urban.

Following this initial step taken by Salomon, my study of comparsas seeks to understand the key role that danza performance as "the site and a means" of "creative tension" and "experimental practice" plays in the redefinition of local distinctions and identities (Comaroff and Comaroff 1993, xxix). More specifically, it attempts to show how this performance creatively mediates between this local redefinition and the regional, national, and transnational processes that affect the life of the people of San Jerónimo. Comparsa performance comments and acts upon processes of migration, urban growth, regionalism, nationalism, the "folklorization" of cultures, and tourism. It does so by giving shape to local distinctions and identities based on experiential categories and values such as modernity, genuineness, and decency.

In this respect, some studies of the negotiation of new identities through dance and music in radically changing contexts in Africa offer a useful source of comparison. In a pioneer work that perceptively analyzed the Kalela dance in the Copperbelt of former northern Rhodesia (today northern Zimbabwe), Clyde Mitchell (1956) showed that this innovative dance form was a central element of the cultural repertoire of migrants to urban contexts. The author argued that the style of dress worn by the dancers (smart European) and particularly the songs incisively commented on the way of life of the Copperbelt Africans. These songs referred to the urban situation, primarily the ethnic diversity of the urban population. They also emphasized the beauty of the land of origin of the migrants and "tribal" unity.

Mitchell attempted to explain the seeming paradox that, while the dance tended to gather people from the same tribe and emphasized tribal differences, the language and the idiom of the songs and the dress of the dancers were drawn from an urban existence that tended to submerge tribal differences (1956, 9). He discovered that, in a context in which people from many ethnic groups (therefore with different cultural repertoires) live together, the most significant category of day-to-day social interaction among Africans is "tribalism." This tribalism in urban areas had become a category of interaction within a wider inclusive system. This sense of tribal unity evoked in opposition to an external group "provides a mechanism whereby social relationships with strangers may be organized in what of necessity must be a fluid social situation" (31). Mitchell's work was pioneering in suggesting the importance that dance groups and dance forms might have in redefining central sociocultural categories that shape relationships between groups in the context of migration and radical social change. He also shows that ethnicity and tribalism are not primordial identities but take on contrastive significance in the inclusive fields of "modern" migrant life. Dance helps mediate the polarities of this existence.

In similar terms in his study of dance exchange in equatorial Africa James Fernandez (1975–1976) has pointed out that the investigation of dances characteristic of a transitional period offers valuable insights not only into the patterns of changing social organization but also into the cultural perspectives of the participants. This author argues that in equatorial Guinea "the flourishing of dance exchange arose in the attempt to capitalize on innovative features made in traditional dances" (2). These innovations seemed to have been stimulated by the new dances that arose under the situation of west African migrant labor. Migrants cohabited in the same area with other local groups such as the Fang. Fernandez points out that the emergence of this dance form responds to important structural changes in the area, the relative tranquillity imposed by colonial authority, and the intensification of trade over the last one hundred years. Again, such forms cut across rural and urban divides to embody new identifications.

It seems apparent that in order to analyze the significance and popularity of dance and music forms, in both the Andean and the African case, one should understand that these forms developed (or were radically transformed) under colonial or postcolonial conditions with which these forms come into continuing dialogue. Emphasizing this aspect, Terence Ranger (1975) developed a sophisticated historical analysis of the emergence and propagation of the Beni *ngomas* (team dances) in east Africa, antecedents of the forms that Mitchell studied. Ranger argued that Beni ngomas, far from being "escapist" aspects of popular culture, were effective ways through which people contested, domesticated, and reworked the signs of domination in their society. Beni provided a significant sociocultural resource in the process through which east African people defined and redefined their identities and relations to colonial society and culture and also presumably to their own past.

Ranger pointed out that in the places in east Africa where the Beni *ngomas* first emerged there were historical and social "ingredients" that encouraged the development of such dance groups into significant cultural forces. These ingredients were a sufficient degree of autonomy from colonial institutions to permit reworking of these cultural schemes, a continued "self-confidence" in the viability of local communal values, and a continuing tradition of competitive communal display (5). Ranger also argued that whatever may be concluded about the origins of Beni *ngomas,* it is clear that *ngoma* dancing (i.e., team dancing) became an integral part of African popular culture under colonial domination, giving rise to many variant forms.

*Ngoma* or *ingoma* dancing is one of the traditions analyzed by Veit Erlmann in his first book about African performance (1991).[46] Building on Ranger's study, he explains how this Zulu-speaking migrants' dance culture "evolved out of the profound transformation of traditional rural

Zulu culture through impoverishment, dispossession, and labor migration around the time of the First World War" (95). Incorporating into his analysis important performative aspects of this popular form, such as the lyrics used in different contexts, Erlmann looks at the transformation of this popular dance-song style in South Africa between 1929 and 1939. He analyzes the attempts of the ruling class to "domesticate" the rebellious and subversive character of this workers' popular culture by turning it into a tourist attraction. Through his study Erlmann sought to understand the dynamic relations among popular culture, socioeconomic change, and political power in the early phases of capitalist development in South Africa.

Erlmann (1991) also examines two other popular performance traditions in South Africa, *isicathamiya* and early "ragtime." He concludes that the practice of these popular cultural forms aims to construct a secure symbolic space within multiple contradictory worlds. Through a historical analysis of all three forms—and with a strong focus on performance—Erlmann's work has furthered our understanding of expressive forms as effective means through which people give shape to and attempt to control their past, present, and envisioned future. This earlier work by Erlmann and his ensuing studies of *isicathamiya* (1992, 1996) are among the most important recent contributions to the study of performance.

In this same line of analysis, and preceding the work of Erlmann, we find David Coplan's study (1987) of *lifela* songs among Lesotho migrants in South Africa. Coplan has argued that these songs "are part of an effort to maintain an integrated, positive self-concept despite the social displacement, fragmentation, and dehumanization inherent in the migratory labor system" (419). Like Erlmann, with a focus on performance, Coplan emphasizes the importance of *lifela* as a "liberating and reintegrative force in a social world of inherent contradiction and dependency" (431).

All these studies of African music and dance have shown the importance this performance has in mediating between the local redefinition of distinctions and identities and the wider sociocultural processes under which this redefinition takes place. Here is where the relevance of the comparison with the Andean case presented in this book is found. In other words, the importance of this comparison resides in the fact that in both cases, the Andean and the African, the studies show how these forms seem to respond to and engage in dialogue with new inclusive colonial and postcolonial situations that create new orders of relations and in which the performers are ostensibly homogenized under the new circumstances, all becoming "migrants," "Indians," or "folkloric."

My research in the Peruvian Andes shows that, in the fiestas and through the danzas, the comparsas address and give form to ambiguous or not clearly defined relationships among local groups as well as between these and the larger context of Peruvian society and transnational ties. In the central Andes the *Avelinos* danza has proved to be a powerful medium through which migrants from the Mantaro valley have explored the meanings associated with the relationship between powerless and powerful local groups as well as between guerrilla bands in the region and the national state (Mendoza 1988, 1989). Throughout this book I shall show how comparsas in San Jerónimo, through ritual performance of danzas and their associations, constantly struggle to redefine and give form to disputed ethnic, gender, class, and generational distinctions and identities. As I have said, danzas and association members comment and act upon key sociocultural categories such as decency, elegance, genuineness, modernity, and folklore, in the process drawing upon and commenting on regional, national, and transnational hierarchies and dichotomies such as rural/urban, white/Indian, highland/coastal, center/periphery, which jeronimianos confront in their everyday lives. Therefore, my analysis explores issues of ethnicity, race, class, gender, and generation in relation to national and transnational phenomena such as urban growth, nationalism, capitalist "modernity," and tourism.

In the ensuing chapters I show that, while jeronimianos' identities may be seen as emerging both in practical activities (i.e., in their occupation as truck drivers or in their school education) as well as in ritual moments, danza performance during the patron-saint fiesta plays a key role in jeronimianos' efforts to locally redefine those identities. In their ritual and through the symbolic frame provided by the two "traditional" local comparsas, the Majeños and the Qollas, as well as by the central figure of their patron saint, the townspeople explore the ambiguities and potentialities of their own identity.

Making bodily adornment (costuming and masking) and dance (patterned or coordinated group movement accompanied by music) the key focus of their actions, the Majeños and the Qollas have invested danza performance with a particularly transforming and creative role within ritual. This kind of bodily praxis or bodily techniques within ritual has transported jeronimianos from their everyday world into a world where experience is redefined through exploring its ambiguities and experimenting with its potentialities. The Majeños, for example, have associated local concepts of decency and modernity with body stiffness, swaying movements, long noses, "white" features, wide-brimmed hats, horseback riding, bottled beer, and brass-band marching music. The Qollas, at the other end, have explored the concepts of genuineness, wit, mischief, and male courage by playing sexual pranks, imitating and carrying llamas (on and with them), singing Quechua songs, engaging in whipping battles, and dancing to the tunes of highland music. Through emphasizing the low body stratum in their carnivalesque performance and playing with extremes, the Qollas not only have associated the concepts mentioned above with "indigenous" identity and the lower social strata but have also provided the fiesta participants with the means to explore and comment upon the ambiguities and potentials of this "indigenous" identity, an identity that, while appealing to cultural belonging and legitimacy, also implies low status and social marginality. In several ways the Qollas performance seems to critique petit bourgeois "order" and "stiffness."

Finally, in some reflections about the young generation of comparsa performers in San Jerónimo, I suggest that the phenomenon of the increasing replacement of Cusco danzas by those from the Altiplano should be understood in light of national and transnational phenomena such as expansion of the national education and communication systems and the role of the international media in promoting certain musical and dance styles as representative of Andeans or Latin Americans. By performing Altiplano danzas and leaving behind cusqueño models of "authenticity," young jeronimianos, especially women, use some elements of cosmopolitan national and transnational "modern" culture to give form to new models of gender relations and to fight against an unequal and prejudiced society.

### This Anthropologist's Perspective

My perspective on the study of Cusco comparsas has been very much influenced by my personal identity as a partial insider to the society I was studying. I am a female Peruvian anthropologist who grew up participating in the kind of fiestas and danzas that I went back to study. My parents are migrants from a highland town who moved to the nation's capital city on the coast, Lima, seeking a better life for themselves and their children. Through the years they have kept alive their links to their hometown, not only going back (and taking the children along) for important fiestas and to visit relatives but, maybe most importantly, by cofounding a migrant association in Lima where fiestas, music, and danzas of the region were re-created. As a result of my participation in these events, not only did I learn about the importance of fiestas and danzas, but I was also able to learn some techniques for the performance of the latter. My early realization of the importance of these festive practices among highlanders for defining individual and collective identities (both as migrants and at home) made me want to understand the larger phenomena of which danza performance in Peru was such an essential part.

Several elements of my personal identity simultaneously made me an outsider to the reality I was studying: although I was the child of highlanders who would be identified by most Peruvians as mestizos, I grew up in the coastal national capital and was exposed to urban cultural practices seen by most Peruvians as more cosmopolitan than those of the highlands. I had become a scholar; therefore I had reached a level of education unusual for cusqueños, male or female, and unusual for Peruvian women of any region. I had gone to study in the United States and had married a North American. In short I spoke, dressed, danced (baile), and generally behaved differently than most townspeople. My "cultural capital" (Bourdieu 1987) was certainly regarded as admirable by most townspeople, but it clearly made me an outsider to the point that some called me by the nickname of "gringita" despite my dark skin (*gringa/o* is the term for foreigner, and in the Andes can be affectionate and not necessarily negative).

My insider/outsider identity marked my research in several different ways. For example, growing up learning some of the techniques that are important for danza practices in Cusco (and in general being an avid dancer) facilitated my investigation by allowing me to perform in an important religious celebration with the most prestigious comparsa of the town, the Majeños, as I was just beginning my study. Although this performance initially caused some conflict with the main competitors of the Majeños, the Qollas, being able to successfully perform with a comparsa gained me recognition as one who was truly interested in learning about those practices.[47]

My personal identity also facilitated my exploration of issues of gender identity with the only women who participated in danza performance, the members of two comparsas of young jeronimianos. I was twenty-nine years old at the time of my research, ten or more years older than the average comparsa member, but because I played sports with them, dressed more like them than like the older women of the town, and did not have children even though I was married, the members of these comparsas considered me young. Because I was a young (in their view) educated *limeña* (woman from Lima) who had lived in the United States, the young female comparsa members saw me as a woman with cosmopolitan views with whom they could discuss their frustration about the conservatism of many of their fellow townspeople.

The female members of one comparsa in particular, the Tuntuna, saw me as a source from which they could acquire some bodily techniques well fitted to their purposes. In particular, they were interested in learning to master shoulder shaking, which is characteristic of the dances (bailes) based on Afro-Caribbean rhythms such as *cumbia* and *salsa*, which these young dancers were interested in incorporating into their danza in order to create an urban, transnational, and cosmopolitan image (see chapter 6). Cumbia and salsa were very popular in Lima among members of my generation, and I knew them well; therefore the young female performers of the Tuntuna took a particular interest in having me participate in their rehearsals so that I could teach them some of these movements and in general judge their bodily techniques.

My gender identity could have been a limitation for my close investigation of the all male comparsas of the town. Nevertheless, my status as a scholar studying in the United States, my identity as a middle-class educated person from the nation's capital city, my style of dress (most commonly sweaters, jeans, and sneakers), as well as my use of sophisticated video and audio equipment and of computers, put me in a sort of in-between gender position. For the male comparsa members of the town, all my personal attributes made me very different from the towns-women and in several respects the incarnation of some of the ideals that they were striving to obtain in order to be recognized as mestizos.

Besides shaping my gender identity, being recognized as a scholar studying fiestas and danzas gave me the status of specialist or authority on what is commonly known as folklore both in San Jerónimo and in Cusco city. It first became clear to me that I had acquired this status when in 1989 the open confrontations between young members of comparsas who performed Altiplano danzas and a coalition of civil, religious, and "cultural" authorities who opposed that performance broke out (see chapter 6). In both San Jerónimo and Cusco city I was asked many times to give my opinion as to whether the performance of Altiplano danzas should be forbidden or permitted.

In San Jerónimo, for example, I was invited to meetings in the town hall where all the comparsas and the local authorities discussed matters relevant to the preparation of the fiesta. There the young performers had to defend their Altiplano danzas, which the members of the adult comparsas wanted to suppress. On these occasions I gave my opinion as to why the "traditional" danzas were losing their appeal to the members of young generation and why they had selected Altiplano danzas (see chapter 6).

Outside of these public occasions jeronimianos, comparsa and non-comparsa members, often informally asked for my opinion on the matter.

If the person was opposed to the performance of Altiplano danzas yet knew that I was sympathetic to that performance, he or she would try to convince me that it was important not to let the young generation perform Altiplano danzas in order to keep San Jerónimo's "tradition." But, probably because of my status as an scholar, even the people opposed to that performance would listen carefully to the explanations that I had to give about the popularity of the danzas among the young people. I believe that in the end I influenced some opponents, at least in making them understand that there was a fundamental problem with the "traditional" Cusco danzas: most of them did not allow for the participation of women in large numbers and leading roles.

In Cusco city I was asked to write journalistic articles about the ongoing confrontations. That led to an invitation to a radio broadcast for the entire departamento. Subsequently, I was invited to give a public talk at the city hall on a topic that I could choose. For that occasion I decided to again talk about the ongoing conflicts. I had realized that it was important for both performers and opponents to keep discussing all the elements involved in the phenomenon and that this discussion would eventually help those who were being repressed, that is, the young performers of Altiplano danzas.

Along with my status as an scholar I believe that being a partial insider, in this case being a Peruvian and not a foreign scholar, allowed me to get deeply involved in arguments about Cusco "traditions." First, I felt that in many occasions being a Peruvian protected my opinions from being dismissed altogether as those of a foreigner "who does not really understand Peruvian culture," an easy and powerful argument that I have heard many times used by Cusco people. Second, and maybe more importantly, from the beginning I felt that as a Peruvian I needed to be assertive and open about what I felt was a problem in many Peruvian traditions. I felt the need to help the people involved in the confrontations to understand where the problems were coming from and perhaps help them to solve them in a peaceful way. Furthermore, as a woman, what interested and bothered me from the beginning were the conservative views about women's public roles that were at the core of these conflicts. Therefore I felt even more compelled to get involved.

This involvement in the antagonisms that emerged over comparsa performance allowed me to meet a series of authorities who organized regional contests of music and dance. As a consequence I was invited to be part of the jury in two annual contests. After my participation in the first jury I became fascinated by the discussion among the members of the jury, by the classification of the danzas under different categories, and by the criteria according to which the performances were considered traditional or appropriate for each category. This led me to investigate many other local and regional contests, something that enriched my understanding of the regional and national context of comparsa performance.

The work of Cynthia Novack (1990) has been helpful to me in thinking retrospectively of my experiences and perspectives for studying fiestas and danzas in highland Peru. Novack was an anthropologist who conducted research in her own culture. Her preoccupation about finding a balance between the insider and outsider perspectives (1990, 21) was not that different from that of many other anthropologists. Nevertheless, Novack and I started from similar positions to find that balance. I do not mean to imply, however, that finding a balance between "empathy" and "removed" observation in the study of dance (Novack 1990, 21) is better done if one starts from the inside. What I want to emphasize here is the value of reaching this balance through paying particular attention to the perspectives and arguments given by the performers. Perhaps guided by my partial insider position, I have let the perspectives and arguments made by the actors about their performances direct my understanding of the special capacity that their practices have for carrying important social action. I firmly believe that the relationship between performance and society can be better understood if the ethnographer privileges in his or her analysis the perspective of the performers, their intentions, and their experience while performing, that is, their agency.

It was the fact that comparsa performers insisted so much on calling their danza practice "folkloric" that led me to study carefully and to take seriously the process of folklorization of cusqueño music, dance, and rituals. The performers' perspectives took me beyond seeing this folklorization as simply a negative effort by controlling elites to take danzas and fiestas out of their original context. The pride and the insistence with which comparsa performers spoke of their practices as "folkloric" led me to understand that this process of folklorization had given danzas and fiestas a powerful new dimension.

In chapter 2 I look at how transnational, national, and regional processes intersect in Cusco, leading to the folklorization of this region's expressive forms during the twentieth century. In chapter 3 I move to the locally situated perspective of the town of San Jerónimo, its patronsaint fiesta, and its comparsas. Chapter 4 analyzes the Majeños danza in historical and regional perspective. Nevertheless, my scrutiny centers on the case of San Jerónimo, showing how the members of this comparsa have constituted themselves as a distinct local elite. In chapter 5 I study the Qollas danza, demonstrating that through ritual performance social contradictions are reflected upon, reworked, and made visible. While I concentrate on the Qolla comparsa of San Jerónimo, I analyze the meanings of this danza in regional and national contexts. Focusing on issues of gender inequality and generation gaps, chapter 6 shows how danza performance can be a key site for the contestation of cultural values and social roles. That chapter centers on the analysis of the series of open antagonisms that pitted young members of comparsas who performed danzas from the Altiplano region against a coalition of civil, religious, and "cultural" authorities who opposed that performance. Chapter 7 brings together the main conclusions reached throughout the book about the relationship between public performance and society.

TWO

# Folklore, Authenticity, and Traditions in Cusco Regional Identity

> The way in which cultural actions come to be called folklore needs to be understood as a historical process, involving changes in the practice both of its producers and of those who seek to interpret and control it.
>
> Rowe and Schelling, *Memory and Modernity: Popular Culture in Latin America*

When contemporary cusqueños, particularly those who live in the valley of Cusco, exalt the central role that comparsas and patron-saint fiestas have in their towns and in regional culture, they categorize them as "folklore." Comparsa members in San Jerónimo use the concept of folklore not only to validate their dances in the eyes of fellow townspeople and outsiders but primarily to define and, during my research, frequently to argue that such practices "traditionally" or "authentically" represent local and regional identity. Comparsa members and their audience label this folklore jeronimiano (from San Jerónimo) or cusqueño (from Cusco) to refer to local and regional repertoires of "traditions."

In this chapter I analyze the efforts of artists, intellectuals, and other members of the mestizo middle class in Cusco city to configure a regional identity based on their idea of folklore and what they create as a repertoire of cusqueño traditions. These urban cusqueños have led what I call the folklorization of Cusco music and danzas, a phenomenon where transnational, national, and regional processes have intersected. This folklorization has had seemingly contradictory consequences. On the one hand, it has been used by national and regional elites to curb the potential threat to established social order posed by some expressive forms, and to foster stereotypes about subjugated social groups. On the other, through this folklorization performers such as comparsa members have gained new spaces and recognition for their creative efforts, providing them the means to rework and contest social values and stereotypes promoted by such elites.

I place the attempt of Cusco city artists and intellectuals to construct regional identity as part of Cusco's social history between the 1920s and the 1980s. My analysis focuses on how the members of this provincial

48

urban class have promoted folklore and have "invented" cusqueño "traditions" (Hobsbawm 1983)[1] through *instituciones culturales*.[2]

The process of folklorization permitted Cusco urban artists and intellectuals to shape the idea of an anonymous "authentic indigenous" identity. This cusqueño elaboration then became instrumental to central state efforts at national-identity construction. Similar to processes elsewhere in Latin America, in Peru images and concepts about an "authentic Indian race" (black in places like Brazil and the Caribbean) have been central in representations of nationhood (Knight 1990; Wade 1993). Moreover, the contradiction that Cusco artists and intellectuals faced in constructing their regional identity, which they responded to by defining their own folkloric practices as mestizo, is at the heart of Peruvian and of much of Latin American nationalism: that is, the ambivalence of trying to define a national particularity (regional in the case of Cusco) based on an "authentic racial" heritage, while also trying to distance such nationalism (or regionalism) from that heritage, which is too easily seen as backward and inferior in terms of global modernity.

The attempt to link contemporary highland-rural society with an "authentic indigenous" ancestry was characteristic of representatives of the intellectual movement that members of the early instituciones sprang from, indigenismo. Indigenismo was a series of intellectual movements on the part of non-"Indians," dating from the 1850s in Lima and in the provinces, that from different social and political perspectives sought to place the "Indian" as a central focus of study, identity construction, and, sometimes, political action (cf. Tamayo Herrera 1980; Deustua and Rénique 1984; Kristal 1987). The efforts of Cusco indigenistas were largely directed toward establishing continuity between a glorified Inca past and the marginal situation of contemporary peasants.

In Cusco and in the Andes at large, the cultural practices that the members of instituciones classified as "folklore"—in particular danzas, music, and religious festivals—had since colonial times been an arena for conflicts over power and ethnic/racial identity.[3] Approximately since the 1920s, folklore has been a realm where cusqueños, including the members of instituciones, have identified their ethnic/racial differences and have tended either to fight against or reinforce the relations of inequality and subordination to which these differences are bound. Moreover, it has been in this context where these ethnic/racial differences have been constantly defined and redefined. In the late 1980s folklore also became the arena of an open generational conflict among cusqueños. In this case it became clear that the definitions of local, regional, and national folklore were questioned because they were unable to contain the phenomena they were supposed to frame.[4]

In defining the boundaries of Andean or cusqueño folklore and traditions, the instituciones culturales have also shaped what cusqueños consider authentic. These three categories, folklore, tradition, and authenticity, have been pivotal for the members of these instituciones in classifying the elements that make up their staged presentations, parades, contests, and other promotional activities (i.e., handicraft fairs). For the Cusco city mestizo intellectuals and artists, the concept of the authentic became particularly important in order to differentiate some of their own folkloric mestizo practices from the practices of those whom they considered indigenous people.[5] This differentiation from "other" cusqueños—most commonly from those who lived in the countryside or in the higher areas of Cusco departamento—should be understood in relation to the regional dynamics between this highland urban center and the rural areas peripheral to it. It should also be explored in relation to the national context in which the highlands, including the cities located in that region, have, particularly since independence, become peripheral to Lima's central state-metropolitan status. Finally, these regional and national processes must be investigated in light of the international processes by which the symbolic or "artistic" practices of the people of third-world countries become known as folkloric.

This chapter emphasizes the role of privately sponsored instituciones because in Cusco the models of folklore, authenticity, and regional traditions that members of these organizations began to crystallize in the 1920s continue to shape ritual dancers' practices and self-perceptions today. While the state supported and promoted the activities of early private instituciones like Centro Qosqo and, especially after the 1950s, indirectly fostered folklore by encouraging tourism in the region, direct promotion of folklore by the state through instituciones or events directly controlled by it did not become widespread until the 1970s. Significantly, the indigenistas and their private instituciones greatly influenced these attempts by the state in recent decades. The models that the members of these private instituciones produced were consolidated more by the development of tourism itself and by the contests and festivals organized by local organizations (i.e., the Comisión Municipal de Festejos del Cusco to which I refer in this chapter) than by the direct state promotion of folklore. Nevertheless, folkloric institutions and events that popularized and spread these models seem to have proliferated as a result of Velasco's military government's promotion of direct state participation in the late 1970s.

Through a repertoire of cusqueño traditions, the promotion of folklore, and the concept of an "authentic" cusqueño, members of these instituciones culturales have without doubt shaped the practices of comparsas inside and outside Cusco city. From their privileged position in the capital city and as authorities in the field of cusqueño "folklore," the members of these instituciones have set certain models that comparsa members have used in their own attempts at identity redefinition. In mestizo towns like San Jerónimo, these models have influenced, in particular but not exclusively, the forms that the danzas have taken (i.e., choreography and costumes), the dancers' perceptions about their roles as representatives of local and regional folklore, and the townspeople's concepts of ethnic/racial identity. Members of this town have long participated in Cusco city rituals and contests and have readily used the models employed in the activities of the instituciones culturales. Although the dynamics of symbolic practice in San Jerónimo ritual and ritual dance go beyond the boundaries that the instituciones culturales have tried to set for the domain of cusqueño folklore, authenticity, and traditions, these concepts have without a doubt shaped such practice. In order to understand the specific meanings and implications of these concepts in Cusco, one needs to begin by scrutinizing how they were shaped by the regional indigenismo.

## Indigenismo, Authenticity, and the Beginnings of the Folklorization of Andean Performance

Analysts of Cusco indigenismo (cf. Tamayo Herrera 1980, 1981; Deustua and Rénique 1984) have examined the development of this nativist movement as part of the expansion of capitalism and the state in Cusco and Peru as a whole, particularly under the presidency of Augusto B. Leguía (1919–1930).[6] Leguía's efforts to gain the support of the proletariat, the peasantry, and the middle class in order to consolidate his position against the old landed oligarchies led him to a populist rhetoric that echoed indigenista thought. Leguía's government established a series of organizations in favor of the peasant population such as the Comisión Pro-Indígena (proindigenous committee), which was made up of well-known indigenistas, and was the first to proclaim June 24 the national holiday El Día del Indio (the day of the Indian), which in the 1940s became El Día de Cusco (the day of Cusco), and finally in the 1970s El Día del Campesino (the day of the peasant).

During the first three decades of this century, Peruvian intellectual and political life flourished in Lima and in the main cities of the country. Migration from the provinces to the capital cities as a result of the development of capitalism and the expansion of institutional education were at the core of this process.[7] During this period members of an emergent middle class of provincial origin struggled for the democratization of Peruvian society, developing both federalist and decentralization political movements.

Cusco and Puno (capital of the neighboring departamento of the same name) were the two cities in which the main indigenista movement developed as part of this effervescent intellectual and political life. Only in Puno did the members of this intellectual movement become actively involved in political struggle and peasant uprisings over land. By the 1920s, when peasant uprisings took place, the split between the ideology of Cusco indigenistas and that of the peasant leaders became evident. The intellectuals in Cusco wanted to direct the peasants' claims to the legally established institutions, preaching for a more flexible society and attempting to soothe the peasant's rage. The peasant leaders, while they used some of the established channels, were much more radical and took into their own hands the organization of protests and uprisings (Deustua and Rénique 1984, 90).

Within Cusco itself, indigenismo was a complex movement whose development may be traced to 1848 and which lasted at least four generations (cf. Deustua and Rénique 1984; Kristal 1987). One of the important early developments was the Centro Científico del Cusco (scientific center of Cusco), created in 1897. This center became the institutional channel through which the emergent upper and middle classes, which developed in the midst of the expansion of the internal market linked to the wool trade, expressed their proposals for the new society. Employing a positivist discourse, the members of this institution attempted to redefine the indigenous peasants as favorable elements of national development. They promoted research, publications, and conferences about the potential for the "modernization"[8] of the economy of the Cusco region based on both its ecological and "social resources," the latter being the indigenous peasantry (Deustua and Rénique 1984, 70).

This preoccupation with what was called the *problema del indio* (the Indian problem) grew among the next generation of indigenistas, who led a radical reform of the universities in 1909. Like the Centro Científico previously, San Antonio Abad University in Cusco became the main promoter of studies and publications about indigenous peasant life, customs, and traditions. The discussion and reflections about the Indian problem were not confined to intellectual and university publications but were also present in the many periodical publications. Deustua and Rénique (1984, 71) have counted twenty-five periodical publications in Cusco between 1890 and 1920. However, the peasantry, the focus of concern and the recipient of legal aid and general support, was rarely involved in indigenista activities.

Representatives of this generation of indigenistas displayed a renewed effort to explain the indigenous present as a function of the glorious Inca past.[9] These indigenistas paid special attention to what they considered the ideology and spirituality of both the pre-Hispanic and contemporary Andean peasants. They committed themselves to "rescuing" music, dance, indigenous languages, handicrafts, customs, and oral traditions that they considered to be expressions of Andean ideology and spirituality in contrast to a Eurocentric modernity. This was best exemplified by the writings of Luis E. Valcárcel,[10] who wrote extensively about Inca life, political principles, myths, and rituals as well as about the contemporary peasant problems.

Valcárcel and other contemporary indigenistas, as Deborah Poole (1988) has argued, worked to resurrect and reinvent the concepts of Indianness, the Inca past, Andean culture, and *cusqueñismo* in their pursuit of regional independence from coastal centralized government. While elevating the utopian socialist and pastoral ideals of the Incaic past, however, they relegated the present-day highland peasants to an essentially cultureless and voiceless situation of partiality and incompleteness. Indigenistas projected their romanticized view of the Inca past onto the rural present and geographically distant. According to indigenista views "[t]he 'authentic' Indian, the true rebel, the 'real' Andean culture is always a bit further away, in the next province, along the frontier" (Poole 1988, 368).

When in the 1920s there was a split between indigenista intellectuals and the peasant political movement, the idealization of Inca culture and society as well as the paternalistic attitude toward the contemporary peasantry became evident. At this point indigenistas were mostly concerned with problems of national and regional identity, and in their search for emblems they granted special attention to "indigenous" music and dance, which provided the clearest contrast with European, U.S., and *criollo* culture (Turino 1991, 267–268).[11] A very specific example of how music, dance, and theater became instrumental to the indigenistas' construction of cusqueño and national identity was the organization by Luis Valcárcel of the Misión Peruana de Arte Incaico (Peruvian mission of Incaic art). The performances of the Misión, which toured Bolivia, Argentina, and Uruguay between 1923 and 1924, displayed a combination of "Incaic" themes—such as the Quechua drama *Ollantay*—with "indigenous" or peasant musical and dance elements. Aparicio (1994, 133–134) transcribes the program presented in Argentina by the misión in 1923. This program includes "Hymn to the

Sun" (the sun being the central symbol of Inca religious life) performed by a symphony orchestra, a piece of music called "*Sumaj Ñusta*" (beautiful indigenous princess) performed by an "*orquesta típica indígena*" (typical indigenous ensemble), "*K'achampa, danza de guerreros*" (*K'achampa*, a dance of warriors), and "*T'ika Kaswa.*" (Below I refer to *K'achampa* and to *kaswas*, or *qhaswas*.)

Indigenistas' transposition of the romanticized past into the geographically distant, rural present gave shape to what continues to be the notion of the "authentic" cusqueño and Andean culture. Today's members of Cusco's instituciones culturales consider a dance or a piece of music more authentic or authentically cusqueño (or by the same token authentically Andean) if it can be linked to the pre-Hispanic past, if it is characteristic of a province distant from Cusco city, or if it belongs to rural life. This notion of the authentically cusqueño derives from the concept of purity, itself a product of the indigenista romantic trend. The city artists and intellectuals' idea of "remoteness" was a product of their cognitive map of modern centrism.

The emergence of the romantic concept of an authentic rural culture in the face of urban growth, expansion of communication systems, and industrialization is not unique to Andean indigenistas or to other elite or intellectual groups in Latin America. In Europe the concept of folklore, which idealized peasant communal life, developed under industrialization.[12] As in Europe, in Latin America, and within it in the Andes, the idea of the purity of a peasant culture, which was soon degraded or forgotten under the pressure of capitalist development, mass media, and industrialization, stimulated the desire to keep the elements of that culture as museum pieces.

This paternalism and nostalgia fostered the assumption that the population whose culture is supposedly being lost, namely the peasantry, has a passive role in society (Rowe and Schelling 1991, 2–3). However, this assumption was for Cusco indigenistas a product of their wishful thinking and was often contradicted by the direct political action of the peasants. During the first decades of this century indigenistas faced a paradox. The cultural elements that they promoted as authentic and vulnerable belonged to a presently living and subordinated majority that, through political struggle, was questioning the legitimacy of the existing power structure—namely, the peasantry.

In light of this paradox, the members of indigenismo who founded instituciones culturales used the concept of folklore.[13] This concept was readily applicable to the conflictual arena of public expressive forms and offered the possibility of reinterpreting and curbing the potential threat posed by these cultural elements. In particular two intrinsically related connotations of folklore, which have continued to be important, became central to the use of the concept by the members of the instituciones: first, that a folkloric element should be, by definition, the product of a decontextualized community, ideally pre-Hispanic, rural, and indigenous; and second, that because of this communal and distant origin, it must be anonymous. In theory these folkloric elements should not be attributable to identifiable individuals. The creation has to come from a hypothetically unified community (folk) that has to be the product of an equally hypothetical common knowledge (lore). In this sense the members of the instituciones have used the concept in an attempt to negate a specific identity and purpose of the phenomena that had been brought within the boundaries of folklore.

The concept of folklore in Latin America, as in Europe, has become highly charged politically. It has been used by national or regional elites to foster the idea of a unitary nation or region where the wide differences between cultural practices of different social groups make that unifying effort not always viable. In regions like the Andes, the cultures referred to as folkloric have upheld their own alternative ideas of nationhood (Rowe and Schelling 1991, 51–63). Therefore, the political charge of the concept of folklore resides mainly in the fact that "the cultures thought of as folkloric" are seen at the same time as "a kind of bank where 'authenticity' is safely stored" and as "contemporary cultures which articulate alternatives to existing power structures" (Rowe and Schelling 1991, 4).

Through staged presentations, contests, parades, and reenactment of Inca rituals, indigenistas invented and reinvented a series of traditions (fig. 1). In their efforts to "preserve" authentic indigenous society, urban artists and intellectuals created idealized models of the cultural forms that were supposed to represent this past and present society. These efforts initiated a trend that since the first decades of this century has furthered a series of stereotypes about the Inca past, indigenous or authentic identity, and cusqueño folklore.

In the first decades of this century, the Centro Qosqo de Arte Nativo (Cusco center of native art) and the Cusco branch of the Instituto Americano de Arte (American institute of art) became the two main entities dedicated to "rescuing" and reinventing cusqueño rituals, music, and dance. The members of these institutions have always referred to their activities as *rescate* (rescue) in their institutional written material, which I have gathered from the archives of these two institutions, and in the interviews that I had with members.

Figure 1. Members of a peasant community performing an "indigenous" dance in a contest. Urubamba, Cusco, 1989. Photo by Fritz Villasante.

## THE CENTRO QOSQO AND THE INSTITUTO AMERICANO DE ARTE: THE INCA PAST AND A FOLKLORIC PRESENT MERGE AS CUSQUEÑISMO

As I explained about indigenismo, the creation of the Centro Qosqo and of the Cusco branch of the Instituto Americano de Arte (IAA) should be understood in a context in which the state promoted the kind of activities to which both these organizations were devoted. In the case of the IAA, the wider international context had a more direct bearing since this institución in Cusco was a chapter of a Latin American umbrella organization.

While the founders of the two instituciones were urban middle-class artists and intellectuals and some of them even participated in both, each organization emphasized different types of activities. The members of Centro Qosqo were more devoted to "preserving," "cultivating," and "promoting" "authentic" music and dance (Centro Qosqo 1988, 1). The members of the IAA, even though they initially participated in the "defense" and "promotion" of "native" music and dance, took more interest in "preserving" the "cultural patrimony" represented by Inca and colonial buildings or monuments, handicrafts, and elements of material culture that they could keep in museums (IAA 1935, October 5). In both cases they were concerned with reconstructing Inca culture and with making it the central symbol of cusqueñismo. In the case of the IAA, its members were particularly interested in instituting newly created and reinvented public rituals. My recent research (1995–1997) on the instituciones has shown that the Centro Qosqo has had from its beginnings a much more mixed membership in terms of ethnic/racial and class background than I originally had envisioned. This exchange between artists of rural and urban origin, I hypothesize, could have led to the very dynamic process of music and dance creation and re-creation that has characterized this institution.

In 1924, around the time of the successful international performances of the Misión Artística, a group of Cusco city "bohemian" friends decided to create an "artistic" organization to perform "vernacular" music and dance: they named themselves the Cusco Center of Native Art.[14] The name stresses their views and makes it compatible with their concept of folklore. The vernacular, or native, practices were revalorized to the point of being called "art" or "knowledge" (the latter when the word *folklore* was used). Among the members of the first *junta directiva* (board of directors) of Centro Qosqo were Luis Alberto Pardo Durant (president), a renowned archaeologist; well-known musicians and composers such as Roberto Ojeda, Baltazar Zegarra, and Juan de Dios Aguirre, three of *los cuatro grandes de la música cusqueña* (the great four of cusqueño music); the now internationally renowned photographer Martín Chambi; and Humberto Vidal Unda, who later through the IAA would become a major figure in the configuration of cusqueño symbols.[15]

In their search for authenticity the members of the Centro Qosqo moved in the two directions that their indigenista trend led them: the Inca past and the rural present. They saw both, and in particular the rural context, as rich fields from which they could select elements to re-create cusqueño regional identity; they modeled this cusqueño identity on their own urban views and aesthetics. The combination of European musical instruments with those associated with the Andean peasantry, the creation of stylized choreographies performed by urban mestizos in staged contexts, and the use of Inca imagery all resulted in new, unique forms that would subsequently influence the production of music and dance in the whole region.

For example, the musicians of Centro Qosqo selected from their contemporary peasant musical repertoire the use of the *kena* (or *quena,* an end-notched vertical cane flute of pre-Hispanic origin) and the *charango* (a small stringed instrument of colonial origin). They combined these instruments most often with guitars, mandolins, violins, and later accordion, to play elaborate pieces that displayed European-influenced harmony, timbres, and pitch ranges, and they juxtaposed all of these elements with Inca imagery (Turino 1991, 269). One of the genres they created was the so-called *fox Incaico* (Incaic fox), which still predominates in today's staged Inca rituals. This Incaic fox and other compositions and arrangements by Centro Qosqo musicians have from the beginning displayed a "softer, less strident sound than is typical of indigenous musical performance" (Turino 1991, 269).

Despite its stylized musical and choreographic production, at least since 1927 members of the Centro Qosqo assumed the role of representative of vernacular Cusco to audiences inside and outside the departamento. In 1927 President Leguía invited highlanders to participate in a contest in Lima that fell on the already-established Día del Indio, to provide the first major public context for highlanders in Lima to perform their own music (Vivanco 1973, 34). Urban Cusco composers such as Baltazar Zegarra, who belonged to Centro Qosqo, participated in that event. An urban Cusco piano and kenas trio won this contest featuring *"yaravíes, huaynos, y danzas de guerra* (war dances)" (Vivanco 1973, 34; yaraví in audio example 12 and video example 7).[16]

The next year, when this event in Lima had taken a much broader national dimension and delegations from around the country arrived in the capital city to compete, Centro Qosqo represented its departamento (Vivanco 1973, 35). As highlighted in a speech by President Leguía, the members of the Centro had become "cultural brokers."

> Gentlemen. Nothing expresses better the *collective psychology* of the *people* than its music. . . . The *race*, the imperial power, the catastrophe of the conquest, the pain of more than three centuries of domination, and the richness of a glorious dawn after this unfortunate event exist in our *Inca* music.
>
> The *vernacular* artists that have come from all corners of the country to take part in this occasion attest to the marvels of our *folklore*, the riches of our musical sources and original choreographic art. This is not a product of study or a maneuver. This is born *spontaneously*, because it exists in the *nature* [*entrañas*] of our *passionate* people.[17]

Leguía's discourse underlines three important elements besides that of granting the role of representatives of the "vernacular" to cusqueño urban performers and composers. First, it makes Inca imagery central to a definition of Cusco and Peruvian national identity.[18] Second, it implies that music and dance as folklore are supposed to represent the Andean and cusqueño ethos or "psychology" of the "people" as a unified communal entity or "race." Third, it notes that the ethos of this "race" reflected at least three characteristics: a victorious imperial past, a long history of defeat and domination, and a "passionate" present that is best represented by its "artistic" sources, which emerge "spontaneously" from its "nature." Leguía's view built on Cusco urban mestizos' reconstruction of their past and the stereotypes they fostered about the contemporary indigenous peasants.

Under the general themes of the Incaic and the peasant life, three sets of characteristics have marked the composition and re-creation of Cusco music, dance, and theater by urban artists who belonged to the Centro Qosqo: the warrior and aggressive spirit of the past that still remains in some distant provinces; the lethargic and bucolic existence of the majority of the peasants during most of the year; and finally the festive and lustful spirit that breaks out when there is a celebration.

As mentioned above, one of the first themes that Cusco urban artists represented through music in Lima was that of "war dances." Among the pieces of the first repertoire of dances that the members of Centro Qosqo presented in Cusco city as well as other cities of Peru and South America were the reconstructed dances of the main Inca ritual for the winter solstice, the Inti Raymi (festival of the sun); K'achampa, a prototypical "war dance" that features men competing with each other through whipping; Los Llameros, representing the llama herders of the high altitudes; and T'ika Qhaswa, a carnival peasant dance that involves celebration of community, fertility, and happiness among the rural population. I expand on the genre of qhaswa or kaswa below because it has become the quintessential example of indigenous dance in contemporary contests and festivals.

In 1933 the Centro Qosqo was the first institución folklórica to be acknowledged in an official decree. By 1950 the Centro had thirty dances and melodies in its repertoire and had presented them in La Paz, Buenos Aires, Santiago, and Valparaíso. In their national and international presentations—and in the same fashion as the Misión Artística had done—the members of the Centro Qosqo put on stage a series of bucolic scenes or skits called Estampas Costumbristas (traditional scenes) and pieces of theater with Incaic themes. One of the favorite estampas was the Awaqkuna (the weavers)—featuring peasant women spinning and weaving in the countryside—and their favorite piece of Incaic theater was the Ollantay drama.

Between the mid-1940s and the early 1960s this institución went through a series of divisions that were in part due to the creation of new nationally and internationally founded organizations. During these years the IAA supported a faction of the Centro Qosqo that adopted the name Conjunto de Arte Folklórico "Kosko" (Cusco's folkloric art ensemble). This faction would later lead the reunification of the Centro Qosqo. Another institution that replaced the Centro Qosqo from its central role of promoter of folklore during this critical period was the Conjunto Folklórico de la Corporación (the folkloric ensemble of the national corporation of tourism), founded in the mid-1940s. By 1964 the Centro Qosqo was again revitalized, producing its first album *Qosqo takiyninchis* (let's sing Cusco). In May 1973 the Centro Qosqo inaugurated its own theater and building on the main commercial avenue of Cusco city, Avenida del Sol.

Today, the Centro Qosqo continues to be the main institución that promotes folklore in the whole region and a central force in Cusco city public rituals. It has become the role model for many mestizo comparsa members who aim to turn their voluntary association into a respected organization. The *Estatuto* (official guidelines or statutes), which contains 112 articles and at least 280 clauses, and the repertoire of this institución shape comparsa members' ideas about their role as cultural intermediaries at the local level, and their models of authentic, indigenous, and mestizo Cusco music and dance tradition.

Depending in large part on local tourism, Centro Qosqo continues to be a private, self-financed institution (see below). It currently has eighty associates, fifty dances, and two hundred melodies in its repertoire. The organization has sponsored a series of local and regional celebrations, conferences, and contests. It has produced eight albums and a videotape as well as written material for the promotion of national tourism and for teaching folklore in schools and universities. Besides sponsoring a series of events in Cusco city and throughout the region, it holds daily presentations of folkloric music and danzas in its theater. Finally, the Centro holds a large collection of dance costumes and attire from the whole region, which they not only use for their own staged presentations and annual Desfile de Trajes Típicos (traditional-attire parade; fig. 2), but they also rent to many folkloric organizations and schools throughout the region.

While Centro Qosqo has sporadically received subsidies from the national government, particularly during the construction of their own building in the 1970s, it has mostly financed itself through its daily touristic folkloric shows. A second important source of income has come from the rental of its gear. Donations from incoming associates, rental of the auditorium and sections of the building, sales of tapes and videos, special shows, and fund-raising activities supplement that income. An example of how important the touristic shows have been for

Figure 2.    Member of Centro Qosqo displaying a "mestiza" Cusco outfit during the Annual Traditional Attire Parade. Cusco city, 1995. Photo by Fernando Pancorvo.

Centro Qosqo is the 1976 budget, when 87 percent of the total income came from that source (Centro Qosqo 1976). This institution has suffered a deep financial crisis since the mid-1980s or so, due to the decline in tourism in the country because of political violence.

The Cusco branch of the IAA was created in 1937 as a result of the participation of Cusco indigenistas in the Americanist Congress that took place in Buenos Aires that year. The renowned indigenista Uriel García, who participated in the congress, gathered a "select" group of other intellectuals of the city, some of whom belonged to Centro Qosqo, and founded the IAA with the primary goal of working for Cusco, defending its cultural values and its cultural patrimony. The words used by a now deceased early member of the IAA whom I interviewed in 1990 were "Uriel García gathered the most select intellectuals of the time and constituted the Cusco branch of the American Institute of Art."[19] The record of the first session of the Cusco branch of the IAA states that its immediate task was to "defend, propagate and give stimulus to the art in Cusco" (IAA 1935, October 5).

The international and local development of the academic disciplines of archaeology, anthropology, and folklore influenced in particular the first kind of activities that this institución advocated. The development of those disciplines also stimulated the creation of other more academically oriented organizations in Cusco.[20] Cusco intellectuals believed that collecting and classifying cusqueño materials could serve comparative purposes within these disciplines, which many of them were interested in developing locally. At the same time, Cusco had the opportunity to become important not only at the national level but also internationally, showing that it had a high cultural development in the past and that it currently had a rich "popular culture." The notion of popular culture that developed then and continues to be valid for this kind of institution is that of "popular" as opposed to that of the educated upper classes of the cities.[21]

First, they collected and/or preserved elements of the material culture such as handicrafts, costumes, and Inca and colonial monuments (most often Inca fortresses and temples and colonial churches). A key example was their work to create the contest within the local Christmas exposition of *Santurantikuy* (literally "purchase of saints"). This local tradition of buying and selling religious statues for Christmas built on the tradition of religious art among Cusco artisans that dated from colonial times. The members of the IAA wanted to promote this "popular art." This institución created a "museum of popular art" where the members collected statues (which they bought at the Santurantikuy), costumes, masks, instruments, and other elements of "popular art" and "folklore." Both the museum and the Santurantikuy continue to be tourist attractions.[22]

Second, the members of the IAA created and reinvented public celebrations and symbols that, centering on the imagery of the glorious Inca past, became distinctive of cusqueño identity. They displayed a desire for "material and tangible" results of indigenista preaching about cusqueño identity (Tamayo Herrera 1981, 172).[23] Humberto Vidal Unda, one of the main leaders of the IAA, had already started to work toward the materialization of the new symbols of cusqueñismo when he led the creation of the *Hora del Charango* (the charango hour) several months before the Cusco branch of the IAA was created.

This weekly radio program, heard by many Cusco city dwellers from speakers placed in the main square, was central to the acceptance of the *charango* as an urban-mestizo Cusco tradition (Aparicio 1994, 136). Charango playing had been identified until the first decades of the century only with the peasantry, but as the urban style "evolved" and the practice of this instrument was more accepted among urban cusqueños, it became emblematic of a mestizo regional identity (Turino 1984). This attempt to find emblems of Cusco "mixed-blood" elements that, as in the case of charango playing, were called "cholo"—stressing the highland in contrast to the coastal—was consistent with a new dimension of the indigenista trend known as *neoindianismo* (neo-Indianism; De la Cadena 1995, 188–241).

Vidal Unda himself was the one within the IAA who came up with the idea of having a special holiday to honor Cusco and a central ritual that would stand for cusqueñismo. Vidal Unda, as vice president of this institución and a member of Centro Qosqo, was the main promoter of the creation of both. He also was the main upholder of the creation of folkloric contests during these celebrations and the one who deserves the credit for stimulating the participation of groups from outside Cusco city in these events. This is evident in the series of communications between the participant folkloric groups and Vidal Unda and between him and the local institutions that funded the travel and the subsistence of these competing groups (Vidal Unda n.d.). He clearly stated his cusqueñista intentions: "It is not a matter of adding another civic holiday to the calendar that passes unnoticed by the people and is limited to a few official acts. Instead, it is a question of promoting *a true spiritual revolution* in the children of Cusco and the people of the country in general about the meaning of our homeland."[24]

Subsequently, in 1944 the formerly established Día del Indio on June 24 and the Inca winter-solstice ritual, the Inti Raymi, which according to chronicles used to take place on that date, were selected as the main symbols of cusqueñismo. A committee organized the celebrations, and the Inti Raymi was staged for the first time in the Inca ruins of Saccsayhuaman.[25] That same year, the national government made not only El Día de Cusco official, but also Cusco's week, the week of June 24. Later, the whole month of June became Cusco's *mes jubilar*

CHAPTER TWO / 64

(jubilee month), and a series of different activities exalting cusque-ñismo, such as contests and parades, was established. The Comisión Organizadora de los Festejos del Cusco (Cusco festivities organizing committee) first organized by Vidal Unda became the main ruling organ for these events.

From 1944 until the late fifties Centro Qosqo was in charge of staging the Inti Raymi. Its dancers, musicians, and other members were the main crew of participants in the presentation of the ritual. This institution designed the script, based on the colonial *crónicas,* and the features of the music and dance to be presented during the ceremony. After the first fifteen years, Centro Qosqo alternated with other instituciones of the city, participating in a selection process organized by the Comisión Organizadora in which the best prospect for the representation of the ritual won the opportunity to take charge of the event. Finally, in the first few years of the 1980s, a forum was held with the participation of local anthropologists, archaeologists, artists, and scenographers in order to design a definite script and unify criteria for the representation of the ritual. After three years the forum designed an official script that continues to be the basis of the representation, although modifications are constantly being made.

In 1990 I participated in a meeting convoked by the committee in charge of the event. There scholars, artists, and scenographers were still trying to improve the representation, making it more "historically" based and more meaningful for contemporary cusqueños. The organizers were worried about the widespread comments that this ritual had become mostly a tourist show and had lost meaning for local people. The ritual evokes the subjugation of the people of the four sections of the Inca empire to their supreme deity, the Sun, and his highest representative on earth, the Inca.

While the IAA still functions as a society that clusters local intellectuals and artists, this institución is not the main organizer or promoter of the activities that celebrate cusqueñismo today. That function has been assumed by a municipal institution to which I refer below. Nevertheless, its members and those of the Centro Qosqo continue to be considered local specialists on folklore and are constantly consulted and required for local and regional public events and contests.

Since the first efforts to promote folklore through contests and stage presentations took place, it has been clear that this endeavor, instead of preserving or recuperating old forms, has generated new styles and models of traditions. Nevertheless, the urban mestizos' belief that they should rescue the vernacular from its inevitable extinction has continued to inspire this type of promotional activities. The members of the

instituciones have thereby turned themselves into the cultural intermediaries between the peasantry and the urban and coastal audiences. The
members of the instituciones became for both audiences representatives
of the vernacular.

## THE NEW CUSCO AFTER THE EARTHQUAKE:
## CONFRONTATIONS, REFORMS, AND THE
## EMERGENCE OF TOURISM

Soon after local artists and intellectuals had initiated and elaborated
the new cusqueño symbols—El Día de Cusco, the Inti Raymi, and even
Cusco's own anthem—a natural disaster added new dimensions to
these prospects.[26] On May 21, 1950, an earthquake destroyed or dam-
aged most of the buildings of Cusco city. The subsequent reconstruction altered the character of the city and accelerated the ongoing
changes in the region. It also attracted renewed national and international interest in Cusco's Inca and colonial monuments, stimulating the
development of tourism in the region.

By 1945 Cusco had entered a second stage in the process of transformation of its social and productive structures, processes related to the
development of capitalism in Peru and the transformation of power relations in Cusco's countryside (Tamayo Herrera 1981).[27] Migration toward the main cities and new areas of colonization in the lowlands of
Cusco departamento, peasant pressure over hacienda lands, pauperization of the countryside, and peasant union movements, had started in
the Cusco region before the 1950 earthquake. However, the reconstruction of Cusco city and the promotion of a regional economy that
followed this natural disaster unquestionably marked this new era. The
national state and international organizations took part in this reconstruction and promotion.

The president of Peru at the time of the earthquake, General Odría,
took a particular interest in the reconstruction of Cusco, providing legal and economic support and promoting international aid for the economic development of the region. In 1951 the Peruvian government
signed an agreement with the United Nations to provide technical assistance for the reconstruction of Cusco. In 1952, as a result of the first
inspections of the North American technical advisers, the Junta de
Reconstrucción y Fomento (reconstruction and development junta)
was created with the main purposes of restoring the city, developing
the industrial potentialities of the region, and promoting the technical
development of agriculture. This regional institution was the first of
the various regional development organizations that emerged in Cusco,

primarily in the 1960s. From the 1950s on, Cusco became a focus of international (especially from the United States) financial and technical aid, particularly after the Cuban revolution in 1959 and the creation of the Alliance for Progress in 1961 (Brisseau et al. 1978, 28–29).[28]

The new character of the capital city as a tourist resort and as an urban center surrounded by marginal settlements started to take shape as a result of the reconstruction after the earthquake. For the first time the souvenir industry was promoted, various museums were created, and there was a particular interest in the restoration of Inca and colonial buildings (Inca temples, fortresses, and streets as well as Catholic churches and convents and old colonial houses of noble families). At the same time, the social and economic differences between the urban bourgeoisie and the growing poor sectors of the city (in large part immigrants from the countryside) increased and became more evident with the appearance of the first shantytowns. The national and international investment in the reconstruction of the city mostly favored the urban bourgeoisie who speculated with these funds.

In 1956 the Junta de Reconstrucción became the CRYF, Corporación de Reconstrucción y Fomento (reconstruction and development corporation). The role of this organization in the economic and political life of the region lasted until 1972. The CRYF, from its beginnings as the Junta, gathered together many Cusco city intellectuals and artists who had been part of the Centro Qosqo and the IAA. In general, the CRYF had a central role in all the different social, economic, and cultural aspects of the reconstruction of the Cusco region, in particular of Cusco city, a reconstruction that emphasized the features of Cusco as a folkloric and tourist center. Therefore the members of both the IAA and the Centro Qosqo sought its support for many of their institutional projects on a regular basis. The CRYF was the first regional corporation of the country. It articulated the enduring cusqueño desire for administrative and economic independence.

Even though Cusco's tourist industry had been growing with state and international support since the 1950s, it was not until the 1970s that Cusco and its increasingly famous Inca ruins of Machu Picchu became tourist meccas.[29] During this decade Cusco city developed into a cosmopolitan city full of hotels, restaurants, and souvenir stores. Between 1973 and 1977 the state took an active role in the promotion of this industry, creating the Peru-UNESCO joint project known as the "COPESCO plan." Under this plan a series of infrastructural projects, such as the construction or improvement of roads, the installation of public electricity and sewage systems, and development of the transportation system were carried out for the areas that were linked to tourism.[30]

Besides this state and foreign institutional support, private capital has contributed since the 1970s to the development of Cusco's tourism. Tamayo Herrera (1981) points out that between 1971 and 1976 a hotel boom took place, financed by local capital that was mostly from the ex-landowning elite (see below). After 1976 a new phase in the development of Cusco tourism began with foreign and limeño investment in hotels, restaurants, and handicrafts export businesses.

During the period of reconstruction of the capital city, Cusco's rural society was on the verge of open, violent conflict. Between 1940 and 1961, because of the poverty in the countryside, thousands of families migrated to the major cities of the country and to the eastern province of La Convención, creating the conditions for peasant political organization (Rénique 1988, 176–177).[31] As a result of this active political life two of the main unions of the region formed, the Federación Provincial de Campesinos de La Convención (peasant federation of La Convención province), founded in 1958, and the Federación Departamental de Campesinos del Cusco (peasant federation of Cusco departamento), founded in 1961. The leaders of the main Peruvian leftist political parties, some of whom were cusqueños, participated in the organization of the peasant struggle against the dominant landowning class in Cusco. The growth of the urban labor unions at the national level, as well as the victories of the Bolivian and Cuban revolutions, along with their subsequent agrarian reforms, provided a favorable context for Cusco peasants to put forth their demands.

By 1963, when the massive invasion of hacienda lands by peasants took place in Cusco, the landowning class had been seriously weakened. As a result of these internal pressures and concomitant external pressures President Fernando Belaúnde Terry established a legislative decree toward Peruvian agrarian reform during his first government, 1963–1968. However, no actual transformation was set in motion until after the military government of General Juan Velasco Alvarado (1968–1975) produced the 1969 Ley de Reforma Agraria (agrarian reform law). Also, in light of increasing pressure from provincial sectors, Belaúnde supported the movement toward a less centralized political and economic administration of Peru. Since at least 1940, Cusco's urban middle and upper classes had lobbied for administrative decentralization. The creation of the CRYF in Cusco was a step toward this autonomy. Belaúnde continued to support organizations of regional development such as the CRYF. He also reinstituted municipal elections banished in the country during Leguía's government. However, these independent organizations and municipal elections were suppressed by Velasco, who sought to undermine the power of regional elites.

The military coup of October 1968 that brought General Juan Velasco Alvarado to power should be understood in the context of a long-term struggle involving the modernization of the Peruvian political system and the desire to transform the dominant power structures (Rénique 1988, 212–307). Velasco's "military revolution" emerged, on the one hand, as an alternative to the failure of the political parties, formed by the emerging national middle classes, to reform the oligarchic system. On the other, it aimed to prevent a radical revolution from below. The military government had as its main aims to change a rigid social structure, to avoid the breakdown of an economic apparatus with an incipient productive capacity, and to eliminate the subordination of the Peruvian economy to foreign capital through the development of national industry. The two principal means to achieve these ultimate goals were agrarian reform and the development of a regional policy strongly tied to the central government. The highlands, in particular Cusco, became a privileged recipient of reformist policies in part because "since the 1960s Cusco's social situation awakened the fear in the military that it might become fertile ground for an attempt at revolution" (Rénique 1988, 212).

In Cusco, as in other parts of Peru, the agrarian reform was drastic but not fast or efficient enough to avoid the decapitalization of the estates and the transfer of this capital to other areas of investment. By the late 1970s the limits of Velasco's "revolution" had become evident as the former landowners managed to recover power through public positions, commerce, and the tourist industry (Rénique 1988, 305–306; Tamayo Herrera 1981, 265–266). By the beginning of the 1970s the investment in tourism, particularly in hotels, became attractive for the former hacienda owners.

During Velasco's government the growth of state bureaucracy and public education, the development of new areas of commerce, and the increase in public and private transportation contributed to enlarging the middle class in Cusco. The number of professionals, petty merchants, schoolteachers, bureaucrats, and *transportistas* (people who work on transportation and/or own the means of transportation) increased in Cusco city between the 1950s and the 1960s. During the 1970s and 1980s this class greatly increased in number and developed in districts of the province of Cusco such as San Jerónimo and in other provinces. Members of this social sector will be the main protagonists in the analysis of dance groups in the following chapters.

The end of the hacienda system in the countryside of Cusco resulting from Velasco's reforma agraria brought down a series of social barriers that had been the base of domination exerted by the landed elites over the peasant majorities. However, the overall attempt of this military leader to conduct a revolution from above failed. The new structures created by the military were rapidly surpassed by popular mobilizations conducted by the leftist parties (Rénique 1988, 305).

The most important nationwide corporatist organization for the development of military policies at the regional level was the Sistema Nacional de Apoyo a la Movilización Social (SINAMOS, national system of support for social mobilization). Created in 1971, SINAMOS had as its stated purpose to promote regional autonomy through the emergence of regional and local government institutions and policies that would be directly controlled by "the people and communities of Peru" (Rénique 1988, 215). SINAMOS participated in "cultural" promotion, organizing folkloric events in Cusco and at the national level. The military government's interest in promoting Andean culture and folklore should not be surprising if we consider its nationalistic and populist ideology. As shown in Velasco's statement, the government conceived of the "Peruvian problematic as a totality. This implies an integral and integrated vision of social, economic and cultural manifestations" (1972, cited by Turino 1991, 273).

Before Velasco took power and launched a renewed effort to promote folklore, regional contests and festivals promoted by Cusco city organizations had started to take a key role in the production of Cusco expressive forms. Although indigenista instituciones since the 1920s had been characterizing and categorizing "traditional" cusqueño dances, these characteristics and categorizations became more defined and their diffusion and influence grew with the proliferation of contests and folkloric festivals toward the end of the 1960s.

## CONTESTS, FESTIVALS, AND THE CONTEMPORARY REPERTOIRE OF MESTIZO AND INDIGENOUS DANCES

The first folkloric contest of wide regional impact in Cusco took place in the capital city in 1967. This contest was organized by the newly founded Comisión Municipal de la Semana del Cusco (municipal committee for the week of Cusco), which from then on replaced the Comisión Organizadora de los Festejos del Cusco in its role as organizer of the celebrations for Cusco's week. Even though this contest was called Concurso Folklórico Departamental (folkloric contest of the departamento), it had participants from the neighboring Puno and Apurímac departamentos. The trophy was named after the central symbol of the celebrations, the Inti Raymi. This contest and subsequent ones as well as the festivals promoted by the state since the 1970s have used, popularized, and developed further the models of cusqueño traditions and folklore promoted by the *instituciones*.

One interesting phenomenon that these contests and folkloric festivals started was that, gradually, a regional repertoire of folkloric dances, some classified as "indigenous" and some as "mestizo," shared by peasant and urban populations, started to consolidate. Urban and rural populations have drawn from this repertoire according to their own purposes. Quechua-speaking peasants perform "mestizo" dances in their local festivities and their regional pilgrimage sites in order to gain popularity and prestige, making themselves less indigenous. Urban, Spanish-speaking cusqueños perform "indigenous" dances in urban settings such as schools, universities, and patriotic celebrations, in order to promote and preserve this indigenous identity as a source of regional identity. Urban and rural groups also draw from this repertoire to represent themselves in folkloric events, that is, the former would perform "mestizo" dances and the latter "indigenous" dances (fig. 1).

Since the beginnings of the dramatization of the Inti Raymi in the 1940s—and thanks to the impetus of wholehearted cusqueñistas such as Vidal Unda—this ritual and the whole week surrounding the event had become an occasion to present "vernacular" or "traditional" music and dances. The most stylized of these expressive forms were presented as part of the reconstruction of the Inca ritual itself by Cusco artists such as those who belonged to the Centro Qosqo. Other folkloric music and *danza* performances, which were presented in the capital city by ad hoc groups often constituted by local town councils, participated in the contests organized by the Comisión Organizadora. In the documentation that refers to the *danzas* that were first brought into the city from the countryside to participate in these celebratory events, the terms *vernacular, traditional,* and *indigenous* are used interchangeably. In the first program of Cusco's day the term used was *típicas* (traditional; Vidal Unda 1944). The celebratory events during the "week of Cusco" also became the backdrop for Andean beauty contests, first to search for the *Qoya* (the Inca queen) and later the *Hatun Acclla* (the great Inca virgin concubine).

As mentioned above, by 1967, when the first Concurso Folklórico Departamental took place, folkloric groups from Puno and Apurímac took part in Cusco's celebrations.[32] By the late 1970s, as tourism grew in Cusco, this contest had gained national popularity, attracting folkloric groups from all over Peru. Finally, in 1989 the official competition was restricted only to representatives of the Cusco, Apurímac, and Madre de Dios departamentos, which are now part of the Región Inka.[33]

The Concurso Folklórico Departamental generated a series of other subregional events that eventually gained regional importance and/or served as the basis of state promotion. For example, this was how the Raqchi festival emerged to become one of the most important folkloric festivals of the whole region. In 1968, in the town of Raqchi (Canchis province), where a very important set of Inca monuments is located, beauty contestants and folkloric groups competed for the opportunity to participate in the Cusco city finals for the title of Hatun Acclla and the Inti Raymi trophy, respectively (*El Sol,* June 15, 1968).

While during these years the private and municipal entities were the main promoters of folklore, the military government of Velasco in the early 1970s fostered its own program to incorporate folkloric music and dance into the construction of a "truly integrated national culture that fully assumes the multiplicity of cultures of the Peruvian reality" (Instituto Nacional de Cultura 1977, 3). Aware of the multiplicity of expressive forms in Peru, Velasco wanted to create "permanent channels for cultural exchange," which, in the same way as his economic and political reforms, he wanted to control through state-administered institutions in order to unify the nation (Instituto Nacional de Cultura 1977, 3). SINAMOS, the educational system, and the newly founded Instituto Nacional de Cultura (INC, national institute of culture) had a central role in the creation of these channels.[34]

Some of the most important folkloric dance events that this government organized at the national level were the Encuentros *Inkarri* (*Inkarri* encounters or meetings).[35] These events encompassed competitions first at the district level, then at the provincial and departamento level, and finally at the national level in the Lima finals. The Encuentros *Inkarri* attempted to make peasant communities perform their own dances without needing cultural brokers such as the members of Centro Qosqo. Nevertheless, this direct state promotion failed in Cusco after a few years and did not transform but rather reinforced the models of cusqueño folklore and traditions promoted by the private instituciones, crystallized in contests such as the Concurso Departamental.

The most long-lasting, nationwide state promotion of folklore remained in the hands of the local INC.[36] During the military governments of Velasco (1968–1975) and Morales Bermúdez (1975–1980) and the following nonmilitary ones, new contests and folkloric events were instituted primarily through this state institución.[37] This state promotion and support of folklore stimulated the creation of new private instituciones culturales and the use of folkloric presentations and contests by almost every institution in urban centers (schools, ministries, sports leagues, clubs, and parishes) and by peasant organizations.[38] The proliferation of local and regional folkloric contests and presentations in the 1970s in Cusco seems to have been influenced by Velasco's attempts to give new value to Andean culture.[39] One of Velasco's most symbolic acts to revalue the status of the highland population was to change the name of El Día del Indio (the day of the Indian) to El Día del Campesino (the day of the peasant) because of the derogatory connotations of the former term. That day, July 24, a year after the coup, Velasco proclaimed the Ley de Reforma Agraria.

In a similar fashion to earlier state efforts to have peasant communities represent themselves at contests, in 1989 the most important peasant union of the region, the Federación Departamental de Campesinos del Cusco (FDCC) organized the Concurso Departamental de Música y Danza Andinas (Andean music and dance contest of the departamento). Although this contest lasted only four years, it was a particularly interesting chance to see, even in the 1990s, the central role that city artists and intellectuals still play in defining cusqueño traditions and folklore. I was able to appreciate the "particularity" of this situation because I was part of the jury for this regional contest in 1989 and 1990. In many instances the peasant leaders of the FDCC, which has been one of the most radical leftist federations of the region, requested that the urban artists and intellectuals members of the jury teach them the "right" way to perform their own traditions.

Based on this experience I became especially interested in participating in local and regional folkloric contests, in gathering information about the criteria for judging the competitors, and in learning about the characteristics expected from proper folkloric performances. I have been able to discuss these criteria and expected characteristics in group situations and in personal interviews with Cusco artists and intellectuals who are called on a regular basis to be part of the regional contests. I have also gathered printed material on the same kind of issues (i.e., guidelines), used since the first Concurso Departamental. Finally, I have collected extensive video and audio material at these events, which I have used in my analysis. Linking this information with the criteria applied by the members of local comparsas to mold their own performance, I determined that the Concurso Folklórico Departamental and subsequent contests established at least two complementary clusters of characteristics that shape how cusqueños produce and categorize folkloric dance.

The first set of characteristics corresponds to the context in which the dances are performed: in a staged competition with time constraints. In order to be competitive, the dances have to display, in a very limited time (a maximum of twenty minutes was the first time limit; Villasante

1989), three qualities: group coordination, appropriate and uniform costumes, and a creative and varied "choreography." The second is a consequence of the ethnic/racial differentiation made by the urban artists and intellectuals on the juries: there are "indigenous" and "mestizo" folkloric dances. In both cases they have to display features characteristic or "traditional" for their places of origin. That is, the performers have to show that the dances are representative of those places.

It is obvious that the organizers of the 1967 Concurso Departamental assumed that the dances they classified as indigenous and the ones they considered mestizo could compete with each other. In other words, even though the urban artist and intellectual organizers conceived mestizo and indigenous dances to be different, the mestizo ones corresponding to the organizers' practices and the indigenous to those of the peasants, both could be considered folkloric under their understanding of the term. Here one of the main contradictions of the use of the concept of folklore by urban cusqueños becomes clear: many of their own current public ritual practices were equated with those of the rural indigenous population from which they tried to differentiate themselves.

For the purpose of the first Concurso, and subsequent ones, indigenous and mestizo dances were considered comparable. Mestizo and indigenous dances are supposed to be able to meet the criteria established for these contests in order to be competitive under the category of folkloric. The guidelines of the first Concurso Departamental explicitly invited the participation of "folkloric dance groups" whose dances could be "indigenous" or "mestizo" (Villasante 1989, 179). Nevertheless, the juries established the criteria to judge what was valid or correct for each type of performance. Here the difference was of degree and theme. Indigenous music and danzas were supposed to be less elaborate, they were not supposed to display traces of industrialized materials (i.e., synthetics) in their costumes and paraphernalia, and preferably they should represent scenes that corresponded to the "authentic" ethos of Andean peasantry elaborated by the indigenista members of the early instituciones: an aggressive warrior spirit, a bucolic and peaceful communal existence, and a festive and lustful spirit.

By contrast, mestizo dances were allowed to display elaborate and synthetic costumes as well as obviously stylized choreographies. They were also permitted to evoke themes that might have become cusqueño through Spanish influence (i.e., colonial themes) or that represented aspects of urban life in the past. In order to be considered folkloric, however, these dances had to be purportedly rooted in local tradition: they had to have been part of cusqueño repertoire for some time and to be able to establish a continuity with the local and regional past. The

Figure 3. *Qhapaq Qollas* dancers of Paucartambo wearing their stylized "mestizo" costumes. Paucartambo, Cusco, 1996. Photo by Zoila S. Mendoza.

musical instruments and the melodies used for the mestizo dances could draw strongly from the *criollo* (coastal) and urban Andean tradition. For example they could use guitars, accordions, and trumpets, and incorporate *marineras*—a coastal music-dance genre (see chapter 4)—or urban-style *waynos*.

The new repertoire that emerged was configured under the parameters of contests and folkloric presentations. In the first place a folkloric dance has to have a noticeable "choreography." That is, in order to be attractive the dance needs a minimum variety of steps and coordinated movement over space, "making figures" (*haciendo figuras*) such as circles or crossing lines. The costumes, more stylized in the case of mestizo dances, have to be uniform. If the dances are indigenous, the three themes mentioned above predominate (the aggressive warrior spirit, the bucolic and peaceful communal existence, and the festive and lustful spirit). This can be seen in dances like *Ch'iaraje*,[40] which displays fights and whipping; *qhaswas* or *carnavales*, where lust and happiness are central (video example 11); and dances that show planting or harvesting (video example 12). The "mestizo" dances that have become particularly popular are those with very elaborate choreographies and costumes, which impersonate themes of Andean history such as the war of the Pacific (i.e., *Aucca Chileno*) or the role of muleteers and llama drivers in colonial and republican commerce (i.e., Majeños [figs. 11–20] and *Qhapaq Qollas* [figs. 3 and 4]).

The qhaswas or qhaswalike dances have clearly become the quintessential example of indigenous dance and musical styles in contemporary contests and festivals (video example 11; audio example 1). The Quechua name *qhaswa* has been used since colonial times to denote an indigenous dance style that is performed in a circle with the dancers holding hands.[41] In folkloric events in today's Cusco the term is commonly used to denote a peasant carnivalesque dance that is not always performed in circles but invariably features couples who play and flirt with each other's partners. The sexual connotation of qhaswas currently staged in contests and on-stage presentations is obvious.

Qhaswas are danced to the music of *kenas* or other vertical or transverse cane flutes like *pitus* and *pinkullos*, accompanied by double-headed snare drums called *cajas* or *tambores*.[42] In contrast to the use of the kena by the Centro Qosqo musicians, these wind instruments are played by Cusco peasants and herders with a dense, breathy tone that is more typical of an indigenous Andean style (Turino 1997, 232). Also in a different way than the Centro Qosqo, Cusco peasant musicians play in highly syncopated rhythms, combining these two instruments with female high-pitched voice and creating a heterophony (audio example 1). This kind of musical style, because of its link to pre-Hispanic antecedents, its identification with peasant culture, and its "rustic" or "less refined" sound as perceived by urban audiences, is still considered by cusqueños, inside and outside the competitions, to be "authentically indigenous."

Figure 4.  *Qhapaq Qollas* dancer of Paucartambo, Cusco, 1996. Photo by Zoila S. Mendoza.

One of the most characteristic elements of the qhaswa music is that the lyrics refer metaphorically and explicitly to fertility and coupling. There is, for example, widespread metaphoric use of ripe fruit or a flower to refer to women, and often a very explicit call for finding a partner of the opposite sex. It is likely that the qhaswa performed in the

1920s by the Misión Artística and the Centro Qosqo contained sexual and reproductive allusions as well, since its name was *T'ika Qhaswa* (qhaswa of the flowers).

In Cusco the mestizo danzas of Paucartambo have gained particular regional recognition. This has been more obvious since they were awarded the Inti Raymi trophy and the title of *Provincia Folklórica* (folkloric province) after having won three Concursos Departamentales. "Paucartambo danzas," as they gradually came to be known regionally, were characterized already at the first Concurso Departamental by very sophisticated music and choreography and very elegant and expensive costumes. This was so obvious that *paucartambinos* (people of Paucartambo) added the Quechua adjective *qhapaq* (which could mean "wealthy," "powerful," or "elegant") to the name of some of their dances. Since at least the 1940s, Paucartambo mestizos who had migrated to Cusco or who were well acquainted with regional and national urban culture had incorporated elements from these contexts into their music and dance for religious festivities. Known as famous artisans and performers, the inhabitants of the town of Paucartambo had turned their patron-saint festivity into a center of attraction for outsiders.

Among the Paucartambo danzas that were awarded prizes or were considered top finalists in the Concurso Departamental were *Saqras* (an allusion to the Catholic devil), the winner of the first contest (audio example 2); *Contradanza* (country-dance or European square dance; figs. 5 and 6), winner of the second contest; *Qhapaq Qollas* (wealthy llama herders and merchants from the Qollao area; figs. 3 and 4); *Qhapaq Ch'uncho* (wealthy or powerful "savage" inhabitants of the rain forest); and *Qhapaq Negros* (elegant black slaves; figs. 7 and 8; audio example 3). Some competitors and some Cusco city residents accused Paucartambo mestizos of being *arreglistas* (someone who fixes up a piece to make it look or sound better) and *arribistas* (arriviste) artisans (Ramos Carpio n.d., 3). These accusations arose because their dances did not appear to be traditional, having too many new elements. However, this novelty seems to have been central to their subsequent regional popularity. "Paucartambo danzas" were also promoted though Paucartambo's own patron-saint festivity, which in the 1970s entered the tourist circuit.[43] Since the 1940s jeronimianos have incorporated Paucartambo danzas into their fiesta. Two chapters in this book deal extensively with the dances that have become "traditional" for San Jerónimo: Majeños and Qollas.

The markers of mestizo and indigenous identity described above have come together with some aspects of bodily practice that are emphasized in the performance of folkloric danzas. Here I want to stress two aspects

Figure 5. Machu or leader of Paucartambo *Contradanza,* a "mestizo" danza representing the European country-dance. Paucartambo, Cusco, 1996. Photo by Zoila S. Mendoza.

of this practice that seem to be central in differentiating the bodies of Indians and mestizos for members of juries and performers alike: the first relates to posture and the second to movement.

I have found not only in contests and staged presentations but also in comparsa ritual performances that an upright posture, slower, sometimes swaying movements, and minimized foot-stomping *(zapateo)*—the last characteristic of Andean dance—is often associated with what is considered mestizo performance (video examples 13 and 14). On the other hand, indigenous dances are often performed hunched over, stooping low to the ground and displaying jerky, quick movements (fig. 1). Also

Figure 6.    Paucartambo *Contradanza* performer during the patron-saint fiesta of that town. Paucartambo, Cusco, 1996. Photo by Zoila S. Mendoza.

Figure 7. *Qhapaq Negros,* a "mestizo" danza of Paucartambo during the patron-saint fiesta of that town. Paucartambo, Cusco, 1996. Photo by Zoila S. Mendoza.

individual and couple twirling is almost always present in indigenous dances. Hard, fast, and marked zapateo as well as short, quick hopping steps are characteristics of this style as well (video example 11). When nonpeasants perform "indigenous dances," these markers are almost always more exaggerated (video example 12).

In the ensuing analysis of the Majeños danza I show how keeping an upright posture inside and outside the dance is associated among cusqueños not only with an air of arrogance and haughtiness but also with tallness and whiteness. On the other hand, hunched-over posture is associated with an attitude of subservience and with agricultural activities, therefore with the indigenous peasantry. In particular I show how the kinds of movements considered characteristic of mestizos are seen by jeronimianos as more controlled and therefore more "elegant" and "decent." In the chapter about the Qollas I reveal that the jerky, quick, twirling movements considered characteristic of indigenous people are seen as uncontrolled and unpolished. In the context of competition and staged presentations in Cusco city and other regional folkloric events these indigenous-like movements, especially stooping over, match very well the themes of agricultural activities and drunkenness of indigenous danzas, making the "Indians" "closer to the earth" (Orlove 1998).

It seems that the use of neckerchiefs or handkerchiefs in mestizo performances and of *warak'as* (woven wool slings) in indigenous performances emphasizes this contrast of movement and posture. The soft, stylized way in which the neckerchiefs and handkerchiefs are used in the mestizo dances emphasizes the slower, swaying movements of the

Figure 8. *Qhapaq Negros.* Photo by Zoila S. Mendoza.

performers (video examples 13 and 14). The use of warak'as to whip or tie down a dance partner in an often quick, unexpected move gives form to the idea of the aggressive, uncontrolled indigenous identity (video example 11).

Throughout the history of folkloric contests in Cusco, conflicts have emerged among competitors, among jurors, between competitors and juries, and between juries and the general public about the criteria used to evaluate the folkloric danzas and to select a winner. At the base of these conflicts has been the vulnerability of the criteria for differentiating the "indigenous" from the "mestizo," the "authentic" from the non-"authentic," and the "traditional" from the non-"traditional." One example of these conflicts is the controversy over the nontraditional form of Paucartambo danzas. Another example is a disagreement that emerged among the members of the jury in one of the contests organized by the peasant federation—of which I was part—over the authenticity of some costumes that used synthetic materials. A final example is the ever-present complaint of the public when the juries select a particularly well-coordinated dance full of stereotypical movements and props representing "indigenous identity," over one which, not as well choreographed, is closer to a performance carried out by the rural population whose identity is purportedly being represented by the other danza.

Although public and private instituciones culturales have attempted to establish boundaries around the forms and meanings of highland music and dance by classifying them as folkloric and modeling them after "invented traditions," these expressive forms have constantly surpassed these boundaries even in the context of contests and other staged presentations. Outside this context the performers who consider their music and dance folkloric have used this concept to validate their creative efforts and to gain new spaces and recognition for their performances. Thanks to this acknowledgment within the regional and national arena, the performers of Andean music and dance have been able to give new meanings to these performances. Even though the concept of folklore has pejoratively marked the performances of Andean music and dance at the national level (mostly because these forms are supposed to represent the highlanders), and many gender and ethnic/racial stereotypes have been fostered through folkloric events, this concept has helped legitimate a field wherein some sectors of cusqueño society can contest ethnic/racial, gender, and social-class identity.

Cusco city intellectuals and artists have confronted a crucial paradox in the attempt to configure their identity: while they wanted to consolidate a regional culture, they also needed to establish differences between themselves and the "indigenous" and peasant population. In the face of this paradox they found effective media to define their identity in the concept of folklore and their idea of authentic cusqueño traditions that idealize and romanticize the Inca past and rural present. In doing so they have shaped new forms and concepts, such as mestizo dances and indigenous dances that address and give specific form to ethnic/racial identity in Cusco and Peru. These forms and concepts have both influenced and been influenced by the symbolic practices at the local level, such as that of San Jerónimo and Paucartambo comparsas, which have been aimed at the redefinition of local distinctions and identities.

# The People of San Jerónimo, Their Lives, and Their Main Ritual in Regional and Historical Perspectives

People of San Jerónimo live neither a thoroughly rural nor an urban life; as the mayor of the town put it in 1994, they "are permanently between the city and the countryside" (Centro Guaman Poma de Ayala 1994, 15). During my research the majority still practiced small-scale, part-time agriculture while having another or more than one occupation that frequently took them to Cusco city, which they could reach in half an hour's bus ride. This in-between-ness and back and forth movement has had important implications in terms of the ethnic/racial and class identities of jeronimianos. In Cusco the rural world, still a strong presence in jeronimianos' lives, is associated with "Indianness" and the urban with "mestizoness" (see chapter 1). This somehow ambiguous ethnic/racial situation of the people of this town seems to have made it even more imperative for members of emergent socioeconomic groups to perform "mestizo" danzas in their most important public ritual. Through this performance, members of the new local petite bourgeoisie have devoted their efforts to blurring the differences between themselves and Cusco urban elites. In doing this, they have also distinguished themselves from the rest of their fellow townspeople, becoming the new local "mestizos."

## THE PARISH OF SAN JERÓNIMO: CHURCH, LOCAL POWER, AND IDENTITY DURING THE COLONIAL PERIOD

The colonial civil/religious organization shaped contemporary Andean social organization and ritual practices. The town or village of San Jerónimo was founded under the civil/religious reorganization of the population by Viceroy Toledo in the 1570s. San Jerónimo was the head (center) of the parish of the same name, one of seven that belonged to Cusco city. The history of the area where the Spanish founded this town had been marked by its closeness to the city of Cusco since the Inca period.[1] The areas surrounding the Inca capital, as explained in chapter 1, were occupied by Incas-by-privilege, conquered groups that were granted land in the valley and that periodically had to be represented at the court of the Inca (Zuidema 1990).[2] The members of the Inca and Inca-by-privilege nobility that survived the drastic population decline after the conquest became members of "Indian" parishes and were resettled in Spanish-style villages, or reducciones.

During Spanish colonialism the parishes of San Jerónimo and San Sebastián were known as the homes of noble Inca descendants (Blanco 1974, vol. 2, 113). Contemporary inhabitants of both districts proudly comment on this noble background, pointing out that they still have Inca last names.[3] Adopting Inca last names and claiming to have been part of the Inca nobility was a strategy developed during the colonial period in order to avoid various burdens imposed on common "Indians" and to have access to various privileges. Nevertheless, the important political posts assigned to indigenous people resettled in those villages, and their children's access to formal education in the special schools that the Spanish created for the Inca nobility, reveal that they were able to establish Inca ancestry (Blanco 1974, vol. 2, 113).

In the period of more than a year that Toledo spent in Cusco, he elaborated detailed *ordenanzas* (codes of regulations), which attempted to regulate almost every aspect of religious and civil life. During the colonial period both realms, the civil and the religious, were closely intertwined.[4] For example, his ordenanzas created structures that combined civil and religious posts in local organization and that came to be known as the "fiesta cargo system" (Fuenzalida 1976; see chapter 1). In every parish the priest was assigned as the main local representative of the "civilizing" mission assumed by the Spaniards. The priests lived among the "Indians" in order to evangelize them, through the Catholic sacraments (baptism, confession, marriage, Sunday mass, and wake) and through public communal rituals (Spalding 1984, ch. 8).

The parish of San Jerónimo was assigned for most of the colonial period (from the sixteenth century until 1759) to the "preaching" order, also known as the Dominicans (Ramos n.d., 5).[5] Besides being in charge of this parish the order had an *estancia* (ranch) named Pata Pata in the jurisdiction of San Jerónimo. According to a report from the parish priest of San Jerónimo, in 1690 there were four haciendas and two estancias in the territory of the parish. The four haciendas belonged to Spaniards residing in Cusco city; one of the estancias was owned by the Dominicans and the other by the Mercedarians.[6] In this same period (1690), the main economic activity of this Indian parish (there were only three Spanish families of a total of 450 people who lived in this parish's jurisdiction) was agricultural production, mostly corn and some wheat and other vegetables (Ramos n.d.). By the beginning of the next century the Dominicans had increased the amount of their property in San Jerónimo, and their estancia became the hacienda Pata Pata.[7]

San Jerónimo was a wealthy parish; the post of *cura* (parish priest) of San Jerónimo must have been very sought after by the local clergy. During the colonial period, becoming a parish priest was generally one of the most effective ways of accumulating personal wealth. The parishes were assigned land, livestock, and Indian labor. In San Jerónimo more than half of the income of the parish came from the production of its land, which was worked by the members of the local communities (Ramos n.d., 6). The priest also collected fees that the parishioners had to pay for ecclesiastical services (i.e., at weddings, funerals, and fiestas) and had personal servants who took care of his properties. The collection of these fees and services seems to have been an important benefit for the cura and for that same reason an opportunity to abuse the local people.[8]

Further research needs to be done on the relationship between parish properties, cofradías (religious lay brotherhoods; see chapter 1), and communal organization throughout the colonial and early republican periods in Cusco. There are indications that during the colonial period members of local communities contributed large amounts of labor and material wealth to the local parish (Ramos n.d., 21). Even though it is not clear how much the local population was forced (as opposed to volunteering) to work on the parish land or to use part of the production of their own land to finance religious festivities, in San Jerónimo there seems to have been massive participation by the local population in the economic activities of the church.[9]

Celestino and Meyers (1981) have demonstrated for the case of the central Peruvian Andes that transferring property to the church, as a gift to the parish or to a cofradía, was used as a strategy by the local communities to keep communal property under their control. These authors have also shown that cofradías offered an important medium for the organization of local collective life and for the reorganization of the previously existing local communities called *ayllus* that were brought together in the colonial parishes. Anthropologists and ethnohistorians have spent considerable effort trying to define the key concept of ayllu, fundamental to understanding Andean social organization over an extensive period of time, from pre-Inca times to the present.[10] Although the concept has definitely changed over time, it is clear now that even since the pre-Hispanic period it has been more flexible than first conceived by chroniclers and early Andeanists.[11] As the most recent studies show, "The social frontier of the ayllu is imminently—and quite literally—political in that it adapts itself to the needs of a given context or situation" (Poole 1984, 146). In San Jerónimo the ayllus, sometimes called *parcialidades* (when their territorial aspect was emphasized), provided the politico-administrative organizational basis for the participation of the local indigenous population in the civil and religious obligations imposed upon by the colonial state.

During the colonial period in San Jerónimo, the relationship between the local parish and the ayllus was not an easy one. To begin with, the resources that Toledo assigned to the local parish had formerly belonged to local ayllus. It is difficult to find documentation that would show how the parish properties expanded during the colonial period; the local parish was not interested in keeping careful records of this process, and in its documents it tended to hide the real amount of property it had (Ramos n.d., 9). Nevertheless, the existence of lawsuits between ayllus and the local parish over the possession of lands and the legal accusations against the local cura for stealing precious jewels from the church (jewels bought with the product of communal work) signal a conflictual relationship between these two institutions in the town of San Jerónimo (ibid., 10, 14).

In San Jerónimo as in other Andean towns the cofradía seems to have been the middle ground or compromising institution that facilitated negotiation between the church and the local population.[12] While the first cofradías were imposed (because according to Toledo every parish should at least institute a cofradía to celebrate the local *advocación,* or name given to the parish after a Catholic "saint"), these religious lay brotherhoods soon proliferated in Andean towns, and San Jerónimo was no exception. These institutions seem to have mediated conflicts not only between church and local communities but also between different local communities. In 1689 there were at least twelve cofradías in San Jerónimo, and this number continued to grow into the beginning of the republican period.

The Catholic festivals themselves, sponsored by cofradías, in particular the danzas performed in those rituals, became an arena of confrontation and negotiation of symbolic practices and identity during the colonial period. As explained in chapter 1, the massive participation of the indigenous population in Catholic rituals through the performance of danzas, and the constant preoccupation with and at times repression of these forms, has suggested to some students of the subject that these

expressive forms channeled the capacity for contestation and accommodation of this population during the colonial period (Ares Queija 1984;
Poole 1990a; Estenssoro 1992).

After independence San Jerónimo parish documentation did not
acknowledge the existence of cofradías. All the property destined to
finance the cult of the images seems to have been collapsed with the rest
of the parish properties under one administration (Ramos n.d., 35).[13]
Nevertheless, as late as 1935 a separate account of the properties of at
least twenty local images celebrated in the town was kept in the parish
records (Parroquia de San Jerónimo 1935, 1956).

## SAN JERÓNIMO AND THE CITY OF CUSCO:
## CHANGES SINCE THE 1940S

Since the 1940s various interrelated processes transformed Cusco region, creating possibilities for the people of San Jerónimo to reshape
their ethnic/racial and class identities. The most relevant have been the
gradual shift of the axis of the region's economy toward the capital city
(most clearly marked after the city's growth and modification following
the 1950 earthquake), the demise of the hacienda system in the region,
and the emergence of new socioeconomic sectors linked to the growth
of the state and to the improvement of infrastructure (i.e., roads,
schools) in the surrounding areas of the capital city.

While independence from Spain had been official for over a century,
and soon after that San Jerónimo was recognized as a district (1825;
Centro Guaman Poma de Ayala 1994, 18),[14] in the early 1940s a
landowning elite still dominated San Jerónimo economically and politically.[15] Seventy to eighty percent of the arable land was owned by either religious orders or *mistis* (also known as *hacendados* or *gamonales;*
Rodríguez 1942, 10–11). The latter landowning class had grown in
this district as in most of Cusco since the end of the nineteenth century.
The members of this new social group, who developed innovative
cultural and economic mechanisms to consolidate their local power,
had expanded their estates, usually at the expense of the local peasantry
(Poole 1988). During this period, although a variety of labor relations
existed on the estates, the notion of a clear division between the powerful hacendado and the subservient peasant developed (Tamayo Herrera
1981, 50).[16]

This picture of San Jerónimo started to change by the mid-1940s.
While the hacendados remained in San Jerónimo until the 1970s, beginning in the 1940s the members of local ayllus, whose rights were

recognized by state institutions promoted by indigenistas, started to fight and win battles against local landowners over the possession of land.[17] At the same time, the members of this district started to diversify their economic activities and a new socioeconomic sector, a petite bourgeoisie, began to grow as the kernel of a local middle class. This sector, still incipient in the forties, developed as a result of the increasingly important role of San Jerónimo in providing goods, services, and labor to Cusco city, which was emerging as the most important market of the region. Even though commerce had been an important activity in San Jerónimo since colonial times, a larger segment of the population became involved in this activity during this and the following decades. Obviously not everyone could profit equally from this growing economic activity. Those who had the means to combine commerce and ownership of motor vehicles (emerging as the most important mode of transportation) could obtain a more advantageous position within the new economic sector.

These local and regional trends became accentuated during the reconstruction of Cusco city after the 1950 earthquake, leading to deeper transformations during the 1970s. The city offered even more opportunities for the people of San Jerónimo to earn wages as laborers (in construction or at state or private institutions) and to offer their services as artisans (i.e., stonemasons, carpenters, and tailors). Jeronimianos had easy access to the city market, where they sold what they produced and bought or exchanged in more remote provinces. The town of San Jerónimo, capital of the district, gained regional recognition through its Sunday market. The town also started to benefit gradually from the infrastructural and sanitary improvements from foreign and state investment in the Huatanay valley.[18]

While economic diversification grew in San Jerónimo during the 1960s, the people of this district continued to fight against the landowning elite. In 1963 there were new attempts to take over some of the lands of Pata Pata and Larapa haciendas, which still belonged to the Dominican order (Centro Guaman Poma de Ayala 1994, 19). By the end of the decade, and under an incipient agrarian reform law enacted by President Belaúnde, the largest current *comunidad campesina* (peasant community), at that point still called *comunidad de indígenas* (Indian community), had been formed by various former ayllus and had received the official possession of a large portion of land and water rights. Also, former sharecroppers of the Pata Pata hacienda had signed a final sale agreement to become the official owners of the well-irrigated land owned by the Dominican order. Finally, during this decade state projects (such as the promotion of credit for the peasantry and the expansion of the educational system) started to benefit the middle class in San Jerónimo.[19]

During the next decade (the 1970s), and under the more radical reforms of president Velasco's government, many of the ongoing changes in San Jerónimo crystallized. The large, privately owned estates ceased to exist in the district, and the land was either sold to private buyers or granted to the recognized comunidades de indígenas, which under a new statute from Velasco were to be called comunidades campesinas. In both cases the former arable land of the valley was apportioned for new housing developments or as small plots of land in the hands of hundreds of small farmers organized in comunidades. During this decade urban economic activities grew among jeronimianos who benefited from the increasing economic importance of Cusco city in the region. The economic activities of this capital city increased during the 1970s with the new booming industry, tourism. By the beginning of this decade the town of San Jerónimo was already providing a wide range of services to the city through commerce, transportation, wage labor, and craftsmanship. Most women of the town were involved in petty commerce, and most men were craftsmen (tailors, carpenters, cobblers, hatters, masons, and so on), truck drivers, state employees, domestic servants, and wage earners. Most townspeople combined these enterprises with small-scale agriculture and limited livestock raising (van den Berghe and Primov 1977, 203).

The sociologists Pierre van den Berghe and George Primov (1977, 204) described the town of San Jerónimo in the early 1970s.

> Were it not for our reluctance to use the term, the simplest shorthand label that we could use to describe San Jerónimo would be *cholo*. The town exhibits most of the characteristics that anthropologists have associated with this term: 85 to 90 per cent of the urban population is neither clearly mestizo nor clearly Indian but somewhere in the middle of the continuum. . . . The cultural character of the town has a hybrid flavor, clearly distinct from both the city of Cuzco and from the remote Indian areas.

While van den Berghe and Primov explain the local status divisions along "ethnic" and "class" lines (clarifying also that *cholo* is a term that jeronimianos use to designate persons of a lower status than themselves), they point out that "categorical, unambiguous, and consensually accepted cleavages are not found anywhere on that wide status continuum" (205). Whereas van den Berghe and Primov's description of the indicators of status is quite accurate, their analysis of local identity in San Jerónimo has at least one main limitation. These authors did not analyze the mechanisms by which local people gave new meaning to and manipulated those indicators to place themselves within local and regional society. In other words, van den Berghe and Primov's analysis is static in the sense that, once they had established the indicators and the categories of status, assigning a certain fixed and objective reality to them, they tried to explain how much the local people fit into those categories. This kind of analysis prevented them from understanding the complex social and cultural reality of San Jerónimo, as evidenced by their saying that the town had a "hybrid flavor."

I argue that for the people of San Jerónimo their patron-saint festivity and their comparsas have been important realms where local distinctions and identities have been redefined. Forming comparsas and becoming the main sponsors of the central ritual festivity of the town has allowed members of emergent social groups to become distinct from each other and from other social groups. It has also allowed the members of these groups to give local meaning to categories on the basis of which this distinction is constructed. By the end of the 1940s members of an incipient local urban petite bourgeoisie made their first attempt to make the patron-saint festivity a place where they could introduce new local values that they impersonated. This group, led by *transportistas-ganaderos* (truck owners and drivers–cattle dealers), formed the Majeños comparsa and performed for the first time a danza in the patron-saint festivity. Only in the 1970s did this festivity itself become an important realm in which the Majeños and other local comparsas could become central ritual sponsors and start being acknowledged as distinct groups within the town through their performance.

## THE TOWN OF SAN JERÓNIMO IN THE LATE 1980S

Various characteristics and trends described by van den Berghe and Primov (1977) regarding the social and cultural reality of the town of San Jerónimo in the early 1970s remained true throughout the 1980s. The people of San Jerónimo continued to live neither a thoroughly rural life (such as that in smaller towns in the more remote areas of the departamento) nor an urban life (such as that in Cusco city). Nevertheless, by the late 1980s the use of Spanish in jeronimianos' everyday life had increased; they had reached higher levels of formal education;[20] a larger percentage of the population had become part of the urban petite bourgeoisie; and the patron-saint festivity of the town was dominated by mestizo danzas. Therefore most cusqueños and social scientists would agree that the best ethnic/racial characterization of the town would be to call it mestizo.

Since the 1970s the role of the town within the district has changed. Until then, the colonial town and its immediate surroundings *(radio urbano)*, all of which I call the town of San Jerónimo, had contained most of the urban population of the district. The rest of the district territory was mostly plotted land and partially cultivated high mountains.[21] But since the 1970s the growing urban population of the district and the Huatanay valley as a whole has inhabited new settlements built on the previously plotted land; these are known as *asentamientos humanos.* In the late 1980s, only about half of the twenty different asentamientos could properly be called urban. This half has access to running water, electricity, and sewage systems (Posta Médica de San Jerónimo 1990: Proyecto Ununchis n.d. a, b, c).

San Jerónimo's asentamientos and those that belong to the district of San Sebastián have formed a chain between the capital city and the town.[22] The great population increase during the urban expansion of Cusco city (which since 1979 officially includes the districts of San Jerónimo and San Sebastián) has resulted from immigration from other provinces of the departamento and, to a lesser degree, from other departamentos of the southern highlands.[23] Although there has been no demographic study of the district of San Jerónimo that considered this aspect, I determined with a survey that much of the population living in the new asentamientos, approximately 30 percent of the population of the district, is not originally from San Jerónimo and has moved there in the last twenty years (Mendoza 1990).

By the late 1980s the town of about 8,000 people continued to contain those who were originally from San Jerónimo or were married to people from this district.[24] Most of the families who resided in this town, approximately 80 percent, were members of one of the four largest comunidades campesinas.[25] However, the fact that these people belonged to a comunidad campesina belies the fact that most of them practiced only small-scale, part-time agriculture. The weight that this activity had in the family economy, of course, varied among the members of these communities and between communities according to the size of the plots or to the access to irrigation.[26] Nevertheless, the great division of the arable land into small plots and the depressed prices for agricultural products made agriculture only a supplementary economic activity for these families.[27] For the approximately 20 percent of this population who practice agriculture, this activity represented half of their income, and for 45 percent only one-fourth or less (Mendoza 1990). While agriculture is not a lucrative economic activity in Cusco or in

Peru, it is more profitable for people such as jeronimianos who are able to directly commercialize their own products. They can easily sell them in their own Sunday market or every day in Cusco city. Women of the town are in charge of most of this commercialization.

Apart from agriculture, in which both men and women participate more or less equally, the other economic activities in the town of San Jerónimo are clearly but not strictly divided by gender. As described by van den Berghe and Primov for the 1970s, by the late 1980s most of the women of the town continued to be involved in some kind of petty commerce.[28] Women are in charge of most *tiendas de abarrotes* (retail stores), *chicherías* (where corn beer *[chicha]* is sold), and restaurants. There are at least 460 of these *establecimientos comerciales* (commercial establishments) in the town.[29] As mentioned above, women are in charge of most of the commercialization of the surplus agricultural products sold in the local market or in Cusco together with other bought goods. A very popular product sold by jeronimianos is meat that is usually bought in another province by the husband or a male relative of the woman who sells it in the market. The women in charge of the establecimientos comerciales also sell their retail products, drinks, and food in the Sunday market of the town.

One of the features that still distinguishes San Jerónimo from Cusco city is the strong and visible presence of market women.[30] These women, known as *cholas* in anthropological literature (Seligman 1989) and by city dwellers, and as *mestizas* by the people of San Jerónimo, have developed a very distinct character over the decades. Because of the key economic and cultural role of these market women as mediators or brokers between rural and urban society (i.e., selling agricultural products from the countryside in the city), they have remained a distinct and visible group. Throughout Cusco, market women "stand out in their tall, white stovepipe hats with wide, black, or colored band; their many cotton or velveteen *pullera [pollera]* skirts; brightly colored polyester sweaters; . . . and money purses bulging beneath their skirts" (Seligman 1989, 703). During my research most of San Jerónimo's townswomen above forty years of age more or less fit Seligman's description (fig. 9); they were also bilingual, and the language they used most was Quechua. In general, adult women of San Jerónimo have had very limited access to formal education; most of them, approximately 70 percent, only have primary education (Mendoza 1990). This necessarily has limited their Spanish competence, because in Peru formal education is carried out in Spanish and school is the medium through which most highland people have improved their use of Spanish beyond the functional level.

These women's economic activities are often not conceptualized as

Figure 9.   San Jerónimo women preparing guinea pigs for a celebration. San Jerónimo, Cusco, 1990. Photo by Zoila S. Mendoza.

work by either men or women. As De la Cadena (1991) has argued, in the gender hierarchies established by cusqueño dominant ideology, the activities of women in the house (which include the management of chicherías, restaurants, and stores) and in the markets are not considered work. According to this ideology women are considered less capable of working or unable to accomplish "better work," because on the one hand "good work" requires physical strength and on the other it requires that the activity be linked to certain urban activities (e.g., driving) and specialized skills (e.g., technical knowledge). In the Cusco region, as De la Cadena (1991) explains, the ideologies about gender and ethnicity come together in one hierarchy that establishes the person's capabilities to work. At the bottom is often the "Indian" woman and at the top the urban man. According to these ideologies urban people know how to work "better" than "Indians" (here synonymous with peasants), and women are not as strong or as efficient as men in accomplishing "good" work (ibid.).

With the increase of formal education among the female population, by the late 1980s women in their thirties and in particular those in their twenties had started to question some aspects of this dominant ideology. Through higher education and technical training, some women, still not the majority, had started to have access to urban, skilled occupations (among them accountants, teachers, and nurses).[31] Young women, first through sports and social clubs (since the mid-1970s) and later through comparsas (since the beginning of the 1980s), have started to participate in larger numbers and more actively in public events. They formerly either were excluded from or occupied a more passive role in these events. It should also be pointed out that, while the generational gap is much more visible among women, it is also apparent among men, who, like women, through easier access to higher education, urban skilled occupations, and the growing influence of national and international mass media have adopted a much more cosmopolitan outlook than the older generations of men. This novel cosmopolitan outlook among men and women is also evident in their comparsas, through which young jeronimianos are struggling to impose their views against the dominant regional ideology about cusqueño traditions (see chapter 6).

The occupations among adult townsmen have continued to diversify since the early 1970s. Nevertheless, throughout the eighties the urban petite bourgeoisie (formed by professionals; cattle dealers; truck, bus, and car owners and drivers, usually combined with wholesale commerce in the case of the truck owners; state and private employees; and technicians) has grown to make up approximately half of the population (Mendoza 1990). Within this broad group a new local elite has consolidated, and comparsas have played an important role in its social and cultural configuration. Since the mid-1970s comparsas and their patron-saint festivity became for the members of this urban petite bourgeoisie an important medium for becoming instrumental in the town's incorporation into regional mestizo culture, for gaining local social recognition, and for establishing distinctions among themselves. The remaining half of adult men who continue to be occupied as craftsmen (i.e., tailors, masons, carpenters, and tile makers) and as unskilled wage earners (i.e., as *obreros* [janitors or laborers] at hospitals, the experimental farm in the district, universities, or municipalities; or as *cobradores* [bus conductors]) tend to have a more limited participation in comparsas for the patron-saint festivity.[32]

Transportation is one of the activities that has grown the most in San Jerónimo since the early 1970s. By 1990, 20 percent of the population of the town worked in transportation as their main economic activity (Mendoza 1990). Of this percentage those who benefit most from that activity, the owners of the means of transportation, are still less than half. It is interesting to note that the four main comparsas of the town, two formed by adults and two by youngsters, tend to contain people who either work in transportation or are young children of these people. During my research three of the four comparsas were clearly conceptualized by townspeople as belonging to transportistas. The Majeños is considered to be the comparsa of the *propietarios de carro,* which means owners of a truck, bus, or automobile. The Qollas is considered a comparsa of some truck owners and mostly truck drivers. Finally, the Tuntuna is considered the comparsa of the children of the bus owners.

The living conditions and the physical environment of the town of San Jerónimo in the late 1980s continued to have both rural and urban characteristics. Two-story houses (characteristic of the city as opposed to the one-story houses in more rural towns) had started to predominate (approximately 60 percent of the total houses of the town), but these houses still reproduced some of the old patterns of space distribution: a large open space, a sort of patio, is in the middle, and rooms are not specialized or individualized (i.e., various children of different ages sleep in the same room and sometimes with their parents). The majority of households raised animals mostly for consumption (85 percent raised guinea pigs and 66 percent chickens), and they alternated between kerosene stoves and traditional wood stoves for cooking (73 percent of the households still used wood stoves and 63 percent alternated between kerosene and wood). Most houses had a rudimentary electricity system (90 percent), a black-and-white television set (80 percent), a radio (100 percent), and a tape player (80 percent). Access to running water varied according to the location of the house, but less than a third of the population had access to running water all day, and most of the houses (75 percent) had only one faucet in the house, which was usually located in the patio.[33]

The town of San Jerónimo is surrounded by extensive areas of unpopulated land (including the slopes of the high mountains located in the district), of which some is cultivated, and, especially to the north, some large areas are planted with pine trees. San Jerónimo is also well connected with the city through private and public bus lines and by taxis, most of which are owned or driven by jeronimianos.[34] The flow of people between both points is constant, although during the week this flow is stronger from the town to the city. On weekends, especially on Sundays, the contrary occurs, since most jeronimianos stay in town and people from Cusco come to the local restaurants, chicherías, and most often to the Sunday market. This market is very popular for the good, cheap meat and vegetables sold there. An intense daily flow of hundreds of trucks, buses, and cars drive through the main avenue of

San Jerónimo, Manco Ccapac, which is also one of the main commercial roads of the region, connecting Cusco city with other important trade centers of the region.

Only since 1980 has San Jerónimo been able to democratically elect its local municipal government and to participate fully in national elections.[35] The political scene started to change in the 1970s when local university students, affiliated with leftist national political parties and with the Cusco University student federation, organized protests and demanded various political and economic reforms from the departmental government and from local elites.[36] At the time of my research the mayor had been in office since 1981 (that year he replaced the mayor elected in 1980, and since 1983 he has been reelected). Between 1980 and 1988 this mayor was a representative of the national leftist coalition Izquierda Unida (united left). In 1989 he became a representative of Izquierda Popular (popular left), the more radical faction that split from Izquierda Unida at the national level.[37] In local elections all the main political parties of the nation have had representatives, but since 1980 Izquierda Unida (and in 1989 both Izquierda Unida and Izquierda Popular) have had the majority of the votes. In the 1990 national elections, however, following the crisis at the national level of leftist parties and a national trend that rejects the traditional political parties of the nation, the population voted overwhelmingly for the current president, Alberto Fujimori.[38]

Even though, as mentioned in chapter 1, the Shinning Path guerrilla movement failed to gain strong support in the Cusco region, during my research, fear of guerrilla attacks and of state repression, as well as worsening living conditions due to the severe economic crisis of the country, were clearly part of San Jerónimo's reality and that of most Peruvians. While I lived in the town I was warned against socializing with one or two young males who people suspected had been recruited by Shining Path. I never saw or heard any proof about such membership; it is likely that those young men were just politically opinionated and supported leftist ideals. There were also sporadic comments about attempts by this guerrilla movement to recruit young people of San Jerónimo as they did in many areas of the Peruvian Andes.

## SAINT JEROME AND HIS FESTIVITY IN THE TOWN

Saint Jerome has been the local patron saint since the foundation of the town of San Jerónimo. The physical representation of this saint that is worshipped during the fiesta, the *imagen* (the icon), is a large, impressive

Figure 10. Imagen of Saint Jerome during the Corpus Christi procession. Cusco city, 1990. Photo by Fritz Villasante.

statue (2.17 meters tall) made by an indigenous sculptor during the colonial period (Rodríguez 1942, 11).[39] In this statue Saint Jerome is portrayed as a middle-aged, tall white man with rosy cheeks, curly dark hair, and a long thick beard. He wears a wide-brimmed hat, gloves, and a long red-and-white gown that reaches his feet and replicates that of a Catholic cardinal. Saint Jerome is standing in a very upright position, holding in his left arm a silver replica of the town's church on top of a Bible. His right hand is raised, holding a golden quill. This imagen is regionally known and admired as one of the most majestic participants in the Corpus Christi celebration in Cusco city (fig. 10). The people of San Jerónimo proudly participate in this regional ritual re-creating the important position that their parish and their imagen had in relation to the colonial civil/religious administrative center, Cusco city. Saint Jerome's imposing figure corresponds to his widely acknowledged and respected personality as a doctor of the church.[40] Contemporary jeronimianos, through their prayers, songs, and miracle and punishment stories, acknowledge this saint as a powerful and potentially dangerous intermediary between the unknown (i.e., death, sickness, good fortune) and their everyday lives.

This imagen is kept during the year on a separate altar on the left side of the church aisle. Along this aisle are various other altars, but the one for the patron saint stands out clearly because of its arrangement and the quantity of flowers and candles lit in his honor. The imagen is brought out of this altar only twice a year, for the Corpus Christi celebration in Cusco and for the local patron-saint festivity. Only selected people— ritual sponsors or people in charge of taking care of the possessions of the temple (i.e., the *ecónomo*)—have the honor of touching the image while changing its clothes or placing it on the *andas* (litter or portable platform).

This imagen has become for jeronimianos a central symbol of their identity as dwellers in that town, and his fiesta is San Jerónimo's quintessential community "tradition." But "traditions" are always kept, "invented," or re-created by particular groups within society. In the case of San Jerónimo, not only have comparsas, like the cofradías before them, become the main sponsors and promoters of this festivity, but their danzas have become the focus of attention of jeronimianos and outsiders during the fiesta.[41] In their discourse about their main role as ritual sponsors and as danza performers, comparsa members of San Jerónimo exalt their key position as intermediaries in a double sense: as representatives of their fellow townspeople to the patron saint of jeronimianos and as the representatives of local "folklore."

During my research in 1989 and 1990, a month and a half before the central date of the fiesta (September 30) clear signs that this celebration was approaching began to appear. Firecrackers, live and recorded loud music of the local danzas, and excitement around the church and the main plaza announced to jeronimianos that preparations for this event were taking place. Townspeople who already roughly knew who the main sponsors of the fiesta were for that year and who were going to join a comparsa began to confirm their information at this time. The local municipality convened meetings at which the leaders of all the organizations of the town (ritual and nonritual) and all the local civil and military authorities, including the parish priest, participated. At these meetings, known as *reuniones multisectoriales,* the mayor tried to establish a general consensus about the rules for carrying out the fiesta in an orderly and nonconflictual way and announced municipal dispositions that the participants had little freedom to question.[42]

One element that became evident in these meetings and that was openly discussed by the participants was that jeronimianos had lost interest in becoming either mayordomo or *lentradero,* which had traditionally been the two most important sponsorship roles. These posts still exist, in the last few years assumed by nonjeronimianos (particularly from Puno), but they have become marginal in comparison to the role that comparsas have assumed in the sponsorship. Social recognition and status is now acquired through becoming the main sponsor, also called *carguyoq* ("cargo holder" in Quechua), of a comparsa for the fiesta. This regional trend signals the increasing importance of the role of comparsas. In San Jerónimo to become a carguyoq one has to be a member of the comparsa. This is not always the case in other Cusco towns, but if carguyoqs are not members of a comparsa, they are often close relatives or friends of a member. Some comparsas are more prestigious than others and assume, according to their possibilities, more or less important roles during the ritual. In San Jerónimo the Majeños comparsa has assumed the role of main organizer and coordinator of the ritual. The Qollas are the main opponents of the Majeños' assumption of leadership and resist their regulations to the extent that they can. Nevertheless, the Majeños is widely acknowledged by the people of the town and by the local authorities as the comparsa likely to do the best job.

During my research, parallel to the reunión multisectorial, the Majeños convened meetings with all the ritual sponsors to coordinate the order of the *novenas* and the *amarre* of the imagen.[43] Novenas, which always take place before a Catholic festivity, are a series of masses nine days before the central date of the celebration. For Saint Jerome, novenas must start at least a month and a half before the central date, because there are various comparsas and a few individual sponsors who want to participate with novenas. Before the novenas, the sponsors must perform the amarre. The mayordomo and the lentraderos used to be in charge of this practice, but now the Majeños have assumed it. The amarre (literally, "to tie down") consists of removing the imagen from its altar, dressing it in one of its festive gowns, and tying it to the andas. Securely attached to the andas, the imagen is moved to the main central altar of the church, the *altar mayor*. When I was there, the imagen was surrounded by colorful, shiny metal paper arrangements, fluorescent lights, flowers, and candles. Firecrackers in the central plaza announced that the amarre was occurring inside the church. When the arrangement of the imagen was complete, participants ate and drank in the atrium. From that day on, the church, otherwise often closed during the day, was usually open for devotees to pray to their patron saint.

The next day the first novena mass took place at 6:00 a.m., announced with firecrackers audible throughout the town. After mass, the sponsor in charge offered food and drink to the participants. Because this particular sponsor had the economic means to pay for it, a live band played for the participants to dance baile in front of the church. The celebration continued in the house of the sponsor until the end of the day.

The Majeños have assumed the role of offering the first novena of the fiesta; they often have a band the day of the first mass. Among the members of any comparsa it is an honor to have the opportunity to offer the first mass of the novena that corresponds to the group. Among the Majeños it is even more of a privilege, because that mass would be the first of the whole community celebration. In turn, all the comparsas sponsor novenas, and the series ends with the novena offered by the mayordomo. The beginning of each novena is a special celebration for the group sponsoring it. Nevertheless, for the sponsor of each of the following eight masses, it is a special occasion for which he or she tries to gather as many friends and family members as possible.

While the novenas began in the town, the comparsas started their more formal organizational meetings and danza rehearsals. The two groups that began to meet and rehearse first were the Tuntuna and the Mollos, the two comparsas of the young generation.[44] Around this time, the carguyoqs of every comparsa started collecting the goods or money promised them by either the members of the comparsa or friends and family who had made that commitment through the *jurk'a*.

The jurk'a is an act in which ritual sponsors visit the house of a friend or family member and offer him or her a drink and a special kind of bread. The sponsor implores that person to promise reciprocation in the form of a contribution for the days of the celebration. The size or the amount of the aid promised through the jurk'a varies greatly, from paying for fireworks or a large portion of the cost of a brass band to a few guinea pigs or half a sack of potatoes to be cooked during the fiesta. At least half of the families currently residing in the town have been *jurk'adas* (engaged through jurk'a) for the patron-saint festivity (Mendoza 1990). Jurk'as for the next year begin soon after the festivity ends. The sponsors carry them out in a few days. The latest jurk'as occur in April or May of the next year. The meetings and rehearsals of comparsas often were hosted by the comparsa member with the most spacious house. Even though organizational meetings at which important decisions were made were exclusively for the comparsa associates, I was invited to all of them because by the time they started I had already been welcomed as a person with a true interest in their danzas. Part of their recognition was a result of my performance with the Majeños comparsa during the Corpus Christi celebration.[45] Rehearsals tended to be a little more open, but the degree to which other townspeople could observe varied from comparsa to comparsa. The two more prestigious groups, the Tuntuna and the Majeños, tended to have closed rehearsals. The amount of practice needed before the fiesta also varied among the comparsas. As mentioned above, the Tuntuna and the Mollos started their rehearsals earliest. They were the groups that incorporated the most innovative choreography every year. These two groups increased the frequency of their rehearsals to every day or every other day in the two weeks before the central day. Most of the rehearsals took place with recorded music. Only the Qollas, whose music for the rehearsal (not for the fiesta performance) required only a flute player and an accordionist or violinist (both easy to find around the town for a minimal or no fee), was likely to practice with live music.

Around September 20 various local institutions started carrying out their annual celebration or some public event for institutional fundraising. Among the most important ones were the celebration of the anniversary of the main local high school, on the twenty-second and the twenty-third, and the *día familiar* (family day) organized by the Mollos.[46] The high-school celebration included street parades and contests of *danzas típicas* (on-stage folkloric dances), a night torchlight parade, and the lighting of the high school's initials at the top of one of the tallest mountains surrounding the town, Ccumu. The día familiar is a sort of carnival or festival in which people play some gambling games but mostly eat and drink and dance (baile). The funds raised are used by comparsas to help finance the fiesta.[47]

The two or three weeks preceding the fiesta was the auspicious period for jeronimianos to open a business, found a club, get married, or baptize their children. Thus, the town's most important celebratory occasion framed many other smaller celebrations. Some sponsors married and some members of comparsas were chosen to be godparents. In addition, the local municipality and parish organized "mass weddings" (in which many couples, about twenty, got married in the same ceremony) in the days preceding the fiesta, facilitating the civil and religious sanction of the common free unions.[48]

On the morning of the twenty-ninth, the official program of the celebration (announced and printed by the municipality) began. This event, like most central fiesta events, occurred in the main plaza, where the church and the municipal building are. The plaza was already lined with food and drink vendors, who remained during the four days of the fiesta. After raising the national flag and the purported Inca flag and singing the national anthem, the speeches began. Local and regionally important personalities were in charge. At the close of the speeches, the *desfile cívico* (civic parade) commenced, accompanied by music from a large military brass band brought from Cusco city.

The local authorities leading the parade included the members of the municipal government, the local governor and judges, the parish priest, and the head of the *guardia civil* (local police). Next came the *policía forestal* (forestry police), an institution that has an important post in the district. In the third place were all the local schools; the two high schools paraded with their own bands. Fourth were all the occupational associations, such as the *habaceras* (market women), *abarroteros* (retail-store owners), artisans, cattle dealers, and others. Fifth were the representatives of all the asentamientos humanos; sixth were all the *instituciones de servicio* (service institutions) such as the local bank, the transportistas, and the *posta médica* (small clinic); seventh were the local clubs such as sports and youth clubs and the mothers' associations (formed around municipal projects). The last contingent was the comunidades campesinas.

While the parade continued, comparsa members, many of whom participated in the parade at one point, rushed around finishing up the last details for the *entrada* (entrance), the formal beginning of the religious celebration which would take place that afternoon. Some comparsas conducted their final rehearsal that day, joined by the live band that would accompany them during the next three days. All the comparsa members gathered at the same place, usually the house of the carguyoq or the house of the rehearsals, and put on their costumes together. This moment was a key transitional point between their individual identities outside this performance and their group identity as danza performers. Through playing, joking, drinking, and eating together, the members started to assume their roles as representatives of one whole social and performing unit, the comparsa.

The presence of the live band and the constant repetition of the melody to which they would dance added to the strong emotions experienced by performers as they donned their costumes and masks. In the case of the Majeños and the Qollas (who wear masks), the transformation was completed when they were fully masked. At that point these performers started exaggerating and joking about the features of the characters they were impersonating. All the comparsas went through a period of intense nervousness before they began their annual performance. This feeling clearly intensified as they put on their costumes. They knew they would be watched and judged from the first moment they entered the streets.

The entrada, closely regulated by the municipality, marked the beginning of the *vísperas* (eve or vespers), the prelude for the main celebration the next day. This parade was again led by the local authorities, followed by the devotees who had made donations to the imagen (i.e., gowns, capes, jewels, and large candles, or *ciriones*), the mayordomo and the lentraderos, and all the comparsas with their carguyoqs in front showing their distinctive *estandartes* (banners).[49] The entrada began in an open field on the outskirts of town, moved along the main avenue (also the main car road of the region), and continued along one of the few wide cobbled stone streets of the town leading to the main plaza. The entrada ended when all the groups had entered the church to salute the imagen, concluding after dark. The comparsas then moved to assigned places around the plaza, eating, drinking, and dancing baile with their friends and family. This public celebration in the main plaza developed into an obvious competition to determine who served the best *chiri uchu,*[50] a special local dish, who could offer more expensive and sophisticated drinks (such as bottled beer, wine, or champagne), and whose band was the best. Some comparsas then continued with private celebrations in a house. Every comparsa had a fixed place for private banquets and bailes, often the house of the carguyoq or a house borrowed or rented by the sponsor for use during the fiesta.

After the comparsa members had removed and stored their costumes safely in their gathering places, they joined the rest of the townspeople in the main plaza to watch the fireworks. To warm up, most people drank *ponche de habas,* one of the specialties of San Jerónimo.[51] This evening spectacle, together with the entrada, constitutes one of the most popular events that attract people from Cusco city and neighboring districts. During my research, each evening of the fiesta, including this one of the víspera, young people, through their high-school association or private clubs, organized *bailes sociales* (social dances) to raise funds. The music/dance genres performed in these events were cumbia, salsa, and chicha, all coastal and the first two originally Afro-Caribbean rhythms, very popular among the young Andean population all over the country (see chapter 6).[52] These forms contrasted clearly with the danzas and the bailes of the adult generation, the Majeños and the Qollas, whose repertoire is still dominated by the more traditional waynos and marineras (see chapter 4).

Starting at 4:00 a.m. on the central day of the festivity, the comparsas took turns offering a mass to Saint Jerome. The first were, of course, the Majeños. Firecrackers awoke the townspeople announcing the *misa de gallo* (literally "rooster's mass") the first mass to honor the saint on his day. Before or after offering mass, each comparsa performed a small excerpt from its choreography in the atrium of the church. Next they traveled around the main streets of the town, dancing with their bands. The central mass of the fiesta occurred around noon. The main sermon of this mass extolled the personality of Saint Jerome, reminding the people why this personage is specially venerated by Catholics and in particular by jeronimianos. His qualities as an erudite scholar, which earned him the title doctor of the church, were pointed out. Jeronimianos were reminded that their protector saint translated biblical writings, dedicating a large part of his life to this kind of scholarly pursuit and to meditation. His dedication to intellectual and spiritual matters, it is said, obtained for him a privileged place in the church hierarchy, and therefore a closer place to God than other human beings.

At the close of the mass, the main processions began. Only on the central day of the fiesta were there two processions. In the first one the priest led, removing the *Santísimo Sacramento* (Holy Sacrament or Host) from the main altar of the church and then carrying this icon around the main plaza (fiesta processions only go around the main plaza, always counterclockwise). The presence of the Santísimo in a patron-saint festivity is not common in other fiestas of the region. In San Jerónimo its role derives from the fact that the regional importance of the imagen of Saint Jerome is very much linked to its participation in the Corpus Christi procession in Cusco, of which the Santísimo is the central icon. The presence of the Santísimo in the local celebration makes it more solemn for jeronimianos and outsiders. The music accompanying this and other processions was religious marches played by a brass band (audio example 4). The icon, like the imagen of Saint Jerome in the second procession, stopped at various times for prayers at the temporary altars placed around the plaza by local institutions and groups.[53] The crowd following the icon was clearly led by a group of authorities, the mayordomo, the lentraderos, the comparsa carguyoqs, and donors of objects for the imagen. After this leading group came the comparsas and then the rest of the townspeople.

After returning the Santísimo to the church, the imagen of Saint Jerome was brought out for the second procession. All the comparsas and other devotees had the privilege of briefly carrying the andas. Comparsas not carrying the imagen formed files called *cadenas* (chains) on both sides of the procession. In addition to stopping at the *altares,* Saint Jerome was enclosed for few seconds inside the *salas,* wooden structures built around the main plaza. These were financed by townspeople who had acquired such a commitment through the jurk'a, at the request of the mayordomo and the two lentraderos. Salas were surrounded by firecrackers, and at the end of the procession they exploded in turn when the imagen faced each of them from the atrium. There were two or three salas in every procession. After all the fireworks had exploded, the most important performance of the comparsas began. The first and last day of the festivity, the imagen was placed outside the church door to be honored by the danzas performed in front of it.

Every year there are quarrels about this central performance. This is one of the important aspects that the mayor attempts to settle at the reunión multisectorial but that can always only be partially agreed on. Every comparsa is supposed to perform in turn in the atrium in front of the imagen. For many years the Majeños (the most powerful and prestigious comparsa) had been in charge of performing first. During my research other comparsas, not willing to wait until the Majeños had finished, started their choreography in another part of the central plaza.[54] Before and after their turns in the atrium the other comparsas also performed in different places around the main plaza. Crowds surrounded each danza performance, and comparsas did their best to attract the most attention from the fiesta participants. This intense moment of the fiesta, with loud live music, danza, laughter, drinking, and big crowds, as well as gossip and other verbal commentaries, was overwhelming, and this is considered by most jeronimianos to be the climax of the fiesta. During this time strong emotions tend to predominate, ranging from a deep sense of camaraderie among comparsa members or between them and their admirers to hatred and anger between different comparsa members or between two townspeople. There is no doubt that the participants' sensual and emotional experience was particularly heightened during this part of the fiesta.

After this central performance the comparsa carguyoqs, the mayordomo, and the lentraderos offered their main banquets of the fiesta in their private gathering places. It is an honor to be invited to any of them, and prestigious townspeople and authorities were invited to various ones. At these private celebrations a great deal of baile, eating, and drinking took place. This was one of the main occasions, similar to that of the night of the vísperas, when townspeople showed their social allegiances. In other words, on these two occasions, spending the most time with one comparsa and accompanying it during its main danza performances and their private gatherings was for jeronimianos the best indication that a person was associated with that social group and identified with it.

When the main banquet was finished, comparsas went out dancing along the streets and performing their danza in the plaza again. In the case of the Majeños and Qollas, a particular part of their choreography was designed for this moment. Music, danza, baile, drinking, and eating continued for jeronimianos in the main plaza and in private until late at night. Comparsa members were careful to put their costumes away before they got ruined during this night of celebration. Another baile social took place during that second evening of the fiesta. These bailes, which were mostly for teenagers, were held in the municipal public saloon or in another locale around the main plaza. These after-dark celebrations at the plaza are considered by jeronimianos to be very dangerous for single women. Townspeople assume that the amount of drinking and social license that occurs during them can make young women an easy target for seduction. Young women who want to avoid gossip make sure either to go home early or to always be accompanied by an adult or a group of female friends.

On October 1, the third day of the festival, the sequence of events developed in a very similar way. The main difference was that part of the morning was dedicated to a visit to the cemetery. The comparsas went to visit the tomb of deceased members of the group or deceased close relatives of one of them. Sometimes a mass was said in front of the tomb; other times it was just a short prayer or speech. Afterward, some comparsas went out to a big open field in front of the cemetery. With their friends and family, they had something to eat and drink, and in some cases they danced baile. This was one of the few opportunities in which Qollas and Majeños fraternized by having a drink together. Nevertheless, particularly on the occasions I observed, the tensions between the two groups soon became obvious, because the Qollas were bothered by the condescending attitude of the Majeños (video example 6).

Also on October 1 members of one comparsa visited those of other comparsas in their homes, and each of them went to visit people who had made important donations to the group or who had been supporters for some time. Late in the afternoon the *arranque de gallos* (literally "grabbing of roosters") took place. This was a very abbreviated and modified version of a practice that used to be done more completely until the end of the 1970s, when the main plaza was stone-paved. Originally, several young men on horseback tried to reach a live rooster hanging down from a rope; whoever got the rooster won.[55] Now a few young men go around the plaza riding horses and holding a chicken in one hand. There is a special sponsor in charge of the arranque, called the *gallo capitán* (video example 10).

The fourth day of the celebration, the last, had as its peculiar features the *bendición* (blessing) and the *cacharpari* (farewell) (video example 10). After the procession the imagen bowed to the four cardinal points (an effect provided by the carriers of the andas) and returned to the church until the next year; after all this, the comparsas did their farewell danza performances. That same evening the imagen was returned to his altar. In the afternoon members of every comparsa and other individual sponsors went to collect their *walqanchis* ("hangings" in Quechua) from the people who had promised them through the jurk'a. The walqanchis are arrangements of fruit and small useful objects such as straw baskets and plastic plates, which, tied together, are put around the bodies of all the central performers of the ritual (i.e., mayordomo, carguyoqs, comparsa members) as a sort of reward for a job well done (figs. 25 and 32).

After all these people have their walqanchis on, they join in a communal dance, baile, in the central plaza. This is the only time that dancers from different comparsas, and comparsas and the general public, blend together in conga lines and circles. The Majeños and the Qollas had a distinctive part of their choreography and music for this occasion, which they performed right before the final communal cacharpari. This farewell, like the main day's climax of the fiesta, was filled with emotions. The predominant emotions among the comparsas were sadness, because the fiesta was over, and happiness and a sense of accomplishment, for having fulfilled their public responsibility.

For jeronimianos, dynamic incorporation into the economy and the urban life of Cusco city as well as the emergence of new local elites have made the patron-saint festivity the main communal celebration of the town. Of all the other Catholic public celebrations in which former comparsas used to perform, the fiesta *patronal* (more clearly since the mid-1970s) has been chosen by the emerging social groups of the town as the main realm where local distinctions and identities are locally redefined through the performance of danzas. In the chapters that follow I show how this redefinition takes place through danza performance and through other ritual and nonritual activities of the members of the comparsas.

Cusco regional ideology and culture support and promote the existence of fiestas and comparsas as positive "folkloric" performances. This regional ideology also allows jeronimianos to become more mestizo through performing mestizo danzas. The process by which people of San Jerónimo have been able to form part of local and regional elites, leaving behind their peasant or "indigenous" background, has not been easy or without ambiguities. Comparsa members have negotiated their public identity and have redefined local sociocultural categories through danzas in the patron-saint festivity. The creative qualities of danza performance within this ritual have been fundamental for the members of these organizations in constituting local distinctions and identities.

# The Majeños Comparsa

*Power, Prestige, and Masculinity among Mestizos*

A s the procession of the central day of the fiesta is coming to
an end and the statue of Saint Jerome is carefully being placed
outside the church door, a group of nineteen fully masked and
costumed dancers makes sure to take over the flat empty space in
front of the church in order to be the first to perform in honor of
their patron. These are the members of the Majeños comparsa.
There is only one woman among them, the *Dama* (lady), whom
the leader of the group is holding by the arm. She is wearing a
knee-length flared skirt, high-heel sandals, and a long embroidered shawl tied across her chest covering most of her long-sleeve
blouse. Her mask has rosy cheeks, blue eyes, and a very discrete
smile; she is also wearing a stovepipe white hat. Two of the male
comparsa members, dressed very differently than the rest, are in
charge of keeping the crowd off the empty space so the performance can take place. The rest of the male dancers, including the
leader, are dressed identically with brown-leather boots, belts, and
jackets; jodhpurs; and wide-brimmed hats. Their masks are striking, with big rosy cheeks, blue eyes, extremely long straight noses,
long mustaches made of horsehair, and a wide smile showing their
teeth. Each of them has a bottle of beer in one hand. As the
marchlike melody played by their brass band begins, they organize
themselves in two lines, with the leader and the Dama going back
and forth in the middle, and they start swaying their bodies gen-
tly, keeping a very upright posture and veering their bodies right
and left. As they do this, they switch the bottle of beer from one
hand to the other. The expectation of the audience grows, knowing what is about to happen. Changing to a melody with a much
faster tempo, the two lines turn into a circle and the Majeños start

spraying their beer upward and outward, getting the front rows of the audience wet; people scream and laugh.

In this chapter I analyze historical and contemporary features of the comparsa that has become the most powerful and prestigious in San Jerónimo, the Majeños. Through their ritual performance of a particular danza and through their association, the members of this comparsa have constituted themselves as a distinct local elite. Placing ritual performance at the center of their group activity, members of this comparsa have used their cultural, economic, and social resources (Bourdieu 1987) to establish a superior position in local power relations, thereby replacing the old elites. Through their ritual performance and their association, the members of this comparsa have redefined and given local meaning to categories such as *decencia* (decency or propriety), *elegancia* (elegance), and *madurez* (maturity) that cut across some regional and national ethnic/racial, class, gender, and generational categories and that refer to a prior sociocultural field. The Majeños have given form to and embodied these categories not only in their ritual performance but also in their everyday lives through their association. In an effort to assert hegemony the members of this comparsa have made their association and their danza a highly condensed symbol of economic power, social prestige, and masculinity.

I regard the members of the Majeños comparsa as successful "bricoleurs" (Lévi-Strauss 1966; Hebdige 1985) who have drawn upon the signifying capacity of ritual symbolism and who have been able locally to give form to and generate new meanings for their danza. By putting together a series of iconic symbols (i.e., leather jackets, brass-band music, wide-brimmed hats, and beer bottles) and through metaphoric comparisons (i.e., to muleteers, landowners, their patron saint, and city dwellers), the Majeños of San Jerónimo have creatively brought together different domains (ethnicity/race, class, and gender) and specific situational contexts (their strategic position close to Cusco city, the demise of the hacienda system, and the promotion of "folklore") to make convincing "arguments" through ritual performance (Fernandez 1974, 1977, 1986; Fernandez and Durham 1991).[1] Through this performance the Majeños have mediated between the ideological and the practical embodiment of those domains and specific situational contexts, shaping local categories that are the basis on which to redefine local distinctions and identities.

By making body adornment (costuming and masking) and dance (individual and group patterned movement accompanied by music) the focus of their ritual action, the Majeños have made danza performance a particularly transformative and creative experience within ritual.[2] This kind of elaborated bodily praxis or bodily techniques within ritual has allowed jeronimianos to explore the ambiguities and unrealized potentialities in their lives. In their rituals, and through danza performance, jeronimianos have been moved to participate in a realm where certain "experiential truths" have been established through actions that "speak louder and more ambiguously than words" (Jackson 1990, 132–135).

Since it first appeared in the town of Paucartambo in the 1920s, the Majeños danza in the region of Cusco has been the vehicle for the "invention" and "reinvention" of local and regional traditions (Hobsbawm 1983). This danza-drama has become part of the cusqueño repertoire of mestizo "folklore" (as defined in chapter 2), and it is now performed in various regional and local rituals by people of Cusco city and smaller towns. The two comparsas that have gained regional recognition as the best performers and have given shape to the contemporary form of the danza are the Majeños of San Jerónimo and the Majeños of Paucartambo.[3] These competing comparsas have made a particular effort to incorporate the characters of their danzas into the reconstruction of their local past. As well-known representatives of local and regional folklore, they have re-created the discourse of the instituciones culturales (explained in chapter 2), assuming the role of defenders of a local "tradition" and teachers of a local and regional past.

The local meanings that the San Jerónimo comparsa has generated among jeronimianos since the time of the incorporation of the danza into local tradition in the late 1940s have been linked to those created by paucartambinos since the 1920s. Beginning in the 1970s, when both comparsas were resurrected after a period of twenty years in which the danza had not been performed in the local fiestas, these two groups have competed for regional recognition. Since then, both groups have considered themselves the best performers and innovators of the costumes and choreography. This rivalry has led each to incorporate almost immediately the elements introduced by the other group. Moreover, while the first jeronimianos who introduced the danza in the town openly say that they brought the danza from Paucartambo, the present jeronimiano Majeños try to negate this fact. One strategy used by these jeronimianos to try to convince me that the danza was originally from San Jerónimo was to describe to me old local danzas, which are no longer performed, as the "real" antecedents of their Majeños danza.

The meanings of the danza that the comparsas have generated in both towns have drawn upon regional and national ethnic/racial, class, and gender distinctions and identities that include dichotomies such as hacendado/servant, white/Indian, and urban/rural. In this chapter I explore how, through their danza, members of both comparsas have given local form and meaning to these dichotomies and have made innovative associations through a series of iconic symbols in ritual performance (i.e., costumes and ways of dancing). The competition established between the two comparsas makes it difficult to determine which group first introduced the different modifications that the danza has undergone. Nevertheless, by following the relative emphasis that the members of the comparsas have put on particular aspects of the danza, these local meanings can be analyzed. Finally, through a close look at the role that the organizational aspect of the comparsa of San Jerónimo has had in its recognition as the most powerful local comparsa in San Jerónimo, I will show the contemporary relevance of this kind of "folkloric" association in the Cusco region.

## THE HACENDADO AND THE ARRIERO MERGE THROUGH RITUAL PERFORMANCE: THE FIRST MAJEÑOS PERFORMERS IN CUSCO

The "invention" of the Majeños "traditions" in Paucartambo and San Jerónimo should be understood in the context of change and innovation that have taken place in Cusco since the first decades of this century.[4] As detailed in chapters 2 and 3, by the 1920s the Cusco region was undergoing many transformations that accelerated after the 1950 earthquake and that developed further in the 1970s. Three interrelated processes had started to affect the whole region: the gradual shift of the axis of the region's economy toward the capital city, the demise of the hacienda system, and the emergence of new socioeconomic sectors linked to the growth of state infrastructure (i.e., roads, schools, and bureaucracy). Since the 1920s, regional traditions were "invented" and the "folklorization" of danzas was promoted by instituciones culturales, leading to the definition of a regional repertoire of "indigenous" or "authentic" danzas, on the one hand, and "mestizo" danzas on the other.

One particular transformation directly related to the third process mentioned above is especially relevant for the analysis of the invention and re-creation of the Majeños tradition in Cusco: the construction of roads and the concomitant gradual replacement of *arrieraje* (transportation with mules) by motor vehicles. This started in the 1920s but gained force during the 1940s. People of towns like San Jerónimo, strategically well located in relation to the main regional commercial routes and close to the new economic axis of the region, could take better advantage of these regional transformations than could people from other towns. At first only a small sector of those privileged towns, such as townspeople who had the economic means and who were more often in contact with urban society, could take advantage of the new emerging economic activity: truck transportation. The people who engaged in this new economic activity were aware that, in San Jerónimo as in other Andean towns, danzas and fiestas were privileged local media for realizing social status, and chose these realms in order to define their local identity.

The danzas of Majeños comparsas in both San Jerónimo and Paucartambo impersonate a particular group of *arrieros* (muleteers) who traded alcoholic beverages such as wine and sugarcane brandy between Arequipa and Cusco departamentos. These arrieros, it is said, were originally from Majes (a valley in Arequipa departamento), thus the name of the danza, *majeño* (person from Majes). Arrieros played an important economic as well as cultural role in South America throughout the colonial and early republican periods (cf. Flores Galindo 1977; Glave 1989). They transported goods and were the main intermediaries in the exchange of news and cultural elements between distant places. These bilingual, physically mobile, and often wealthy members of society were frequently innovators of local culture in small Andean towns through the introduction of new elements (i.e., liquor, food) brought from the metropolis or from coastal valleys.[5]

During the colonial and early republican periods, Cusco was one of the most important centers of production and exchange in the southern Andes (including what is today Argentina and Bolivia). Cusco produced coca leaves, wool textiles, sugar, and foodstuffs consumed in the urban and mining centers (Mörner 1977). The valleys around Paucartambo had a particularly central role in the trans-Andean market. Between 1860 and 1920, the flow of arrieros who went from Arequipa to Cusco increased because of the boom in the wool trade (Flores Galindo 1977). It is likely that, until the 1920s, the arrieros from Majes had a central role in the trade that took place in Paucartambo and that they passed through that town on a regular basis.

Beginning in the 1920s, when these arrieros started to be displaced by the new kind of transportation, the local hacendados of Paucartambo appropriated the memory of this merchant group that had gained regional recognition. It is difficult to know if the landowners had participated in danzas before, but by the 1920s they had an important presence through the presentation of their Majeños comparsa (Villasante 1989). Certainly since the 1920s, urban mestizos had started to participate actively in the performance of folklore, appropriating old and creating new expressive forms that could be defined as such. The hacendados of Paucartambo were part of Cusco's urban culture because as members of the regional elite they had many links with the capital city. Some hacendados even lived in Cusco city part of the year, and they certainly sent their children to high school there. Some children of hacendados became part of the indigenista nativist movement and became involved in the promotion of regional folklore.

At least since the 1920s these Paucartambo hacendados associated themselves with the re-created figure of the arriero through their ritual performance. All the information indicates that the first Paucartambo Majeños was a hacendado comparsa. Paucartambinos who witnessed the fiesta in the first decades of the century said that the danza was performed only by *potentados* (potentates). The concept of *potentado* is centered on the idea of social, economic, and political power, three attributes that the hacendados definitely had. Informants have even used the word *omnipotentados* to describe the people who performed in the Majeños comparsa of Paucartambo in the 1940s. The prefix *omni* emphasizes even more the attributes mentioned above. One of the best-known Peruvian anthropologists, José María Arguedas (1987, 113), described the Majeños danza of Paucartambo in 1941 as one in which only wealthy, elegant, and Spanish-speaking mestizos participated.

These hacendados succeeded in establishing a continuity between their ritual performance and the reconstruction of local history, a characteristic of invented traditions. The landowners were able to blur the line between the memories of what the "actual" muleteers did in the fiesta and what they themselves, through their comparsa, started to re-create when the arrieros did not come anymore. The following testimony of a paucartambino who witnessed the comparsa in the 1940s and who led the reinvention in the 1970s is representative:

> Well, the history of the Majeño, as far as I know, is: it is said that actually some muleteers came from Majes, and on their way to Q'osñipata [a tropical valley in the departamento] they brought along to sell here some wine and *alfajores* [pastries], everything they produce there in the Majes valley. They were on their way to Q'osñipata, where in those times, I am not sure when exactly, there were 360 haciendas, most of them producing sugarcane brandy, coca leaves, and all of that stuff, right? And when leaving Q'osñipata, the majeño muleteers—of course there was no road but just horse trails—entered Paucartambo. . . . And, I mean, they timed their return to coincide with our patron-saint fiesta in honor of the Virgin of Carmen . . . that is the way it is told. Well, since at that time Paucartambo, like other provinces and departments, was mainly haciendas, so the hacendados, well, they did

the danza, the Majeños didn't come anymore for some reason and they, the hacendados, danced.

With nostalgia, the hacendados invented the Majeños danza glorifying the memory of these arrieros, choosing an appropriate image of beneficent travelers. It is likely that the hacendados identified with the arrieros because they had many common traits. Like themselves, the arrieros rode horses, spoke Spanish, and were economically powerful; most important of all, they were reciprocally interdependent in economic terms. The appropriation of the idealized reconstruction of the arrieros through ritual performance allowed the local hacendados to capitalize on new symbols of power. This appropriation was facilitated by the iconic relationship that the hacendados were able to establish with the arrieros. Therefore, and as exemplified by its characteristic melody with its evocation of drunkenness (see below), establishing iconic relationships seems to be a principle that has guided the performance of the Majeños danza since its Paucartambo beginnings.

In the 1940s a small group of truck owners/drivers who traded cattle, in local terms a group of transportistas-ganaderos, emerged in the town of San Jerónimo. In an attempt to gain social recognition as a distinct local group, this sector of the petite bourgeoisie selected the Majeños danza, a prestigious symbolic element from the main ritual of the town of Paucartambo (with which they had contact through their commercial activity), and introduced it as a local tradition in their own patron-saint fiesta. This group of jeronimianos considered this danza "decente" and "elegante" for reasons that I analyze below. Besides being performed by prestigious members of Paucartambo society (the hacendados), the danza was itself an impersonation of another regionally prestigious and economically important group of the near past with which these jeronimianos identified: the muleteers from Majes. The motivations that the transportistas-ganaderos had for selecting the Majeños danza as their main vehicle for defining their local identity leads to an understanding of the elements that made this danza particularly suitable for their purposes.

## THE FIRST MAJEÑOS IN SAN JERÓNIMO:
## THE RE-CREATION OF THE CONCEPT OF
## DECENCIA IN THE EMERGENT MESTIZO IDENTITY

Several crucial ethnic/racial and class differences in San Jerónimo, Cusco, and Peru are defined around the concept of *decencia* (decency or propriety). Almost any study about Andean towns has found that local elites are often defined as the *gente decente* or *los decentes* (decent people; cf. van den Berghe and Primov 1977; De la Cadena 1995). This implies that members of local elites are the ones who are able to conduct themselves in the most decent or proper way within society. Decencia is then a concept through which one can explore aspects of the hegemonic or "commonsense" level of sociohistorical constructions that are labeled "propriety" or "decency."[6] In San Jerónimo the concept of decencia is defined in terms of ethnic/racial and class hierarchies. In this town a person is decente if she or he dresses and behaves like the local or regional elite. For comparsa members their danza is decente if it is acknowledged, through its music, costumes, or choreography, as representative of a high-status group. Decencia has become a central concept that powerful social sectors have tried to shape and appropriate in an effort to assert hegemony. The moral judgment of clean, upright, and good behavior implied by the term legitimizes the status of those who control the signs of "decency."

The study of the Majeños comparsa permits the analysis of some of the specific meanings of the concept of decencia in Cusco and Peru and how a particular group of jeronimianos has constructed and appropriated these meanings through ritual performance. It also allows the exploration of how the members of this particular group have tried to define themselves as decentes in their everyday lives. The highly condensed and elaborated symbolism present in the ritual performance of the danza, such as the emphasis placed on certain aspects of the costumes, the music, body movement, posture, and paraphernalia, is central to disentangling those meanings.

While by the end of the 1940s San Jerónimo had begun to undergo important transformations and a petite bourgeoisie had started to emerge, the hacendados still existed as a local elite, the local "decentes." Local hierarchies were apparent in the patron-saint fiesta of the town, of which the decentes had most of the privileges of sponsorship. They were in charge of the salas (large fireworks temporary structures) and of the main plaza altar (the *Wiracocha* altar) for the processions (which they also led), and they enjoyed the music of the brass band hired for the occasion. Wiracocha is the Quechua name of a pre-Hispanic deity that became synonymous with *caballero* (gentleman). For this fiesta all the ayllus (indigenous peasant communities) were obliged to put small altars around the plaza for the procession. Also, the ayllu authorities, the *varayoqs*, had to pay for the band, which played only for the bailes of the local elites.

Old townspeople remembered this patron-saint fiesta as a very solemn ritual. They said "it was like a Corpus," alluding to the magnificent and hierarchically structured Cusco city ritual. One main element, however, differentiated this fiesta from the other two important ones in honor of local "saints." The patron-saint fiesta did not have danzas. In San Jerónimo the performance of danzas was not a tradition of local decentes but instead of those who were largely excluded from the privileged sponsorship roles of the decentes. In fact, the performance of danzas was excluded from the central fiesta of the town.

The leaders of the first group of Majeños in San Jerónimo, the transportistas-ganaderos, openly say that they selected the danza from Paucartambo because it was decente. Moreover, for their first performance toward the end of the 1940s (the old dancers' recollections fluctuate between 1947 and 1949), they chose the arena where the decentes, the caballeros of the town had the preeminent place, the patron-saint fiesta. The following statements indicate the elements that, for the leaders of this first comparsa, made the danza decente, one that only decentes performed:

> We saw that the danza was very elegant, with their sashes, pockets, hats, and brass-band music . . . we saw their entrance; they were all on horseback, among them was a mestiza . . . they arrived with their mules and their kegs of liquor . . . so it came to us: "how about if we get together for the patron-saint fiesta" . . . It is a danza for caballeros, with decencia, the best people danced, the music itself is pretty, decente, [the dancers wore] boots, [and were] well dressed.

> I liked it, so I said to myself: "why couldn't I do it in San Jerónimo?" . . . because it was danced with a brass band, it was more decente, the other comparsas had bands with kenas, their [the Majeños'] costume was more decente, their entrance was on horseback.

In these accounts, as in others of the members of the first Majeños comparsa of San Jerónimo, the dancers highlight the same elements that made this danza particularly attractive: brass-band music, riding on horseback, riding clothes (i.e., jodhpurs, boots), wide-brimmed hats, and above all that it was performed by the Paucartambo decentes, the hacendados, and impersonated prestigious personages of the recent past, the arrieros. These entrepreneurs found a danza whose central symbols were, inside and outside ritual, associated with two regionally prestigious male groups, the hacendados and the arrieros. Also, the fact that the danza had as one of its central choreographic elements the consumption of liquor made it even more attractive in the eyes of these jeronimianos. The Majeños always had a bottle of sugarcane brandy in their hands, and their mules carried this liquor in kegs that they then offered the fiesta participants. Also, their patterned movements simulated drunkenness. This "ethylic" aspect of the danza added an element of masculinity to the danza, because male public behavior was, and continues to be, associated with drinking.

The Majeños danza in Paucartambo, and as it was also performed by the first comparsa in San Jerónimo, was much more of a dance-drama than it is today. The fiesta participants were also more directly involved in the performance. The Majeños used to dance and play "with" the fiesta participants, much more than "for" them. Most of the performance replicated the activities and personality of the arrieros as they were remembered. The performers simulated the arrival from Q'osñipata, the unloading of the mules, and the camaraderie of the arrieros with the townspeople. In this reconstruction the generosity and the liveliness of these personages were emphasized. This was clearly an idealized impersonation in which these arrieros were presented as local benefactors. The performance of the danza emphasized the correct costuming and paraphernalia.

The Majeños *pasacalle* (coordinated group movement along the streets), done mostly on horseback, was accompanied by a characteristic "staggering" melody that is maintained today (see below). When they had reached the central plaza and had finished the reconstruction of the arrival of the arrieros, the Majeños danced mestizo waynos and marineras with the townswomen (see below for definitions of these two genres). When the Majeños appeared in Paucartambo, marineras were still a novelty in Andean fiestas, mostly performed by Spanish-speaking urban dwellers. In San Jerónimo the Majeños were also the first to make the marinera part of the repertoire of the local danzas.

Another central symbolic element of the Majeños danza that made it decente in the eyes of the transportistas-ganaderos was the place of origin of the arrieros. This is particularly important because it highlights the element of ethnicity and racism in this construction of local distinctions and identities. As mentioned above, the arrieros were supposed to be from Arequipa. This Peruvian departamento has been known by Peruvians and social scientists not only as one of the centers of regional economic power throughout the colonial and republican periods but also as one of the "whitest" and most "aristocratic" centers of the country. This was a result of pre-Hispanic (there were fewer indigenous people in the area), colonial (a large Spanish population concentrated there), and early republican settlement patterns (many other European immigrants settled there) as well as of the economic development of the area (Flores Galindo 1977). "Whiteness" continues to be acknowledged as a characteristic of *arequipeños* (people of Arequipa), despite miscegenation and migration characteristic of this and other Peruvian economic and political centers. Arequipeños' historically constructed identity is still defined in reference to the phenotypic characteristic of "white," which for most Peruvians is a sign of superiority.

If one were to make a regional hierarchy based on dominant cusqueño ideology about the relative prestige of southern Andean departments, Arequipa would be at the top, Cusco next, and Puno at the bottom. Racism as well as economic and political power play a central role in this classification. Many Peruvian popular jokes refer to Arequipa as a foreign country and to the purported haughtiness of arequipeños. Being a foreigner in Peru is often a source of social prestige, especially if the foreigner has white phenotypic features. According to regional and national hierarchies a "white" is much more decente or proper than an "Indian" or a cholo. Cusqueño elites consider people from Puno to be more "Indian" than themselves. This has a direct implication in the symbolic elaboration of the Qollas comparsa, which impersonates a group from Puno (see chapter 5).

The appropriation of the Majeños danza (one with decente characteristics and impersonated by the decentes of Paucartambo) and their ritual performance in the patron-saint fiesta (one dominated by local decentes) was one of the main vehicles for the members of the local petite bourgeoisie to become gradually acknowledged as local decentes. Through the ritual metaphoric association of their group with the arrieros and the hacendados, the members of this comparsa redefined their local identity as decentes. As James Fernandez (1977, 101–102) has argued, "metaphors provide organizing images which ritual action puts into effect. This ritualization of metaphor enables the pronouns participating in ritual to undergo apt integrations and transformations in their experience."

By making metaphoric comparisons and bringing together different domains in creative ways, the Majeños have made use of "the argument of images." Fernandez argues that one of the missions of our argumentative powers is to persuade others to recognize our performances and our place in the world (Fernandez 1974, 1986). This has been true of every Majeños comparsa in San Jerónimo, whose members have always striven to be recognized as decentes and caballeros.

The first performance of the San Jerónimo Majeños comparsa had a particularly strong impact in the town because the patron-saint fiesta was a privileged arena where local hierarchies were annually re-created and where the former elite groups asserted their predominance. The first Majeños opened a space for danza performance in this exclusive realm. All this was helped by shifting notions of national and regional identity that fetishized folklore and its artistic performance.

Not just anyone from San Jerónimo could have appropriated this danza and successfully performed it in the fiesta. Many challenges were involved in this performance, but transportistas-ganaderos of the town could withstand them because they had the necessary social, cultural, and economic capital (Bourdieu 1987). Performing a danza in the patron-saint fiesta was a challenging innovation for this first group of economic and cultural entrepreneurs. They defied those who opposed the performance, such as the parish priest who wanted to keep the fiesta from becoming "paganized." According to these old dancers, people of the town thought that this performance could be a bad omen and that it could lead to a bad agricultural year. But, as they put it, they "became obsessed" *(nos encaprichamos)*. They were identified with the danza and were convinced that they could successfully carry out the performance.

Thanks to their economic activity, this emerging petite bourgeoisie had frequent contact with the hacendados of Paucartambo and San Jerónimo. Through the trade of cattle and other products, they were intermediaries between them and the urban regional markets. They dealt with these elites on much more equitable terms than local ayllu members because of their ownership of the means of transportation and because of their skills, such as the mastery of Spanish (although their mother tongue had been Quechua) and the knowledge of dress and behavior codes of these elites. This role of economic and cultural intermediaries was another element of identification with the danza. They said that owning a truck and shipping products with it made them the equivalent of what the arrieros had been in the past.

Knowing the decentes of Paucartambo made it possible for this group of jeronimianos to ask members of the Majeños comparsa there to teach them their danza. A couple of paucartambinos even performed in San Jerónimo for the local fiesta. The access to good horses and, of course, knowing how to ride them were crucial for that performance. This was not difficult for these ganaderos, who could easily borrow horses from local hacendados and who knew how to ride them very well because cattle-dealing involved riding. Also, some of these entrepreneurs or their fathers had worked on local haciendas as *capataces* (foremen) and had learned how to ride. Because of this association with riding and haciendas, they also had access to the special kind of boots and belts that the Majeños of Paucartambo had for their performance. Finally, performing the Majeños required money to hire a brass band and to buy liquor. This was possible for these jeronimiano entrepreneurs.

The first group of Majeños in San Jerónimo succeeded; in their words, "*cayó bien*" (it was well received). People from Cusco city went to watch them. "They all liked us" and "we were admired" are common expressions the members of this first comparsa used in referring to their first presentations. This is also the opinion of many other residents who watched those performances. They also pointed out that this danza was different from the other local ones. Both groups agreed that the presence of the Majeños in the patron-saint fiesta was a major innovation not only because there were no comparsas in that fiesta but because the danza contained many novel elements.

Besides the arriero/hacendado-like costuming and paraphernalia, one feature of the danza that attracted many townspeople was the brass band. Up to that point, all the other comparsas in San Jerónimo were accompanied by pitu or kena and tambor ensembles, which were associated with the peasantry and which by then had already been sanctioned by instituciones culturales as "authentic" and characteristic of "Indians." As is still true today, brass-band music was a symbol of status because it was associated with economic power and European bourgeois and Peruvian urban/coastal culture. It made the danza even more decente. There was one additional characteristic of the Majeños band, however, that contributed to the comparsa's popularity.

The first Majeños said that their band became very popular because "anybody" could dance with it. Before, as mentioned above, only the local *elite* danced with a brass band during the fiesta. Performing a danza with brass-band music was a bold strategy to gain townspeople's attention. This was not only because it made the danza more decente but also because the comparsa took away one of the exclusive rights of the main sponsors of the fiesta. With this act, the Majeños seem to have introduced a new kind of status that was based on the possibility of incorporating into the fiesta groups formerly marginalized. The Majeños initiated the participation of the town's emerging socioeconomic groups in the sponsorship and ritual performance in honor of the patron saint.

The Majeños took the first and crucial step for the comparsas of San Jerónimo to gradually gain the central sponsorship role that they now have in the main ritual of the town. But more important for Majeños comparsa members was that their pioneering performance has awarded them a preeminent place in local ritual performance. Because of its unprecedented ritual action, this group has obtained a series of privileges within the patron-saint fiesta and for the Octava of Corpus Christi that other comparsas have not been able to take away from them. By bringing closer to the majority of the townspeople various privileges previously held by the former elite, the Majeños established supremacy over other local groups.

The popularity that this comparsa had gained among jeronimianos was shown when it was sent to represent the town in a very important regional celebration. In 1953, after three years of mourning brought on by the earthquake that destroyed much of Cusco city, instituciones culturales and the municipal government of that city decided to reinitiate local festivities with a grandiose Carnival celebration. Municipal governments of the departamento received invitations to send a "queen" and a comparsa representative of their district to the capital city for the occasion. For San Jerónimo residents, as the old townspeople recalled, it was a major event because it was the first time that they had a Carnival queen (before, the queens were selected only in Cusco city). They also considered that celebration the best opportunity to make a regional impression with their local folklore. They therefore selected the Majeños comparsa to escort the queen because it was the most appropriate and decente.

The selection of the Majeños as the local representative was an indicator that this danza appealed to a new local mestizo identity emerging in the town and in the whole region. This identity was given form in San Jerónimo by the first members of the Majeños comparsa, converting them into the "new mestizos," the new decentes of the town. The elements that the danza introduced in the ritual performance (i.e., new music repertoire played by a brass band, horses, riding clothes and paraphernalia) were seen by jeronimianos as innovative and as less indigenous than those that characterized old danzas. Performing the Majeños in the special Carnival celebration in Cusco city was an effective way for San Jerónimo people to make the rest of the region acknowledge them as mestizos and decentes. They accomplished that by using signs that were more recognizable as part of a national repertoire, with metropolitan elements (e.g., dancing marineras and urban-style waynos with a brass band).

After successfully introducing this tradition into San Jerónimo and the Cusco valley at large, and maintaining its popularity until the mid-1950s, the first Majeños comparsa of San Jerónimo stopped its ritual performance. It remains unclear why other townspeople did not continue the performance. But the fact that only the relatives of the old Majeños and other successful transportistas could in the 1970s re-create the danza reveals that already in the 1950s this danza was seen as exclusive property of a new local elite. According to the old dancers, there was "nobody" who could replace them when they got too old and tired to perform. Their socioeconomic group was still small in the town, and their children were too young to perform this danza, which, as I explain below, is suited only for "mature" males.

The members of the first Majeños comparsa had started to perform their danza when they were already middle-aged (most were around forty years old) and economically stable. They were part of an emerging regional social group that was leaving behind an indigenous identity marked by rural life. These transportistas-ganaderos, economic and cultural intermediaries between the rural and urban Cusco poles, took the lead in the exploration of new local identities. They gave local form to powerful symbols that they appropriated from former elites and that they re-created through ritual performance in their town. Townspeople continued to perform other danzas in other local fiestas and occasionally for the patron saint, but nobody performed the Majeños.

Also in the mid-1950s the hacendados of Paucartambo ended their performance of the danza in their patron-saint fiesta (Villasante 1989, 144–145). The disappearance of their comparsa coincided with the demise of the hacienda system in the region and with the hacendados' new focus of interest in the emerging areas of economic investment in Cusco city after the earthquake in 1950.

### THE REINVENTION OF THE MAJEÑOS TRADITION: THE REGIONAL CONTEXT AND THE NEW PAUCARTAMBO MAJEÑOS

In both Paucartambo and San Jerónimo, the Majeños tradition was reinvented after the mid-1970s by members of the growing regional petite bourgeoisie (i.e., merchants, transportistas, and state employees), a sector that greatly expanded in Cusco from the 1950s on (see chapters 2 and 3). In San Jerónimo this reinvention by a group of transportistas displayed a continuity in the social sector that originally performed the danza in the town. In Paucartambo, however, there was a change—the hacendados no longer performed. Schoolteachers, state employees, and petty merchants took the place and the ritual symbol of this landowning elite. These petit bourgeois members of the Paucartambo comparsa, however, did not become a local elite. The new local elite was constituted by professionals and by people who worked and lived in Cusco city and who still participated very actively in local affairs, mainly in the patron-saint fiesta.

Many ongoing transformations of the region accelerated during the period of reconstruction of Cusco city and the promotion of the regional economy following the 1950 earthquake. Migration to Cusco city and the new areas of colonization in the jungle (within the departamento), peasant pressure over hacienda lands, pauperization of the countryside, and peasant unionism increased during this period. Another regional change was the reforma agraria carried out during General Velasco's government (1968–1975), which marked the end of the hacienda system in the region, symbolically underscoring the end of the domination of the landowning elite over the peasant majority. During Velasco's regime the growth of the state bureaucracy and public education, the development of new areas of commerce, and the increase in public and private transportation enlarged the middle class in Cusco. The number of petty merchants, schoolteachers, bureaucrats, and transportistas increased greatly during this particular period in other provinces and districts outside Cusco city.

Also between the 1950s and the 1970s the new character of the capital city as a tourist resort and as the new axis of the economy crystallized, enhancing the performative spaces for enacting local identities before an audience. These spaces were bolstered by the mid-1970s with the private and state promotion of folklore that had become widespread in the region. The state had taken a particular interest and directly intervened in this promotion through local, regional, and national folkloric contests and festivals (see chapter 2). The schools had also become a channel through which "folklore" was taught as a way to construct national identity. In this context the preoccupation of the state and private instituciones culturales with the construction of regional and national identity merged with those of the emergent social groups in the towns of San Jerónimo and Paucartambo, concerned with the redefinition of their own local and regional identity. Fusing the memories about an idealized group that had already been gone for some time (the arrieros) with that of another prestigious sector that was waning at the time (the hacendados) allowed the two new groups of Majeños to re-create and to make "arguments" (Fernandez 1986) about their local identity. This identity re-created the three central principles that were emphasized by the old comparsas: power, prestige, and masculinity.

By the mid-1970s, in the context of regional folkloric contests and presentations, various danzas performed by paucartambinos had gained regional popularity. Urban dwellers of that district appropriated a series of danzas from Paucartambo and from other districts of the departamento (including San Jerónimo), to the extent that they became regionally known as the "danzas of Paucartambo." Paucartambinos put substantial effort into innovating their danzas (i.e., composing music and creating costumes and "choreographies" for them) and popularizing their patron-saint fiesta (which has now become a mecca for tourists and cusqueños) to the point of being called "arrivistes" by other cusqueños.

Paucartambo danzas have emerged as the main representatives of regional "mestizo" folklore. Mestizo danzas, as explained in chapter 2, are differentiated from "indigenous" or "authentic" danzas by the instituciones culturales. Mestizo danzas usually display elaborate and synthetic costumes as well as obviously fabricated and stylized choreographies. In 1972, after winning awards in the regional contests organized by Cusco city instituciones culturales, Paucartambo obtained the title of Provincia Folklórica. The "danzas of Paucartambo" have since then been profusely incorporated into local traditions in an effort to re-create local identity using the "mestizo" model propagated by paucartambinos.

The paucartambinos who resurrected the Majeños danza considered themselves part of a group that had achieved the important role of defenders not only of a local folklore but also of a regional one. The choice of the Majeños danza, however, was shaped by local motivations of a group of townspeople. They explained their stimulus: "A class sentiment [una emoción social], a class sentiment that led us to this . . . because until then we had lived subjugated to the hacendado. . . . the three of us [the promoters of the reinvention] didn't like that. We said, 'If the hacendados used to have the best horses, why can't we? Why can't we have the best horses, the same horses? Then, let it be reborn.' Therefore the Majeño was presented that first year."

As highlighted in this testimony of one of the leaders of the reinvention of the Majeños tradition in Paucartambo, the group who decided to perform it saw it as an opportunity to take over a symbolic element that had been the privilege of the hacendados. This formerly powerful group, after the agrarian reform, had largely vanished from the area. Most of its members had migrated to Cusco city, and the few who remained had lost their former preeminence. The new Majeños, a group of local middle-aged schoolteachers, small merchants, and public employees, did not attempt to question or transform the hacendado-like characteristics of the danza; on the contrary, they wanted to emphasize these characteristics. These members of the local petite bourgeoisie, who when they were younger had witnessed the old comparsa, were also attracted by the features of the old comparsa because it had been performed by adult, "mature" males. The appropriation of the Majeños danza, then, would allow them to re-create their local identity as prestigious, mature males.

The new comparsa in Paucartambo, like the comparsas in San Jerónimo (both the one of the 1940s and the one of the 1970s), had two personages of local history that its members sought to impersonate:

the arrieros from Majes and the local hacendados. They wanted to in-
terpret this danza as well as, or, if they could, better than, the hacendados. Moreover, they even tried to look physically like the hacendados.
In this process of re-creation, the phenotypic and other ethnic/racial
characteristics of the former landowning elite became desirable to imitate: the body, the masks, and the costumes of the dancers were designed to resemble characteristics of both the arrieros and the hacendados. In this manner, by "arguing" successfully through their ritual
performance, the members of the new group of Majeños could re-create
their own local identity.

One initial preoccupation that these new Paucartambo Majeños had
was that the bodies of the performers resemble those of the hacendados.
Paucartambinos, particularly the ones who re-created the danza, agreed
that most men who used to dance the Majeños were tall and corpulent.
The new comparsa needed to gather men who had that kind of body
but, aware that this was not going to be possible, they required at least
that the leader of the danza, the Caporal (the equivalent to the San
Jerónimo Machu; see below), fit this archetype. In other words, the
Caporal, through ritual performance and the use of metaphor and related tropes, became the hacendado, the arriero, and the representative of the whole group. The following testimony manifests their preoccupation: "Our first concern was to find a person who could be the
Caporal. The Caporal had to be taller than us. He had to stand out because of his height; height above all, a corpulent man who had the air
of being the owner, the owner of the situation and so on. So after this
conversation we went to see Señor Luis Vargas, the only prototypic
man for being the Caporal, a captain, . . . Fortunately, he didn't turn
us down."

Height is seen in Cusco and in Peru in general as one of the desirable phenotypic characteristics of Europeans and North Americans, or
people of that descent. According to local views, the characteristics that
marked the "whiteness" of hacendados was their height and their physical strength. As re-created in local imagery, the prototype of a hacendado or *patrón* (master) was that of a tall, strong male. On the other
hand, the prototypic Indian or servant was small and weak. He was impersonated in the danza by the personage named Maqt'a.

In the elaboration of the masks for the danza, the purported "white"
phenotypic characteristics of both the people from Arequipa and the
local hacendados were emphasized. One of the Paucartambo dancers
who reinvented the danza explained the origin of their masks in the
features of local hacendados. "In the past, landowners had that face . . .

that's where they [the mask makers] got it from . . . for example the Trujillos, the Palominos; the mask maker copied their faces."

During my research it became obvious that the Majeños mask is one of the central pieces in the costume and that it has become one element of distinction between the comparsas of Paucartambo and San Jerónimo. While in both places the masks had light-colored eyes (often blue), white skin, facial hair (mustaches and beards), big, rosy cheeks, and a wide smile, the noses of the Majeños of Paucartambo were smaller and less phallic than those of the Majeños of San Jerónimo (figs. 11 and 12). The masks of San Jerónimo resembled more the Caporal mask of Paucartambo, which is supposed to have a longer nose and a longer mustache.

The Majeños mask is also supposed to resemble the face of an older man, a *maduro* (mature) man. In Paucartambo masks this was a clearer feature than in San Jerónimo because they had grayish mustaches and goatee beards, which made the face more like those of old men. Here another peculiarity of the Majeños comparsas, both in Paucartambo and San Jerónimo, becomes clear. The characters impersonated and the dancers themselves are *hombres maduros,* mature, full-grown males. The concept of *madurez* (maturity) must be understood not only in reference to age but mainly to social status. A mature male is he who has a strong economic base and/or stable economic activity that allows him to carry through all the demands involved in ritual performance and sponsorship. Also, a man acquires social maturity when he marries and establishes his own nuclear family.

In Paucartambo and San Jerónimo the Majeños danza was often referred to as the one of mature, serious people. Here the characteristics of the dancers, the danza itself, and those of the personages incarnated intertwine. As a paucartambino who had performed in both the Qollas and the Majeños comparsas put it, "The Majeño isn't so characteristically funny. In Qolla you've got to be funny, more agile, whereas the Majeño is like a mature danza; that's what it is." During the performance of the danza, the gentle, unhurried but at the same time firm movements of the dancers made the danza in the eyes of townspeople seigniorial and characteristic of maduro males.

Paucartambinos agree about the stages that dancers go through as they grow up and become fully socialized or maduro males. At high-school age they join danzas that are considered much more playful, funny, satirical, and athletic. These danzas often lack any sort of enduring organization. Then, as men become more maduro, they can join a more organized comparsa or the ones that require a strong economic

Figure 11.   Majeño of Paucartambo on horseback at the entrada of the patron-saint fiesta. Paucartambo, Cusco, 1996. Photo by Zoila S. Mendoza.

status. Qollas, as mentioned in the above testimony, are considered both in Paucartambo and San Jerónimo as more playful and less mature danzas than the Majeños (see chapter 5 and 7). Female performers do not go through these stages. In the early 1990s there was only one comparsa in Paucartambo that had a group of women dancers, and they all had to be single.[7] Married women do not perform in comparsas, nor do people talk about "mature" women.

Another major preoccupation that the paucartambinos who reinvented the Majeños had about their danza was that, because of its mainly dramatic characteristics, it "did not have a choreography." To

Figure 12. San Jerónimo Majeño donning his costume the first day of the patron-saint fiesta. San Jerónimo, Cusco, 1990. Photo by Fritz Villasante.

have a "choreography" was a prerequisite for making the danza attractive locally and regionally. Choreography is understood locally as a sequence of group-coordinated figures over space such as circles or crossing lines. The incorporation of this prerequisite for the Majeños danza may be seen as a result of the development of models of folklore and regional traditions in Cusco. The Majeños received the advice of local specialists on the subject. These specialists helped the Majeños add new melodies to the danza and create their choreography. Majeños from Paucartambo said that they introduced the section of the *taqracocha* and the cacharpari (detailed below). The local artists even composed lyrics for the danza, but it was impossible to sing in the Majeños mask.

This new comparsa re-created many of the old features of the former, such as the simulation of the arrival of the arrieros from Q'osñipata and the offer of liquor to the townspeople. This comparsa put a lot more effort into giving an air of realism to this part of the performance than did the comparsa of San Jerónimo. They took the road that connects the town with Q'osñipata (which was the one purportedly used by the muleteers when it was just a trail) for their entrada. They brought along various mules with kegs of liquor. When they arrived at the main plaza, they offered wine to the people around them and then invited the fiesta participants to dance with them. In contrast to the performance in San Jerónimo (detailed below), the basic step of the Paucartambo danza simulated drunkenness, purportedly emulating the condition in which the muleteers of the past had danced. In most of my interviews with the Majeños of Paucartambo they criticized those of San Jerónimo for dancing "too straight."

As re-created in Paucartambo, the idealized personalities of the arrieros and the hacendados condensed many characteristics of a successful male whose power comes from his phenotypic features, his economic status, and his privileged position over his subordinates. Establishing a connection between the features of the characters impersonated and those of the performer facilitated the process by which through ritual performance the comparsa members could become acknowledged as local maduro decente males.

### THE RE-CREATION OF THE MAJEÑOS IN SAN JERÓNIMO: A "MODERN" COMPARSA OF "CABALLEROS" AND THE PERFORMANCE OF AN "ELEGANT" STYLE

By the end of the 1970s the transportistas of San Jerónimo, a local sector that had grown since the 1950s (along with urban expansion and the development of public transportation), had taken over the sponsor-ship of the local patron-saint fiesta. Truck and bus owners had started to perform the role of mayordomo (traditionally the main sponsor of the fiesta) and lentraderos (traditionally secondary sponsors of the fiesta), and other truck owners and drivers had formed comparsas performing Paucartambo danzas: the Qollas and the *Saqras*. Other local fiestas that used to have danzas waned during this period, and the patron-saint fiesta became the focus of comparsa performance. In this context, in 1978 the relatives and close friends of the old Majeños, perhaps stimu-lated by the reinvention of the danza in Paucartambo, and surely en-couraged by their identification with the danza and the memory of the successful performance of their predecessors, decided to re-create the local Majeños.

Since its re-creation the new Majeños comparsa tended to include jeronimianos who stood out from the rest of the townspeople not only in economic terms but also in social, cultural, and symbolic terms. All the transportistas who formed the first group were owners of motor ve-hicles (truck, bus, or automobile). This comparsa became known from that time on as that of *dueños de carro* (vehicle owners) because that was one of the primary attributes of its leaders. Education was another dis-tinct feature. Among the members of the new comparsa, most had com-pleted high school and some had even had a few years of higher educa-tion or technical training. They were all members of well-known San Jerónimo families. A couple of them had moved to Cusco city or had married into families of that city. They all spoke fluent Spanish, and sev-eral drove personal automobiles in addition to the trucks or buses with which they made a living. Their economic activity often took them to main cities of the country, including Lima. Later on, as explained be-low, this group started to incorporate the town's professionals. When this comparsa was officially made into a "folkloric association" in the 1980s, it became clear that this organization had become for these jero-nimianos one of the primary means toward constituting themselves as a distinct local class, a new elite.

According to the re-creators of the Majeños in San Jerónimo, none of the danzas that had begun to be performed by other transportistas was adequate or decente enough to honor their patron saint. Those danzas were not at the level of the elegant Majeños; their danza, they argued, was the most suitable to accompany the imagen because the Majeños was a danza of *caballeros* (gentlemen). This group identified with the danza because, as they said, "it was in them" (*les nacía*). This expression "it's in me" (*me nace*, literally "born in me") was often used by members of other comparsas to explain why they identified with the danza they performed. In the case of the Majeños, however, this identification was often explained as if "they had it in their blood," as if they had inherited it as a privilege from their relatives (two of the wealthiest and most powerful members within the new comparsa were children of one the leaders of the first comparsa of the 1940s). The members of this new comparsa have continued to feel since the reinvention that this danza is the one that goes best with their personalities because it is decente and suitable for caballeros.

When they re-created the danza, they wanted to do it "*a la moderna*" (the modern way). This statement had various implications. First, as in Paucartambo, it meant to implement a "choreography." However, two other aspects of "modernity" were more important for the members of the San Jerónimo comparsa than for those of the Paucartambo comparsa. First, jeronimianos introduced new symbols of mestizo power and prestige, several of which represented urban culture; this is typical of an "invented" tradition that uses metropolitan criteria to capture the assumed dignity of "antiquity."[8] Two elements were particularly important: the introduction of bottled beer as one of the central symbols of the danza and the innovation of the costumes.

The second aspect of modernity for the new comparsa members was to develop a long-lasting, strictly organized institution that would allow them to establish continuity between their ritual performance and their social life outside of ritual: the Asociación de Comparsa los Majeños (Majeños comparsa association). They were legally acknowledged as such in the Registro de Asociaciones (associations record) of Cusco city around 1985. Although it took them approximately five years to consolidate the Asociación, this institution has become an essential mechanism for maintaining the power and social prestige that the comparsa has gained in the town. At the same time that the Asociación serves to tightly control the group membership, it gives them respectability because it is the only officially acknowledged "folkloric" institution in the town. This Asociación has given its members a social identity outside of ritual based on the three main principles that the danza condenses: power, prestige, and masculinity. Their performance of the danza in the ritual is what actually makes these principles or values visible and tangible, making them real and part of the performers' personality.

Since the invention of the Majeños tradition, alcoholic beverages have been one of the central symbols of the danza. By metonymic association, this element had made the Majeños an even more masculine danza. Besides carrying mules loaded with *aguardiente* (sugarcane brandy), the members of the original comparsas in Paucartambo and San Jerónimo also carried a bottle filled with this liquor in their hands.

Aguardiente was the liquor that the muleteers from Majes shipped and traded. Nevertheless, the Majeños of San Jerónimo decided to replace it with bottled beer. Aguardiente was not, according to them, an alcoholic beverage characteristic of caballeros. Instead, it was a liquor commonly consumed among peasants, for example, during agricultural work. Bottled beer, an expensive industrial product originally from urban Cusco, as opposed to aguardiente or chicha (corn beer, another drink associated with rural culture and produced locally), had become the most expensive and prestigious drink consumed in private and public celebrations in Cusco towns. In San Jerónimo both the bottle and the beer itself have become important in the performance of the danza. In Paucartambo only the bottle, filled with sugarcane brandy, is sometimes part of the paraphernalia of the danza, because this comparsa considers it important to remain faithful to the old tradition.

In San Jerónimo one of the most garish and expected parts of the Majeños choreography was the *jaleo,* briefly described at the end of the introductory snapshot and detailed in the next section. In that portion of the danza, unique to the performance in San Jerónimo, the Majeños made a show of their ability to manipulate the bottle of beer. In Paucartambo the dancers splashed some of the aguardiente on the surrounding crowd at the end of the pasacalle, but this was not part of a coordinated section of the danza and it was not nearly as showy as the performance in San Jerónimo. Most of the jeronimiano fiesta participants and the Majeños were aware that the jaleo was a controversial part of the danza because it could be taken as proof of both the aggressiveness and the haughtiness of the Majeños. In their organizational meetings before their performances, the ambivalence of the Majeños toward the jaleo became evident. While they were all aware that the spraying of beer could make some people uncomfortable or angry, they were also aware that it would get the attention of most townspeople.

The attitudes of the other fiesta participants about the jaleo were equally ambivalent. While they often criticized the Majeños for splashing beer all over people, they enjoyed this part of the performance and admired the ability of the Majeños. Whatever the reaction of the crowd about the jaleo, it became clear during all the public and private performances of the Majeños (i.e., in their banquets during the fiesta, in their visit to the cemetery, and during danza performance) that bottled beer had become a central symbol of their economic power and their masculine abilities.

Since the re-creation of the danza, the new group of Majeños in San Jerónimo has also emphasized the innovation of the costume. Three central prototypical figures of a prestigious male have had a central role: the hacendado, the mestizo urban male, and the imagen of their patron saint. All three have served as sources of inspiration to re-create the old and to introduce the new elements of the Majeños costume. The Majeños of San Jerónimo called their danza "*tipo hacendado*" (hacendado style) when they referred to their costumes. As in Paucartambo, they wanted to impersonate the hacendados but "*a la moderna*," meaning that their costumes should make them look like contemporary prestigious mestizos. The new markers introduced into the costume and into the danza as a whole, they felt, had to make them "elegant" according to current urban culture.

The former Majeños dancers had worn wool ponchos which the new Majeños replaced with hip-length leather jackets. In their different qualities and shapes, ponchos have been worn in the Andes by peasants, mestizo townspeople, and hacendados. Gradually, however, because of its association with highland and rural culture, the poncho had nationally become a marker of Indianness and a symbolic icon associated with the peasantry (i.e., it had started to be used as a symbol for political and folkloric events organized by the state). Cusco city mestizos put ponchos on during the annual parades and celebrations organized to exalt cusqueñismo. As explained in chapter 2, the construction of cusqueñismo has been based on idealized and romanticized ideas about the pre-Hispanic indigenous past and the rural present.

A leather jacket, on the other hand, was an expensive piece of clothing not commonly worn by peasants. It was seen by the Majeños as a sign of elegance because it was distinctive of urban mestizos. Leather, itself a nonindigenous material (cattle were originally European), was also seen as characteristic of the clothing of arequipeños (considered in regional dominant ideology as the "whites" and "aristocrats" of the southern Andes). Arequipeños have been known for their cattle-related industries (i.e., milk and fine leather work) since the beginning of this century. Leather, therefore, could also become associated with the place of origin of the impersonated arrieros.

Jeronimianos said that replacing the wool poncho with the leather jacket would make the danza even more historically accurate because what the arrieros "actually" wore were leather jackets. They also said that the local hacendados used to wear leather jackets. Whether or not the arrieros from Arequipa or the hacendados "actually" wore leather jackets (which is likely), this piece of clothing had ethnic/racial and class connotations of which the new Majeños were very aware. Even for the contemporary comparsa members, the hip-length, high-quality leather jacket necessary to perform the danza is expensive and difficult to get. It is definitely one of the most precious pieces of the costume. New comparsa members often have to borrow a jacket for a few years from retired dancers until they can have their own.

The new markers of social status and "modernity" introduced by the Majeños of San Jerónimo as part of an elaborated ritual costume have taken an exaggerated form. For example, they have been changing the colors, the patterns, and the materials of their jodhpurs and shirts. During my research their jodhpurs were not made of natural-color wool as were those worn by their predecessors and by the Paucartambo comparsa. The new jodhpurs were made of bright, mustard-colored, expensive corduroy. Corduroy pants are, like leather jackets, considered elegant pieces of clothing in today's Cusco. The material itself is representative of urban dress. Their shirts, also different from the plain, white cotton shirts worn by the Paucartambo comparsa, were made of shiny, colorful, patterned polyester. It was clear that these elaborate flashy shirts and pants were meant to be worn as ritual costumes and would not be worn outside of ritual by the comparsa members. Nevertheless, the obvious industrial and synthetic origin of the materials and colors marked the urban and cosmopolitan character of the danza, making it more elegant than those that use handmade and natural-color materials in their costumes.

The Majeños of San Jerónimo have also modified some of the characteristics of the hat. The hat that had been worn before was a wide-brimmed straw hat still popular today among Paucartambo Majeños. In San Jerónimo the brim has been extended to the point of making the hat look like those of the Mexican *charros* (figs. 13 and 14). From the beginning, the wide-brimmed hat has been seen as a sign of elegance. For those who first brought the danza to the town, it made the danza decente and elegante because this kind of hat was distinctive of hacendados and urban mestizos in general. For the re-creators of the danza in the town, the exaggeration of the brim made the hat even more elegant and masculine. Thus, to make the hat look like the hat of the Mexican charro made the danza more elegant and masculine. The figure of the "macho" elegant Mexican charro has been very well known in Peru for a few decades through television. The association of the Majeños with the personality of the charros was also evident when the band played the melody of the *jarabe tapatío* (known in the United States as the Mexican hat dance) when the Majeños practiced with

Figure 13. San Jerónimo Majeños showing equestrian prowess during the fiesta entrada. San Jerónimo, Cusco, 1990. Photo by Fritz Villasante.

their horses before the entrada. The Majeños of San Jerónimo have also added to the hat some embroidered material that makes it look more like the Mexican hats. In Paucartambo only the hat of the Caporal looks like those of the San Jerónimo Majeños. Finally, the Majeños of San Jerónimo refer to their hat as a characteristic that makes them look like their patron saint. This confirms once again that this hat is a symbol of elegance.

The identification of the Majeños comparsa with the imagen of their patron saint has had an important role in the re-creation of the danza in San Jerónimo. As explained in chapter 3, this icon is regionally known and admired as one of the most majestic components of the Corpus Christi celebration in Cusco city. The commentaries about this imagen by other cusqueños during this celebration and in the local literature about this ritual make this evident. These sources indicate that the people of San Jerónimo are very proud of their elegant and powerful-looking patron saint. His expensive and finely embroidered gowns and capes, his very wide brimmed hat, and his white facial features make this imagen, in the eyes of cusqueños, a decente gentleman. Majeños often referred to their hats and masks as elements that made them similar to their patron saint.

Saint Jerome's fame as a doctor of the church, a reference to his scholastic accomplishments as the translator of biblical writings, and as an acknowledged figure in the church hierarchy in which he became a

Figure 14.   Detail of San Jerónimo Majeño's hat and mask profile. The hats are made to resemble Mexican charros. San Jerónimo, Cusco, 1990. Photo by Fritz Villasante.

cardinal has made this particular imagen an even more highly condensed symbol of decencia and power. This saint's fame as a doctor and cardinal of the church has been emphasized not only by evangelizing preaching but also by the particular characteristics of this cusqueño icon. The imagen holds in his left arm a silver replica of San Jerónimo's church on top of the Bible, and his right hand is raised, holding a golden quill, a symbol of his erudition (video example 1; fig. 10). Jeronimianos admired the scholarly accomplishment of Saint Jerome. People of the town call their patron saint the "doctor" (always in the scholastic sense and not in the medical one) as a sign of high respect. This characteristic of the saint has given force to the idea of power that this imagen conveys, because these townspeople have throughout their lives learned that in Cusco and Peru formal education is an important vehicle for transcending their position of subordination.

It is interesting that, while Saint Jerome was dressed like a cardinal, the style of his hat did not match the customary outfit. The hat looked more characteristic of a wealthy Andean mestizo. The upright posture of Saint Jerome as portrayed in this imagen also adds an air of superiority and arrogance to the icon. This posture and the air of arrogance are both very important elements that the Majeños emphasized during their performances. This posture and attitude differentiated them from the Maqt'as, their servants, who were always portrayed as hunched over as a sign of subservience. The Majeños' arrogance and haughtiness is also highlighted by two other elements during their performance of the danza. First, they showed their control of the bottled beer during the jaleo, always holding this symbol of economic power in their hands. Second, as described in the next section, while dancing, they pushed back their jackets and put one hand at the waist, imitating a male posture of defiance.

The Majeños said repeatedly that their danza was the one that went best with the imagen of their patron saint. Here their local elaborations of the concepts of decencia, elegance, and power have served to make a convincing "argument" through metaphorical association between the patron saint and the Majeños. The gender element has also been central for the identification of these jeronimianos with their patron saint. From the metaphorical association with their patron saint, the Majeños have taken yet another step toward becoming the prototypes of respectable, decente, local caballeros. Furthermore, this symbolic association has helped them defend their privileged position in the ritual performances in which the imagen is involved, the Octava of Corpus Christi and the patron-saint fiesta. In both, the Majeños act as if they were the leaders of the ritual and the official escort of the imagen.

For the Octava the Majeños comparsa was the only group that performed its danza to escort the imagen from Cusco to the town (video example 1). They had started to do this in 1983, and no other comparsa has been able to get organized to do the same. They led the procession back to the town, performing their pasacalle and abbreviated versions of the jaleo (without the showering of the beer) on the main avenue that connects the capital city to the town. When they reached the neighboring town of San Sebastián, they performed their complete choreography for the local townspeople and then continued leading the procession toward San Jerónimo. When they arrived there, they performed the danza for the jeronimianos and had their own banquet and celebration in the plaza. In the Octava in the town, the Majeños were also the only comparsa to perform and the only one to have a big celebration. They also stood out among the other sponsors of that local ritual performance by having the most sumptuous celebration in the main plaza.[9]

With respect to the patron-saint fiesta, as detailed in chapter 3, the Majeños have assumed the lead in various preparatory events and a privileged position during the central performance of the ritual. For example, they have assumed charge of the *amarre* (placing and arrangement of the icon at the main altar of the church) of the imagen, of the first *novena* (series of daily masses) and of the *misa de gallo* (first mass on the central day). The Majeños have been able to establish the local tradition of being the first comparsa to perform in front of the imagen after the processions. Whenever the Majeños' privileged position in this ritual was questioned by other townspeople, they recalled the fact that their comparsa was the first and, for a few years, the only to perform in the patron-saint fiesta.

The Majeños have also designated themselves the defenders and main representatives of folklore in the town. This is one of the main reasons it was difficult for them to admit that their danza had come originally from Paucartambo. In the late 1980s and early 1990s, during regional controversies about the so-called invasion of *danzas foráneas* (alien danzas), they have led the fight against the local popularity of these danzas among the young jeronimianos. These danzas are originally from the Altiplano region (Puno-Bolivia) and were performed for the patron-saint fiesta by the two comparsas formed by the younger generation. In chapter 6 I discuss the confrontations between the young generation defending their danzas and groups like the Majeños who held chauvinistic views about local and regional folklore.

The authoritarian attitude of the Majeños was often criticized by other comparsas, local authorities, and townspeople. Nevertheless, most of the privileges that they have obtained in the main rituals of the town have been conceded to them because of the local recognition of them as authorities in the matter of folklore, a recognition gained largely through their organization. This comparsa is clearly the most organized, strict, and therefore respected of the town. Their ability to construct and maintain a solid Asociación is acknowledged as proof that their economic, social, and cultural resources have converted them into a local elite. Their Asociación has clearly consolidated the local power of the Majeños as the main comparsa of San Jerónimo. This institution has also become an important vehicle through which the Majeños have maintained their identity as a distinct, superior group. The other comparsas and voluntary associations often mentioned the Majeños as a model in their own attempts to become respected institutions in the town. This local reputation of the Majeños was strengthened when they became the only local "folkloric" institution officially registered in Cusco city's public records of associations approximately between 1984 and 1985. Since then they have assumed the role of local authorities in folklore and the local equivalents of instituciones culturales in Cusco city.

This strong Asociación was one of the main elements differentiating this comparsa from that of Paucartambo. In Cusco it was clear that having an Asociación that not only allowed the preparation of a good performance for the fiesta but that also provided a structure for comparsa members to become part of a distinct social group outside of ritual, was the most effective way to obtain local recognition and power. In Paucartambo the two most powerful local comparsas were those that had constituted solid Asociaciones. In Paucartambo, as in San Jerónimo, it was evident that belonging to one of the two well-organized comparsas—the *Qhapaq Negros* or the *Contradanza*—was proof of substantial economic, social, and cultural resources. Membership in one of these groups defined a paucartambino as a member of a distinct local elite. In Paucartambo that elite was mostly constituted by professionals, most of whom worked and lived in Cusco city and a few in other major cities of the country. Some of them were relatives of the old landowners of the area. Both comparsas carried out a series of social gatherings (i.e., organized parties and banquets) in Cusco city throughout the year. Forming and maintaining a well-organized folkloric or "cultural" institution in Cusco is taken as a sign of an urban and cosmopolitan attitude toward local expressive forms.

The Majeños of Paucartambo did not have a "folkloric" organization that carried out activities during the year. All of them lived in the town and were members of the petite bourgeoisie there. While in order to perform Majeños in that town the men had to be acknowledged as maduro paucartambinos who could face the responsibilities of the ritual performance, it was clear that during the fiesta they did not stand out as the local elite. The old people of Paucartambo, among them some of the current Majeños, often complained that those who lived and worked outside the town had taken over the patron-saint fiesta and monopolized the realm of local prestige. However, they also applauded those comparsas' sound organization and sumptuous performances because they strengthened Paucartambo's regional fame as "folkloric province of Cusco."

## THE PERFORMANCE OF THE SAN JERÓNIMO MAJEÑOS DANZA

The Majeños of San Jerónimo performed on two occasions each year in 1989 and 1990. One was the Octava of Corpus Christi (a one-day celebration in June), when the townspeople brought back the imagen of Saint Jerome from Cusco city to the town (video example 1). On this occasion the Majeños was the only comparsa. The second, a larger and more complex performance, was during the four days of the patron-saint fiesta described in chapter 3. The following description is based on the fiesta performances.

On the four days the danza was performed by nineteen men and one woman, all fully costumed and masked. The music was played by a brass band composed of wind instruments such as tubas, trumpets, and trombones and percussion instruments such as drums (among them one bass drum) and cymbals. This band was hired for the performance and was not part of the comparsa. Three characters were physically distinct in the danza: the Majeño, performed by most of the men (figs. 12–17); the Dama (lady), performed by the woman (fig. 15); and the Maqt'as or Cholos, performed by two men noticeably smaller than the rest (figs. 18 and 20). Most of the masks worn by all the personages were made of a sort of papier-mâché and painted with bright-colored, shiny varnish. Few were made of plaster.

Among the Majeños were one named the Machu ("old man" in Quechua) and two Caporales ("chiefs" or "foremen" in Spanish) who were not distinguishable by their appearance but by their position in the danza. The Machu was the leader of the whole group and the only one who danced with the Dama (fig. 15). Each of the Caporales led one of the two lines that formed the basic structure of the danza (video example 1). All the Majeños wore matching costumes: brown leather boots with spurs, jodhpurs, wide brown leather belts (*cinchos*), long-sleeve button-down shirts, hip-length brown leather jackets, wide-brimmed straw hats (like Mexican charros), and four colorful neckerchiefs (figs. 12

Figure 15. San Jerónimo Machu, the leader of the danza, and the Dama dancing on his arm. Octava of Corpus Christi, Cusco city, 1990. Photo by Zoila S. Mendoza.

and 14). Among these neckerchiefs was one covering the hair, the second worn as a tie, and the other two hanging down from their belts. Their masks had big, rosy cheeks, and most had blue eyes; their noses were extremely long (up to ten inches) and phallic, with a bulky black birthmark almost at the end. Coming out of their nostrils they had long mustaches (approximately seven inches long) made of horsehair. All the masks had extremely wide smiles extending almost across the whole face, showing their shiny white teeth and a gold one, and their bright red lips (fig. 16). Gold teeth are a symbol of status among Andeans. Birthmarks and facial hair are considered characteristic of white people. Each Majeño carried a bottle of beer that he switched from hand to hand as he performed the danza (video example 1; fig. 17).

The Dama wore a very stylized San Jerónimo market-woman outfit. The market woman is known in San Jerónimo as *mestiza* and not as *chola*, the term often used in Andean literature (cf. Seligman 1989). This Dama wore high-heel ankle boots or sandals; transparent hose; a knee-length *pollera* (flared skirt) with various *centros* (petticoats) underneath; a long-sleeve embroidered blouse; a long, silky shawl; a tall, white stovepipe hat with a wide, colored band; and two colorful neckerchiefs (the same kind as the Majeños'): one to cover her head and the other in her right hand to dance. She had two long braids tied with wide-ribbon bows. Her mask resembled the face of a light-complexioned white woman with blue eyes, a medium-sized perfectly straight nose, and rosy cheeks with a small birthmark on one. She had a very discreet smile showing absolutely even teeth, one of which was gold (fig. 15). The Dama outfit was very similar to the ones worn by women who perform mestizo folkloric dances in the events promoted by the instituciones culturales (fig. 2).

The two Maqt'as, also called Cholos, were dressed the way that "Indians" or peasants are portrayed in folkloric staged presentations (fig. 1). They wore *ojotas* (rubber sandals made out of tires, worn by peasants to work in the fields) without socks, black knickers made of *bayeta* (coarse wool material), colorful handwoven wool sashes, long-sleeve shirts, bayeta-embroidered vests, colorful *chullos* (hand-knitted hats with ear flaps), and *warak'as* (handwoven wool slings) tied around their waists and across their chests. While the colors on their masks were

Figure 16. San Jerónimo Majeño's mask with wide smile showing shiny white teeth and a single gold tooth. San Jerónimo, Cusco, 1990. Photo by Fritz Villasante.

Figure 17. San Jerónimo Majeños holding a bottle of beer, a central symbol of the danza. Octava of Corpus Christi, Cusco city, 1990. Photo by Zoila S. Mendoza.

not too different from those of the Majeños' masks, the complexion of the Maqt'a face differed greatly. The Maqt'a face exaggerated two main features considered characteristic of an "Indian" phenotype: the hooked nose and the prominent cheekbones. Their curved noses contrasted with the long, straight, phallic noses of the Majeños. Their faces were smiling, but their mouths were smaller than the Majeños' and they did not show any teeth (fig. 18). Furthermore, they did not have any facial hair. Through the contrast between the characteristics of the Majeño and the Maqt'a, the comparsa members enacted the exaggerated alternatives—the polarities of the marking system—and situated themselves in an unambiguously dominant position.

The complete performance of the danza was designed for the different sequences of the patron-saint fiesta. On the afternoon of September 29, the day of the entrada, the Majeños gathered at the house of the president of the association. To the background music of their band, they donned their costumes and masks and drank some beer. When they were ready, they went to the local stadium, where their horses and two mules had been stationed. Every Majeño and the Dama rode a horse, while the Maqt'as went on foot, each pulling a mule that carried two big kegs and were adorned with *walqanchis* (hangings; figs. 19 and 20). The group joined the other comparsas for the entrada, where they showed their equestrian prowess by swaying side to side on their horses as if they were dancing while riding (video example 2; figs. 11 and 13).

On the 30th, the central day of the fiesta, the Majeños had their misa de gallo at 4:00 a.m. When it was finished, they had drinks and appetizers in the atrium of the church. When the Qollas comparsa finished its own mass and came out of the church, its members were invited to join the Majeños for a drink. At noon, the Majeños performed their complete choreography in the church atrium. This was done when the procession ended and the imagen of Saint Jerome was placed outside the church door. The same day in the afternoon, the Majeños went out to the main plaza of the town carrying huge bottles filled with *cambray* (a sweet, winelike liquor made of sugarcane), and after performing part of their choreography they offered cambray to some fiesta participants who had watched their performance.

On October 1, the third day of celebration, the Majeños made their visit to the cemetery and held masses in front of the tombs of deceased comparsa members, relatives, close friends, and followers. Afterward they went to the open space outside the cemetery and started to drink beer. After the Qollas comparsa arrived, the Majeños invited the Qollas to join them for drinks (video example 6). At that time, some speeches were made about the importance of always being united in their common cause of keeping San Jerónimo's folklore alive. Here, as in the Majeños' invitation after the misa de gallo, tensions emerged between the two comparsas. These were often a result of the Majeños condescending attitude toward the Qollas, that is, showing off their abundant and expensive drinks. After the procession of that day, the Majeños

Figure 18. San Jerónimo Maqt'a, who represents the indigenous servant of the Majeños. Octava of Corpus Christi, Cusco city, 1990. Photo by Zoila S. Mendoza.

performed their complete choreography again. Finally, on the fourth and last day of the celebration, October 2, after performing their complete choreography following the "blessing" that the imagen gives to the townspeople, the Majeños performed their cacharpari or *despedida* (farewell).

The choreography of the danza had the following distinct parts: pasacalle, jaleo, taqracocha, and marinera with wayno fuga.[10] The pasacalle was the coordinated group movement along the streets that the comparsa performed in two parallel lines, always led by the Machu and the Dama with their arms linked (video example 1). These lines were hierarchically organized by height and seniority. The tallest and the ones

Figure 19.   Dama of Paucartambo Majeños danza riding a horse during the entrada. Paucartambo, Cusco, 1996. Photo by Zoila S. Mendoza.

Figure 20. San Jerónimo Maqt'a pulling a mule that carries the purported kegs of sugarcane brandy to simulate the arrival of the muleteers in the past. Octava of Corpus Christi, Cusco city, 1990. Photo by Zoila S. Mendoza.

who had been in the comparsa the longest tended to be in front. Therefore, the Caporales had both these characteristics: they were definitively the tallest and some of the oldest members. The order of the lines was never lost during the performance.

The basic danza step used in the pasacalle and in other sections was a swaying, gentle body movement accompanied by long and firm steps. The Majeño veered his body right and left following the call-and-response structure of the accompanying melody. This triple-meter marchlike melody of the danza is known locally and regionally as characteristic of the Majeños danza (audio example 5; video examples 1 and 2). As mentioned earlier, this melody has an iconic relationship to the suggestion of drunkenness in the movement of the Paucartambo performers and can be called a "staggering melody" (Turino 1997, 227). As the Majeños turned to the right and stopped briefly before turning to the left, they raised their left arms holding the bottles of beer. At the same time, they put their right hands on their waists and pushed back their jackets. Then they turned left and made the same gestures with the opposite arm. While the dancers bent their bodies slightly as they turned, they tried to keep a very upright posture giving the danza a distinct air of arrogance. After they reached the place where they wanted to continue the choreography, they kept doing the same kind of movements in place. With a change of melody, they started the next section, the jaleo.

The melody of the jaleo (celebration) was played at a considerably faster tempo than that of the pasacalle (audio example 6; video example 3). In the jaleo the two lines formed a circle that turned counterclockwise. After a full 360-degree turn, they turned clockwise once. While they were making the circle they started spraying the beer upward and outward, in a coordinated way, giving the impression of an erupting geyser, which caused the crowd to open up. They made this effect by making a little hole on the lid of the container and shaking the bottle. While the circle was formed, the Machu and the Dama, always with their arms linked, went in and out of the circle. The body movement of the Majeños while performing the jaleo was still controlled and slow, as they shifted their bodies from one place to another by dragging or sliding their feet on the floor, barely lifting them. After the two turns were finished, the circle broke up and the dancers returned to their initial two-line formation. With a change of melody, the taqracocha started.

*Taqracocha* is the name of the wayno that accompanies this part of the choreography (audio example 7; video example 3). Wayno (also *wayño* or *huayno*) is one of the major mestizo song-dance genres in Peru and other Andean countries (Turino 1993, 1997).[11] The basic dance structure of mestizo cusqueño wayno consists of a *paseo* (slower dance) followed by a *zapateo* (foot-stomping or tapping) performed by couples (as opposed to group dancing) (Roel Pineda 1959).[12] Wayno music in Peru "wavers ambiguously between a duple and a triple feel within a 2/4 or 4/4 meter" and is characterized by sung stanzas often mixing Spanish with one of the two main indigenous languages, Quechua or Aymara (Turino 1993; 1997, 233).

With its various subsections the Majeños taqracocha resembled a very stylized mestizo wayno. There was no singing in this performance of the wayno. The two lines of Majeños faced each other and began with a slow front and back foot movement, repeated about eight times each foot. Then they carefully turned their bodies 360 degrees with a very fast, almost imperceptible stomping of their feet; this turn was accomplished with a swaying movement. In the second subsection one line approached the other, with the dancers again almost dragging their feet, until they met: this kind of flattened out movement of the feet is supposed to give an impression of refinement. In the meeting, each couple put their noses together and made a 360-degree turn in place. Then the line that had made the initial movement went back to its place and the other line repeated the movement. This second subsection clearly highlighted the size of their noses, which served as the axis of their turn in the middle. In the third subsection they formed a circle and, as in the jaleo, made a complete turn in both directions. During this subpart, as in the jaleo, the Dama and the Machu went in and out of the circle, as did the Maqt'as.

Finally came the marinera with wayno fuga (audio examples 8 and 9; video example 3). The marinera is a genre that originated in the coastal tradition known as criollo around the end of the nineteenth century (Romero 1985). It is, like the mestizo wayno, a couple dance, whose music usually has a 6/8 meter and which has as one of its typical features the manipulation of handkerchiefs. The two genres, the marinera and the wayno, have been gradually fused by Andeans into various combinations, the most common of which is now the marinera with wayno fuga. As it is typical of fugas, this final section of the Majeños marinera contrasted with the main piece and was played at a much faster tempo.

The Majeños performed their marinera and wayno in the two-line structure, at times approaching and crossing each other. For these parts they put their beer bottles in the pockets of their jackets and performed with one of their neckerchiefs, at times waving them with their right hands and at times holding them with both hands. The Majeños did not link arms or hook their neckerchiefs to perform the wayno, both of which are characteristic of Cusco-style wayno (Roel Pineda 1959). Their stomping, as in the taqracocha, was very soft and gentle, and they always moved in a very slow, controlled motion. When the wayno ended, the Majeños hugged their partners, imitating very deep-voiced laughter. Then they did the pasacalle back home or to another point of the town, where they performed again.

The cacharpari, performed the last day of the patron-saint fiesta, was also accompanied by a waynolike melody. As in the pasacalle, the two lines of Majeños moved along the streets and mainly around the central plaza. The basic step, however, was different. It was a trotlike step done at a faster tempo than the characteristic Majeños step. The Majeños waved their neckerchiefs good-bye to the fiesta participants, and the lines approached and separated without crossing.

During all the Majeños performances, the Maqt'as played a marginal, servant/buffoonlike role. They pulled the mules, cleared the space in the crowd for the performances, teased the audience to make it laugh, and mostly remained outside the choreographic figures made by the

Majeños (such as in the circles formed in the jaleo and the taqracocha) without taking a particular role. They moved their bodies in a way that contrasted with the Majeños: they made jerky, quick, sudden, and uncontrolled movements such as jumping up and down, pushing and shoving each other, as well as exaggerating their stomping when performing wayno. Always hunched over as a sign of subservience, the Maqt'as' posture also contrasted to that of the Majeños. In every respect they marked out differences and acted as foils to Majeños dignity, emphasizing some of the stereotypes used in indigenous staged folkloric performance.

## THE IDEAL MAJEÑO OF SAN JERÓNIMO

San Jerónimo Majeños considered their comparsa exemplary not only in the matter of local folklore but also in terms of local decencia and urbanity. The members of this comparsa were always very careful to guard their public image not only during the ritual and other group public performances but also during their everyday lives. They considered themselves members of an exclusive "family," a closed elite that had to set an example for the rest of the town. They were obliged to help and support each other in any case of need. Each member was made responsible for behaving, according to their institutional rules, as a respectable, proper social being who would not dishonor the name of the institution. This responsible behavior in all circumstances was one of the main criteria given by the members of the comparsa when asked about their strict process of selection of new comparsa members. Each new member had to be carefully chosen, tested, and endorsed by two senior members of the comparsa. These two members had to ensure that the candidate fit the characteristics of the "ideal" Majeño inside and outside ritual performance.[13]

The first important characteristic of the Majeño performer (not of the Maqt'a) necessary to become part of the comparsa was that he had to prove a very secure economic base—a good income—that would allow him to cover all the expenses required not only for the ritual performances but also for all social activities held by the comparsa throughout the year. The Majeño had to be able to afford the expensive costume, the large amounts of beer drunk during the danza performances, the quotas for hiring the brass band, and, when his turn arrived, a sumptuous *cargo* (sponsorship role). It was clear that to be the carguyoq of the Majeños comparsa was one of the most prestigious sponsorship roles of the whole fiesta because of the great economic expenditure involved. In their Asociación meetings, soccer games, barbecues, and other social gatherings during the year, the Majeños always had to have cash ready to spend.

As mentioned, several of the re-creators of the comparsa were prosperous truck owners. By that year, 1978, although the group of jeronimianos whose main economic activity was transportation (bus, automobile, pickup, and truck owners or drivers) had grown, owners of motor vehicles continued to be an economic elite within the town. The most prosperous of them had been able to combine this activity with other wholesale and retail commerce, such as in lumber and hardware stores. Like the first group of Majeños in the town, transportista members of the comparsa today see themselves as having the same role as the old arrieros. They said that owning the means of transportation, working in commerce, and being wealthy makes them modern-day counterparts of the arrieros. In fact, in a conversation I had with two Majeños transportistas, using a very explicit metaphoric comparison to these merchants, they referred to the pickup truck in which we were riding as "the horse." Their control over space through constant movement between commercial points and in general their key role as intermediaries between the city and the countryside, as well as among the jungle, the highlands, and the coast, give them a privileged role in the society. Like the arrieros were during colonial and early republican times, they are intermediaries in economic as well as cultural affairs.

After the first few years, the comparsa started to incorporate members of a new emerging elite in the town, the professionals, a sector that in San Jerónimo continues to be very small. A professional in San Jerónimo is one who has completed a college education or has acquired some technical training. In the Majeños comparsa today, professionals have taken on some central roles. The president of the Asociación during the years of my fieldwork was an architect, the secretary was an electrical technician who had his own shop, and the former president was a forestry technician who worked for a state institution. Despite the incorporation of these professionals and other successful employees of state or private institutions, the comparsa continues to be known as that of the dueños de carro.

During my research, membership in the Majeños comparsa was determined not so much by occupation as by other criteria. A stable economic activity with a strong income was considered, as in Paucartambo, one of the main indicators of madurez. Also as in Paucartambo, a Majeño had to be a maduro male. Nevertheless, in San Jerónimo much more emphasis was put on the members' ability to display wealth inside and outside the danza. For jeronimianos, belonging to the Majeños comparsa became a clear indicator of economic power. Some townsmen commented that they would like to be Majeños but that they still did not have enough money to do it, that they were still saving. On many occasions jeronimianos said of a member of that comparsa, "He is a Majeño, he has money." But to be a Majeño also had other implications for townspeople. They were very aware that it was not easy to become a Majeño, that this comparsa was very closed and exclusive and its members were very strict about whom they admitted. The townspeople knew that even with respect to their internal hierarchies the Majeños were very rigid. Among the main reasons the members that performed the Maqt'as were not considered maduro enough to be Majeños was that they lacked the economic resources. Interestingly enough the literal translation of the word *maqt'a* is "adolescent boy, young man" (Hornberger and Hornberger 1983, 126).

A second main criterion for admission into the Majeños was membership in a "traditional" San Jerónimo family that had resided in the town for several generations. This criterion has become central in the context of a strong migration into the district of people mainly from other provinces of the departamento and some from other departamentos (see chapter 3). During my research the few nonjeronimianos who were members of the comparsa were close relatives of one of the local families (i.e., one was married to a jeronimiana and another was the cousin of a senior member). Kinship played an important role in membership. Among the members of the comparsa there were sets of brothers, cousins, and some in-laws. Also, as mentioned above, two of the main current leaders are sons of one of the founders of the comparsa in the 1940s.

A third important characteristic of the ideal Majeño was showing the capacity to behave like a *patrón* or *jefe* (boss) in all situations. A Majeño, inside and outside ritual performance, had to maintain an authoritarian and patronizing posture. During ritual preparations and performances, and with respect to other comparsas and local authorities, the members of this comparsa often took a condescending attitude. As mentioned before, with a paternalistic stance, they designated themselves the defenders of "traditional" San Jerónimo and cusqueño folklore, drastically opposing the introduction of Altiplano danzas by the two comparsas of young jeronimianos. For a couple of years they even performed another cusqueño "traditional" mestizo danza briefly during the fiesta in order to "teach" the young generation the model they should follow.[14] Outside ritual performance they also carried out public activities to show their institutionalized generosity to the townspeople. In these events they tried to demonstrate that they were a beneficent local elite. For example, they organized a *chocolatada* (offering of hot chocolate) for the poor children of the town at Christmas.

Within the danza performance this institutionalized generosity was shown when the Majeños offered the cambray (the liquor they carried in big bottles the afternoon of the main day) to the fiesta participants. With this act, they reconstructed the idealized memories of the arrieros and at the same time showed their fellow townspeople that they, the contemporary Majeños, also knew how to share their wealth. The invitation to drink the cambray was not a simple "representation" or "emulation" of what the arrieros did. It was an act that clearly showed that, thanks to their economic power, the members of this comparsa could afford to put on this kind of expensive performance. In other words, by means of iconic symbolism and metaphoric comparison, the members of the Majeños comparsa became, through ritual performance, a local beneficent elite.

During the four days of the fiesta, the Majeños performed a series of condescending public acts to establish their superiority and chivalry, or what they called their "caballerosidad." The main target of these performances was the other comparsa of adult men in the town, the one that has also become a "traditional" San Jerónimo comparsa, the Qollas. Composed mostly of truck drivers and butchers, this comparsa emphasized many of the opposite characteristics of the elegante, decente, and caballero characteristics of the Majeños comparsa, through carnivalesque and grotesque danza performance. Every time these two comparsas crossed paths during ritual performance, they teased each other. The Qollas called the Majeños "patrón" and "hacendado," and the Majeños called the Qollas derogatory names such as "cholo," "servant," or "Indian." During the ritual, these comparsas treated each other as absolutely opposite social and ethnic "others" (see chapters 5 and 7).

There were several moments in which the Majeños tried to show the Qollas and the whole town that they were "caballeros" and that they could share with another group with less wealth and power. One was when the two comparsas met after their masses for the central day of the celebration. The Majeños invited the Qollas to their spot in the atrium to have some champagne, *ponche de habas* (described in chapter 3), and pastries. Another moment was in their meetings outside the cemetery on October 1 when the Majeños took the first step and treated the Qollas to some beer. At both times the tension between the groups was evident, particularly on the side of the Qollas, who were bothered by the Majeños' condescending and authoritarian attitudes during the fiesta. While a few short speeches showed that several members on both sides believed that the two groups should be allies in order to keep their fiesta regionally popular and traditional (i.e., performing cusqueño danzas instead of Altiplano danzas), the overall performance during the fiesta clearly showed the competition and the differences between them.

The asymmetrical relationship and the contrasting characteristics between a master/hacendado and an indigenous servant/peon are also manifested within the Majeños danza through the relationship Majeño-Maqt'a and in particular Machu-Maqt'a. As pointed out in the description of the danza, masks, costumes, and postures (white facial features/indigenous facial features, expensive urban clothing/cheap handmade or coarse peasant clothing, upright, arrogant posture/hunched-over, subservient attitude) emphasized the ethnic/racial differences between the Majeño and the Maqt'a. During the entrada in the patron-saint fiesta and on the way back from Cusco city in the Octava, the Maqt'as were in charge of loading, unloading, and pulling the mules, which purportedly carried the aguardiente. The Maqt'as also cleared the way for the Majeños to ride their horses, to march along the streets with their pasacalle, and to perform their choreography in the plaza. The Maqt'as did not ride horses or form part of the coordinated group movement. Most of the time they remained marginal, either clearing the way or marking the borders during the performance of the choreography (sometimes going inside the figure made but most of the time keeping out). They also often acted like buffoons, making the public laugh while always keeping a marginal position within the performance.

The Maqt'a personage should be analyzed in a wider regional context. Many danzas all over the Andes, and certainly most cusqueño danzas today, have Maqt'as or personages with aspects or functions in the comparsas similar to those of the Maqt'a in the Majeños (the more peasantlike dances have *Ukukus*). These characters usually play the role of figures on the borderline between domesticated and undomesticated who at the same time have humorous and subversive features. In Peru entire comparsas may be seen as having these characteristics (Mendoza 1989). Among them is the Qollas, which I will analyze in chapter 5.

Within the Majeños comparsa, the Maqt'as' performance emphasized more the domesticated, harmless, funny, and servantlike side of this borderline personage. The Maqt'as are also often called "cholos" by the Majeños. This national ethnic/racial term has been conflated in the Majeños performance with that of "Indian." While through their clothes, masks, and postures the Maqt'as are portrayed as the prototypical "Indian-peasant" of folkloric presentations and school textbooks, because of their subordinate relationship with a decente personage, they are called "cholos." As explained in chapter 1, *cholo* has become a pejorative ethnic term that implies low social status and cultural incompleteness; in Peruvian dominant ideology, it suggests incomplete assimilation to urban coastal culture. When Majeños described the role of the Maqt'as within the danza they often said, "They are our servants, our cholos,"[15] and often called them "cholos" when giving them orders.

Compared to other Maqt'as or Maqt'a-like characters in other danzas of the region, the Majeños' Maqt'as demonstrate a more respectful attitude toward the main characters. In other danzas these buffoonlike personages harass the main leader of the danza (the Machu or Caporal), pinching, punching, and attempting to outsmart him. Maqt'as in the Majeños comparsa minimized this role. Most of the slapstick play that took place to make people laugh was between the two Maqt'as and not between the Maqt'a and the Machu. Although some playful harassment took place, the respect that the Maqt'a owed to the Machu was emphasized. For example, instead of trying to steal the woman of the Machu, as takes place in the *Aucca Chileno* choreography, the Maqt'as respectfully escorted and protected this female character. The attempt to minimize the grotesque and subversive characteristics of the Maqt'as was evident during their rehearsals, in which the Maqt'a performers were advised to be funny but not disrespectful.

In Paucartambo the relationship between Maqt'a-Majeño and Maqt'a-Machu was similar to that of San Jerónimo. Nevertheless, in Paucartambo the Maqt'as of all the comparsas had a very important role, which was to harass the fiesta participants and make them laugh with obscene statements. The Maqt'as of all comparsas moved more or less freely and at moments formed groups to improvise a funny act. Therefore, although the Maqt'as of the Majeños in Paucartambo maintained a subservient role similar to that of San Jerónimo, in Paucartambo they tended to be more grotesque and playful than in San Jerónimo.

As they did in ritual performance, during the year the Majeños of San Jerónimo tried to exercise and talk about their power over other social and ethnic/racial sectors of society, including women. During their institutional meetings (once a month and, during the months of the central performances, two or three times a week) and informal gatherings (i.e., a private party or a conversation in a cantina), the Majeños often recounted situations in which they were able to use their economic power or their social connections. In these meetings the more powerful position of some members over others was also evident. This power was most clear with the members who impersonated the Maqt'as, who were ordered around, were sent to do the hard work, and served the rest (i.e., they carried the cases of beer and served the food and drinks).[16] They were clearly considered second-class members of the comparsa and treated like servants. The Maqt'as of San Jerónimo admitted that for them it was difficult to be "promoted" to become a Majeño because they lacked the qualities required to perform in that role within the danza and in the Asociación; they were not maduro enough.

The Majeños' configuration of gender distinction, within and outside the danza, may also be understood as part of their attitude as "the masters of all." In their private meetings the Majeños often commented about the importance of being *el hombre de la casa* (the man of the house)—the boss—and of remaining independent of their wives. They made fun of members (absent or present) who had shown themselves to be in any way under the dominance of their wives. While the wives were included in a few of the activities of the comparsa, mostly such as being in charge of the food and attending to the guests, they were excluded from association meetings, rehearsals, and decisions. The only woman who participated in the performance of the danza, the Dama, was also excluded from those realms. She participated in only a couple of rehearsals. The Dama was the niece of one of the members of the old local Majeños comparsa. She was twenty-five years old and single. As anticipated, in Cusco the ideal is that if a woman is allowed to perform in a comparsa at all, she should be unmarried. This has started to change in San Jerónimo, as will be discussed in chapters 6 and 7.

According to the Majeños the Dama dancer did not need to practice much. She only had to follow the movements of the Machu. Obviously, her role within the danza, as in the Asociación, was very passive. The Majeños said that her main task was to dress like an elegant mestiza and to behave and dance like a respectable "dama" (lady), as the name of her danza role implied. What that meant was, first, that she was never free from her "husband" (she was supposed to be the Machu's wife): the Machu always took her by the arm and all she had to do was follow him and be gracious. Second, it meant that, as a *patrona,* the wife of the patrón, she was always protected and served by the Maqt'as, her servants. She acted most of the time like a beautiful, passive adornment to the danza. Her status as an elite woman, the wife of the Majeño, was bolstered by the leisure she incarnated.

I was able to experience the passivity of this female role because I performed this character with the San Jerónimo comparsa in the 1989 Octava of Corpus Christi celebration. In rehearsals and public presentations, I was constantly discouraged from taking any initiative in the dance or from leaving the arm of the Machu. During our ritual performance and when we were not dancing, I could not just go anywhere; I was always escorted by the Maqt'as, who would constantly check on me to see if I needed some service from them.

The Dama character has changed since the 1940s when it was performed by a man who impersonated a much more risqué and flirtatious woman, something that the present Majeños did not consider proper. Some danzas in San Jerónimo, such as the Qollas, and in other parts of Cusco have kept this transvestite feature to retain a grotesque and playful character in their danzas. The Majeños did not approve of this role-reversal aspect of the danza, because in their eyes it was not decente and made the danza less elegante. In this context, as in other aspects of the danza, the belief that this carnivalesque aspect of the danza would make it less decente and elegante meant two things. First, this carnivalesque feature has become associated, through folkloric presentations and contests, with the peasant population of Cusco. Second, this characteristic would counter Majeños' efforts to keep the character of the personages of the danza consistent with those of the comparsa members outside ritual. Inversion and grotesque images, in contrast to the Qollas performance, are minimized by the Majeños in an effort to stress continuities between the characteristics of the danza and their everyday life. Nevertheless, elements like their long, phallic noses and some aspects of the Maqt'a character give the danza a certain carnivalesque quality typical of many other Andean ritual dances.

The reconstruction of the role of the Dama may be seen as an effort by the Majeños to link the principles of masculinity and propriety that the comparsa advocated. Giving the role to a real woman made the danza more decente because, according to the Majeños, no respectable townsmen (as opposed to peasants), not even in ritual, should dress like a woman. Here, the attempt of these comparsa members to make their danza consistent with what they considered the correct social code became apparent. Besides, eliminating the burlesque character of the Dama diminished the possibilities of this personage's challenging the Majeños. The beautiful, chaste, and dependent Dama, in a way similar to the subservient Maqt'a, reaffirmed the superiority of the powerful male that the Majeño and in particular the Machu personage embodied. For the Majeños the new, respectable Dama became at the same time aesthetically proper and a reassuring confirmation of their control over women.

The members of the San Jerónimo Majeños have condensed many symbols of masculinity in their danza. A particularly graphic one was the most salient feature of their masks: their long, straight, phallic noses (figs. 12 and 14). The regionally known artist who makes most of the masks for the Majeños of both San Jerónimo and Paucartambo has explained the particular intentionality of this feature for jeronimianos.[17] He recalled that the dancers of San Jerónimo always demanded that he make their noses particularly long and phallic like those of the Machu personage of various danzas in the region (fig. 5). This nose style then became the "San Jerónimo style," as the artist clarified, together with the long horsehair mustaches hanging down. While the Caporal of Paucartambo had a mask like that of the San Jerónimo Majeños, the rest of the dancers in Paucartambo had smaller noses, not as phallic, and their facial hair (shorter mustaches and some goatee beards) was drawn on the mask itself (fig. 11). A regular-shaped, big nose, together with facial hair, rosy cheeks, and light eyes, was considered in Paucartambo characteristic of the white arrieros and hacendados.

In the case of the Machu (sometimes called Caporal) personage of cusqueño danzas, the long, phallic nose clearly symbolized his status as the oldest, most fully accomplished male of the danza group. The underlying concept was that, as a man gets older, he becomes more accomplished socially, economically, and sexually. In other words, the Machu nose was a central symbol of the madurez of this character, a symbol that emphasized the sexual connotations of his fully realized social features. The Majeños of San Jerónimo appropriated this particular symbol, making their own performance of the danza a more condensed symbol of male madurez. This symbol reasserted their sexual and social superiority.

The reference to their long noses as phallic representations was made overt by the Majeños of San Jerónimo on many occasions. They joked among themselves about their different sizes. During the fiesta they approached women, trying to scare them with their noses or asking them while touching their long noses, "Do you like it?" One of the characteristics of the nose is that it had a big, lumpy birthmark almost at the end. Once a Majeño said to me while pointing to the birthmark, "This is what gets in the way," an obvious sexual allusion. Because I performed for the comparsa I gained the confidence of the members. This factor, added to the fact that they considered me closer to their male personalities than any other cusqueña or even Peruvian female (i.e., my knowledge, my traveling experience, my way of dressing and behaving) allowed them to make explicit sexual references in front of me or directed to me. Long noses represent "symbols of the whole proud ethos of the males" in ritual performance in other areas as well (cf. Bateson 1958, 164). In the case of the Majeños, the exaggeration of this particular male feature may be seen as an effort to highlight their reproductive capabilities through ritual play. These capabilities, by means of metonym and synecdoche, are made symbolic of the Majeños' social superiority.

A fourth important characteristic of the ideal Majeños comparsa

member was that he should be tall. As discussed in the case of the Paucartambo comparsa, height was an important phenotypic characteristic
that marked "whiteness" and, therefore, the ethnic/racial superiority of
the idealized hacendado and arriero. It was a characteristic that became
central to impersonate in the danza, at least through the person who
performed the Caporal. In San Jerónimo, however, this marker of ethnic superiority has taken on a stronger relevance. It was not only that a
tall dancer was aesthetically preferred to a short one but that, since the
Asociación became officially institutionalized, tallness has become a prerequisite for entering the comparsa. As the president of the Asociación
explained, all the members who have been incorporated into the comparsa in the last few years are tall. The short dancers in the group were
those who had reinitiated the danza at a time when the requirement had
not been strictly enforced, or the ones who impersonated the Maqt'as.
The two Maqt'as were noticeably shorter than the average Majeño. The
comparsa members who performed the Maqt'as mentioned their height
as one of the main reasons why it was almost impossible to be "promoted" to perform the Majeño character.

The height of the Majeños performers was also one of the main criteria to determine each one's position in the line structure of the danza.
This criterion was supposed to be combined with that of seniority,
because the senior members were supposed to be closer to the front as
the years passed. Nevertheless, at the time of structuring the lines,
height was the aspect most emphasized. There were some senior members who, because they were short, remained almost at the end of the
line. To put the tallest dancers in front was a deliberate strategy to
give the visual impression that they were all tall, a strategy that worked.
Jeronimianos often commented that the Majeños were all "grandazos,"
"altotes" (huge, tall). This characteristic added an element of excellence
and elegance to the danza. This aesthetic element, based on the purported superiority of the white male, continues to be zealously guarded
by the Asociación. When I performed with them, and every one of the
many times in which they have tried to convince me to dance with them
again, they emphasized how well I fit their danza because I am so tall. I
am 5 feet, 8 inches, which is taller than the average Peruvian male, and
certainly much taller than the average Andean woman.

Another comment that San Jerónimo townspeople repeated about
the physical aspect of the Majeños was that they had huge bellies because they drank too much beer. This was another characteristic that,
through ritual performance, symbolically united the arriero, the hacendado, and the Majeños comparsa member: the three were purportedly

heavy drinkers. This characteristic highlighted both the socioeconomic superiority of the group (their capacity to consume) and their masculinity. Liquor drinking is associated with male public behavior. Nevertheless, in San Jerónimo the Asociación has tried to regulate this potentially disruptive element, demanding that its members display inside and outside ritual a good *conducta etílica* (behavior under the influence of alcohol).

While drinking the Majeños had to be careful not to make public disturbances, get into fights, or pass out, commonplace behavior in San Jerónimo, particularly during the fiesta. The Majeños considered these acts to be indicative of bad taste and characteristic of indigenous people. Their good behavior while drinking had to be displayed during the days of the fiesta and particularly while wearing their costumes. While they were having their public banquets in the plaza or other public gatherings that involved drinking (i.e., outside the cemetery), they were not allowed to break away from the group and drink with other friends. They were all controlled by their comparsa fellows. They had the rule that, if one member had to go to the bathroom or do any important errand while these public gatherings were taking place, he should be accompanied by one or two other members of the comparsa who would be made responsible for his behavior. When they went to their private gathering places, they were able to get more loose and drunk, although many of them were later sanctioned and criticized if they had gone beyond the acceptable behavior. The conducta etílica of a potential member of the comparsa is always carefully tested and observed before he is officially accepted among the Majeños.

Finally, in order to judge if a townsman could become a good Majeños dancer, the comparsa members verified his ability to keep a correct posture and to make what they considered "elegant movements," both essential to performing the danza. Always keeping a very upright posture, with an air of haughtiness, the dancer had to be able to take long, firm steps while swaying his body in a very unhurried, controlled, and almost stiff manner. This kind of body control is another element that differentiated the performance of San Jerónimo Majeños from that of paucartambinos, who staggered and emulated drunkenness. This imitation of intoxication through body movement was eliminated by the jeronimianos because, according to their codes of conducta etílica, it took away the air of superiority and majesty that they wanted to give to the danza.

The Majeños believed that their gentle, unhurried, and controlled movements distinguished them from the characteristic peasant ways of dancing. While performing the wayno, for example, they minimized the zapateo. In the most widespread traditional peasant-indigenous style of performing the wayno, as portrayed in the regional repertoire of "authentic" folklore, the zapateo consists of very quick foot movement, raising the feet high (one at a time) and stomping very heavily on the ground. When the Majeños performed the zapateo, they barely lifted their feet from the ground and put them down very softly in a slow motion. This zapateo was even more subtle and stylized than the mestizo style of regional folklore. In the rehearsals the older members of the comparsa corrected the new dancers when they stomped too hard or made quick and jumpy movements. They taught them how to control their bodies to make slow, swaying movements and take gentle steps. They taught them how to move from one position to the other, almost dragging their feet. The new dancers were not the only ones corrected. Other comparsa members who were caught making the wrong movements were sometimes criticized by being told that they were dancing like "cholos."

Following their Indian-cholo identity, the Maqt'as exaggerated the indigenous-style wayno, making funny jumps and shaking their bodies and especially their buttocks. In his analysis of Cusco wayno Roel Pineda (1959) pointed out that among the rural popular classes in Cusco there was more body movement while performing the wayno than among the elites and the middle classes in the city. As discussed in chapter 2, folkloric staged performances, especially those done by mestizos, emphasize the stereotypical "Indian" way of dancing by making uncontrolled jerky movements and keeping a hunched-over posture (video example 12). Other elements differentiated the choreography of the Majeños danza from those of other cusqueño ones and from the more peasantlike wayno style of dancing. For example, with the exception of the Machu and the Dama, the Majeños did not hold hands or hook each other with their neckerchiefs, warak'as, or *varas,* and they did not perform a zigzag pattern or the *yawar mayu,* typical of more peasant-style comparsa performances (Roel Pineda 1959; Poole 1990a).

Not all members of the Majeños comparsa had equal wealth, family connections, authoritarian and patronizing attitudes, physical characteristics, conducta etílica, or dancing skills. Nevertheless, there were some ideal attributes that these performers consciously guarded, highlighted, or tried to attain if they did not have them. Some of the comparsa members were in fact considered by the rest of the group as incarnations of all of these ideal qualities. These particular Majeños tended to have more power over the other members and became leaders of the comparsa, imposing their views on organizational and performative aspects of the comparsa. All the Majeños, however, were, for the rest of the towns-people, members of a powerful, prestigious, and closed male elite in the town.

With the example of the Majeños comparsa, I have shown how, through ritual performance, jeronimianos and paucartambinos have been able to give shape to local distinctions and identities. The Majeños have redefined and given local form and meaning to central categories such as decencia, madurez, and elegancia, drawing upon regional and national ethnic/racial, class, and gender distinctions. They have done this by inventing and reinventing a danza based on the idealized memory of the muleteers from Majes and the landowners and associating it with an emerging mestizo identity. Through using "arguments of images" (Fernandez 1986) in ritual performance—in other words, through the Majeños performance in the fiestas—jeronimianos and paucartambinos have experienced physically and conceptually the redefinition and negotiation of local identities around the categories of decencia, madurez, and elegancia. These three categories, which the Majeños performers have re-created and appropriated, have strongly drawn upon and given local reinterpretation to the reality of "whiteness" in contrast to that of the "Indianness" and "choloness." Using those two poles of reference, the danza has come to embody male mestizo identity for members of an emerging petite bourgeoisie.

In San Jerónimo the successful performance as well as the strict and organized Asociación has enabled the Majeños to become a distinct local male elite, a group of "new mestizos." This mestizo identity has meant leaving behind an indigenous/rural identity and acquiring a more advantageous position in local and regional ethnic/racial and class relations. The Majeños have obtained their superior local status not only through ritual performance but also through group and individual behavior outside of ritual. Establishing a connection between the features of the Majeños characters impersonated and those of the performer allowed comparsa members to assimilate desirable aspects of their performance into their own identities. Their performance of the danza in the ritual, especially their use of symbols such as masks with phenotypic white features, horse-riding, bodily stiffness, upright posture, swaying movements, bottled beer, mestizo-style waynos and marineras performed by a brass band, allows comparsa members to embody principles such as decencia, elegancia, and madurez, thereby making them real and part of the performers' personality.

*FIVE*

# Genuine but Marginal

*Cultural Belonging, Social Subordination,*
*and the Carnivalesque in the Qollas Performance*

It is early afternoon of the main day of fiesta, and the members of the ever-growing crowd in the main square can hardly keep their places around the opening left in the middle for the next dance group to perform. Three trumpeters, a trap-set player, and an accordionist quickly enter and start playing a familiar pentatonic, syncopated melody that has a dense timbral quality. About seventeen male dancers wearing knitted ski masks, rectangular flat finely embroidered hats, wool vests, small stuffed llamas tied to their backs, blue slacks, and heavy work boots take their places in the open space. When the group gets organized in two lines, the dancers start to spin a piece of wool they carry in their hands, and they begin to make slow trotting steps, leaning their bodies right and left. At the same time they start singing a series of stanzas in Quechua in a very tense voice; one of them says, "Now father [Saint Jerome], please count us, we, your wild children, we are only Qollas, we are only llama drivers." Suddenly the melody changes to another familiar one with a faster tempo, and the dancers quickly take their hats off and make a circle holding hands. One of the most popular skits or games of the many that the Qollas would perform during the several days of the fiesta has begun: the leader of the dance chases the only female character, a role performed by another member of the all-male group. During this chase and the several following skits the crowd cheers the Qollas and roars in delight at their ingenious pranks.

The Qollas danza is one of the most popular and widespread in contemporary Cusco. The performance of this danza has become for cusqueños a vehicle for exploring "indigenous" identity, which appeals to

164

cultural belonging and legitimacy but also implies low status and social marginality. While in this chapter I concentrate on the Qolla comparsa in San Jerónimo, currently one of the two "traditional" groups in that town,[1] I analyze the meanings of this danza in regional and national contexts. My analysis of the Qollas danza demonstrates that through ritual performance social contradictions are reflected upon, reworked, and made visible and that this creative activity embodies key discourses of social order and notions of personhood.

The Qollas performers impersonate llama drivers/merchants from the Qollao region, a high plateau outside of Cusco departamento whose population, according to dominant ideology, epitomize the rustic, poor, but "genuine" or "authentic" people of the highlands. Emphasizing the carnivalesque during their public performances and appealing to the audience's identification with highland culture, the Qollas performers in Cusco, by the late 1980s, had associated indigenous identity with the ambivalence of the lower strata of the body and of society (Stallybrass and White 1986) and the unfinished or ever-changing character of human life (Bakhtin 1984).[2]

Cusco people have identified the personality of the Qolla characters with those of ethnic/racial categories such as Indian, peasant, and cholo, all of which are used pejoratively to designate the populations of indigenous/highland background in Cusco and Peru. Moreover, as can be deduced from the performers' statements about the status of the characters they impersonate, Qolla has itself become an ethnic/racial category, condensing various meanings associated with these other pejorative categories.

Because the Qolla characters impersonate the "genuine" indigenous people and the autochthonous culture, the performers have been able to appeal to and to creatively articulate a wide cultural repertoire shared by the majority of Cusco people. Through this identification with what is shared by most cusqueños, and through the use of dynamic grotesque images, the Qollas have also been able to invoke and explore during their fiesta performance the deepest sentiments and desires of these Andean people. But precisely because the Qollas embody and explore this autochthony or genuineness, they make evident one of the main contradictions or paradoxes at the heart of Cusco regionalism and of Peruvian and much of Latin American nationalism (Knight 1990; Wade 1993). That is, the source of "authenticity," the "Indian race," is too easily seen as backward and inferior in terms of global modernity.

During my research in the town of San Jerónimo the members of the Qollas comparsa were particularly aware of this paradox. They highlighted it by emphasizing even more the ambivalent and carnivalesque nature of the danza and by starting a process of destylization. In doing the latter they have gone against the current promoted by instituciones culturales in the context of folkloric contests and presentations (see chapter 2). Furthermore, in some sections of their performances and by emphasizing the subversive, resourceful, and witty personality of the Qolla, jeronimianos subvert stereotypes about "indigenous" identity fostered by regional and national elites.

San Jerónimo Qollas best explain their character through a contrast with the Majeños characters. The Qolla is seen as the incarnation of the low level or low side of a hierarchical society in which the Majeño epitomizes the high extreme. While the Majeños have seized various signs of economic power and social superiority in an attempt to define themselves as the local elite, the Qollas have created their own "bricolage" (Lévi-Strauss 1966; Hebdige 1985) by incorporating signs that, according to the same dominant ideology, correspond to the dominated but nonetheless skillful and resourceful indigenous population.[3] In their performances, members of both comparsas define their masculinity along with other social and ethnic/racial categories. But while the Majeños emphasize their social and bodily stiffness and self-controlled "decency" and "elegance" in the performance of their male identity, the Qollas have emphasized transgression and physical confrontation to define, according to them, their "sinful" and mischievous yet courageous manhood.

The Qollas are similar to the very popular characters of many danzas all over the Andes which, under different guises, incarnate ambiguous figures who as occupants of the borderline between human and animal, domesticated and undomesticated, have both humorous and subversive features (Salomon 1981; Mendoza 1988; Poole 1990a, 1991).[4] The ambivalent and unfinished nature of these Andean characters seems to give ritual performance a sense of transformation and renewal (Poole 1991) and to make evident some social contradictions and historical paradoxes (Mendoza 1988). These double-nature personages sometimes embody opposite but complementary ideal sexual behaviors (i.e., male/female), and make visible associations between gender and ethnic identities (i.e., female/indigenous) (Harvey 1994).

During the fiesta the Qollas combine and play with extremes and borderlines; they impersonate faithful pilgrims as well as subversive sinners; they play at the margins of the human and the animal, of the social and the wild; they make people laugh and cry; they impersonate bodily pleasures as well as pain, birth, and death. At the core of this exploration of opposites and boundaries and under the central theme of the Qollao llama drivers/merchants, the Qollas bring together in each performance a series of concepts (i.e., indigenous, autochthonous, genuine, low social strata), iconic symbols themselves already freighted with cultural significance (i.e., llamas, Quechua, whipping, nonmonetary exchange or barter), and deep sentiments and desires (i.e., faith, fear of death, sexual pleasure, pain, reproduction, sadness). Therefore, through the Qolla ritual performance, comparsa members as well as fiesta participants explore the relationship between these different levels of social, cultural, and personal experience.

## OF TRANSPORTISTAS AND LLAMEROS

As detailed in chapter 4, by the end of the 1940s the first San Jerónimo Majeños comparsa, a group led by cattle dealers/truck owners and drivers had made their first attempt to make the patron-saint fiesta a place where they could introduce new local values that they embodied. By the early 1970s two other comparsas of transportistas had formed. The first, the Qollas, in 1973, was mostly composed of truck drivers, a few owners, and several assistants.[5] The second, formed a couple of years after the Qollas, was the Saqras (an allusion to the Catholic devil), which was composed solely of nonowner truck drivers and assistants.[6] Only the Qollas has continued to have a steady presence in the fiesta. From the moment the Majeños comparsa was revived in 1978, the Qollas and the Majeños have had a competitive relationship, developing reputations as the "traditional" comparsas of San Jerónimo.

By 1973 the Qollas danza in its stylized Paucartambo version of *Qhapaq Qollas* (wealthy or elegant Qollas) had been widely acknowledged through regional folkloric contest and festivals as a salient representative of regional "mestizo" folklore (figs. 3 and 4). Nevertheless, this danza drew upon themes that, as opposed to that of the Majeños muleteers and landowners, could be traced to the pre-Hispanic period and in many different ways embodied "indigenous" identity as sanctioned by instituciones culturales. The Qollas impersonate *llameros* (llama drivers/merchants) from the *punas* (the highest and most arid plateaus of the highlands, normally more than 3,500 meters above sea level), more specifically from the Qollao plateau, who exchange products with the valley people.

Ethnohistorical studies about the Andes have shown the importance of the well-established and necessary exchange between the Andean valley agriculturists and the puna pastoralists, an exchange that has existed since the pre-Hispanic period. They have shown not only the economic aspects of this symbiotic relationship but also its ritual and ideological ones. Moreover, they have pointed out the central role that this opposition and complementarity between the high- and the low-altitude economic, social, and cultural identities has had in the configuration of the concept of duality in Andean cosmology (Duviols 1973).

Llameros, like the arrieros (muleteers) portrayed by the Majeños, played an important role in the transportation of minerals, foodstuffs, and other goods during the colonial period and into the nineteenth century in different parts of Peru (Glave 1989; Deustua n.d.). By the seventeenth century in the southern highlands, the muleteers dominated the important commercial routes that went through Cusco. Nevertheless, the llameros continued to exist into the twentieth century, moving along the routes that the muleteers did not cover. Since colonial times there have been several distinctions between the roles and identities of arrieros and llameros. These distinctions derived from the different types of beasts of burden that they used, the routes they covered, the different products that they tended to commercialize, and their different cultural and social backgrounds (Deustua n.d.).

Llameros tended to travel intraregional routes and provided the valleys with products from the puna, such as *auquénido* (native cameloids such as llamas and alpacas) wool or wool products, *ch'arki* or *cecina* (jerked or dried auquénido meat), and clay pots. They were also known for maintaining strong ties with their communities of origin, which identified them as indigenous. The muleteers, generally more disengaged from their place of origin, traveled long-distance and interregional trade routes, for which their horses and mules were better fit. They were generally identified by the highland population as mestizos.

The Qollas performers not only impersonate the llameros but also, through many aspects of their costumes and choreography, the llamas themselves. Chroniclers have documented the impersonation of llamas in Andean ritual performance since pre-Hispanic times. They have described performances called "llama-llama" that took place in the context of celebratory occasions. The descriptions do not explain whether these "*comedias*" (comedies), as the chronicler Santa Cruz Pachacuti called one of the performances (Jiménez Borja 1955, 115), represented the llameros or only the llamas. Nevertheless, in one of those descriptions it is obvious that the people from the lower Andean valleys and the coast, the Yungas, were the ones who performed the llama-llama (Jiménez Borja 1955, 115). From either the perspective of the residents of lower regions or that of the inhabitants of the punas, the association of llameros with their animals is very close (Flores Ochoa 1979). This metonymic relationship is enacted in several aspects of the Qollas performances.

In the 1930s a "folkloric" dance called *Los Llameros* was part of the repertoire performed by the main Cusco institución cultural, the Centro Qosqo. In Paucartambo a danza called *Qollas* existed at least since the last few years of the nineteenth century (Villasante 1989, 75). As is characteristic of "invented traditions" (Hobsbawm 1983), the origin of this danza is linked by paucartambinos further back into colonial times, when, according to local accounts, the Qolla merchants brought the imagen of their patron saint to the town (Villasante 1989, 118–121).[7] In 1967, already in its stylized version of *Qhapaq Qollas*, this dance performed by paucartambinos finished third in the most important regional folkloric contest, the Concurso Departamental. In the following years this dance continued to be selected as a top finalist in this event. Today the *Qhapaq Qollas* forms part of the repertoire of folkloric dances of Centro Qosqo's daily presentations in Cusco city. This dance is also always present in the parades that annually celebrate the week of Cusco.

Whereas the stylized *Qhapaq Qollas,* with its elaborate costume, complex songs, and stereotyped movements, has shaped most of the contemporary Qollas comparsas in Cusco towns, the variety of dimensions involved in the performance of this danza has allowed local groups, as will be shown in the case of San Jerónimo, to emphasize, discard, and add new elements in their own performances. The Qollas danza seems to stimulate its performers to take full advantage of the potentials of ritual as a realm where all participants, performers and audience, are engaged in different ways in highly elaborated symbolic practices through which they explore several aspects of personal, social, and cultural experience. On the one hand, the Qollas revive a dimension of the pre-Hispanic taquies (chapter 1) that was almost lost in most mestizo danzas: they combine song, music, and dance in one performance. On the other hand, the performers fully develop the carnivalesque side of the fiesta using, in Bakhtinian terms, a "grotesque realism" that in a "gay and gracious" manner shows the "cosmic, social, and bodily elements" as parts of an "indivisible world" (Bakhtin 1984, 19).

What many cusqueños have found particularly appealing in the Qollas has been the carnivalesque dimension of the danza. Much of the Qolla performance can hardly be called a danza even by comparsa members themselves. These dancers call many parts of their performance *juegos* (games), *números* (acts or skits), or simply *travesuras* (pranks). What the Qollas of San Jerónimo tend to emphasize the most in their performances and what townspeople find the most appealing about them are these mischievous games or acts in which they show their skills, wit, and courage, and above all their ability to involve celebrants.

## The Beginnings of the
## Comparsa in San Jerónimo

I really liked it, I became fond of it, I loved the fact that they have acts [números], the acts that they perform, the acts that they perform to amuse the public; it is beautiful. In the atrium the people always wait for the Qollas' pranks [travesuras], because the Qollas are mischievous, very mischievous, and the public gives them an ovation.

When asked about the beginnings of the Qollas comparsa in San Jerónimo, comparsa members and townspeople unanimously pointed out one person as the founding father and main promoter of the comparsa in its initial years, a man I will call Mr. Martínez.[8] When Mr. Martínez, whose testimony is quoted above, led the formation of the Qollas comparsa in San Jerónimo in 1973, he and the other jeronimiano transportistas who joined him in the first comparsa had for a few years witnessed the recognition that Paucartambo danzas had gained from Cusco city audiences. These jeronimianos had watched several Paucartambo danzas, but the Qollas attracted their interest for reasons other than the regional popularity of this danza. Mr. Martínez, a truck owner and driver who often traveled through Paucartambo because of his business in Q'osñipata (a district in Paucartambo province), and other jeronimiano truck drivers who also traveled that route were close friends of Qollas comparsa members of that town, several of whom were also truck drivers. Therefore, the choice of the Qollas danza for this leader and his followers had two intrinsically related motivations. The first, explicit in Mr. Martínez's testimony quoted above, was that they were particularly attracted by the carnivalesque character of the danza. The second was that the people who performed it were part of their own social and cultural world, transportistas who spoke fluent Quechua and who identified with the informal, playful, and participative character of ritual performance.

Following a common pattern in the way in which cusqueños introduce new danzas to their patron-saint festivities, jeronimianos invited their friends from the Paucartambo comparsa to perform with them in their first presentations.[9] As described in chapter 4, San Jerónimo had had a successful presentation of a danza in the local patron-saint fiesta. That festivity, an exception in relation to other local and regional fiestas, had not had comparsas until a group of transportistas-ganaderos formed the Majeños in the late 1940s. Encouraged by that antecedent, which awarded social prestige to that first group of jeronimianos, by the recognition of the *Qhapaq Qollas* at the regional level, and by personal identification with this danza performed by his work comrades, Mr. Martínez led the formation of the first Qollas comparsa in San Jerónimo.

Although by the 1970s transportation had grown as an economic activity in San Jerónimo, different groups of San Jerónimo transportistas had then, as today, in Bourdieu's sense (1987) of the concepts, different economic, social, and cultural capitals. Some of these transportistas owned the means of transportation, while others were just drivers or assistants; some had more formal education than others; some belonged to more prestigious local families than others; some spoke fluent Spanish and used it more frequently in their everyday lives, while others, although bilingual, spoke mostly Quechua in their work and at home. Finally, and linked to the last difference in their language use and lifestyle, some transportistas traveled to metropolitan centers more often and in general lived more thoroughly urban lives (i.e., driving private automobiles to the city of Cusco and marrying Spanish-speaking city women), while others traveled more rural routes toward the jungle and were more tied to the local rural life (i.e., they participated more in agricultural activities, and their wives were only functional Spanish speakers and market women).

In contrast to the Majeños, which became known as a comparsa of dueños de carro because from the beginning it had a high number of vehicle owners, the Qollas comparsa became known as one of *choferes* (nonowner drivers) or *ruteros* (nonowner drivers who always cover a particular route). Even though there were a few owners among the members of the first comparsa, such as Mr. Martínez, truck drivers who drove to Q'osñipata and later on the Maldonado route (both in the eastern tropical lowlands) predominated in the group. Several assistants were also part of the first comparsa.

In the first few years that Majeños and Qollas interacted in the fiesta, the distinctions between the socioeconomic strata of their leaders and of the majority of the group were subtle. Into the mid-1980s, when the Majeños officially constituted their folkloric association and when jeronimianos from other occupations joined those comparsas, the association of members of both groups with different economic, social, and cultural backgrounds became more accentuated. Even in nonritual contexts the members of the Qollas comparsa became known as belonging to a lower social stratum.

The symbolic element that both groups of jeronimiano transportistas, the Qollas and the Majeños, chose in order to define their local identity revealed their economic, social, and cultural alliances. Both the Qollas and the Majeños impersonated merchants, therefore choosing a danza iconic with their own role as local entrepreneurs in symbolic as much as in cultural affairs (i.e., they took danzas as well as material goods from one town or place to another). The Majeños, however, chose the images of the powerful, wealthy, "white" horse-riding muleteer who came from a prosperous valley and traded liquors. The Qollas selected the images of the "coarse," walking llama driver from the punas who sought to exchange his limited, rustic, "indigenous" products such as blankets, jerked meat, and clay pots for valuable valley products.

The Qollas, like the Majeños of the 1940s, sought to gain social recognition and prestige through their comparsa performance. Alluding to a pre-Hispanic theme in Andean history, namely, the exchange between valley people and the puna inhabitants through the llama drivers/merchants, using indigenous instruments such as kenas, and singing in Quechua, the Qollas performance appealed to a "genuine" Andean indigenous identity. Qollas comparsa members in San Jerónimo could easily tie this newly introduced "tradition" to their own local history and indigenous cultural heritage. Even though the *Qhapaq Qollas* danza was considered by most cusqueños a mestizo danza, to Cusco city folklore promoters as well as to jeronimianos, it appealed to a genuine or autochthonous cultural tradition. Here the paradox of having the ultimate validation of a regional "tradition" in the highland pre-Hispanic "Indian," even if that "Indian" is stylized and transformed into a "mestizo" "*Qhapaq Qolla*," becomes evident.

Nevertheless, the Qollas of San Jerónimo sought to obtain local prestige and recognition not only by appealing to a notion of legitimacy or autochthony that the central theme, the paraphernalia, the musical instrumentation, and the Quechua lyrics of their danza helped them to achieve, but mainly through the technique of a carnivalesque performance. They saw amusement and mischief, based on Quechua and indigenous highland culture as well as on grotesque, unpolished bodily images, as the keys to their success. In order to achieve that engaging dimension that made the Qollas danza so attractive to them, the leaders had to find performers who could give an informal, mischievous, and playful character to their performance. It was in that spirit that Mr. Pinto became part of the comparsa and soon its main innovator and promoter of the destylization of the danza.

As Mr. Pinto himself states, they wanted him as part of the comparsa because he was known as a *cómico-satanás* (a devilish/prankish comedian). At the time not yet a transportista, Mr. Pinto was extremely popular in his role of Maqt'acha for a comparsa of jeronimianos that performed *Contradanza* for the regional pilgrimage of Qoyllurit'i. This danza used to be known as traditional in San Jerónimo until its popularity waned with the emergence of the Qollas and Majeños comparsas and the assumption of the central roles of sponsorship of the patron-saint festivity by the transportistas.[10] The Maqt'acha of *Contradanza* has a role like that of the Maqt'a of the Majeños but is more subversive and grotesque. He constantly tries to trick the Machu, or leader, and to outsmart him. The Maqt'acha engages in obscene pranks, harassing the Machu and making the public laugh; he tries to subvert every coordinated movement that the Machu leads in the danza. Mr. Pinto takes great pride in the fact that he was a genuine *satanás* at performing this role and that the whole town and even the Cusco archbishop acknowledged his skills.[11]

All the leaders and Mr. Pinto himself recalled that he made it difficult for the comparsa members to convince him to perform with them. In fact, he reminisced that it was the wives of the comparsa members who, in his own words, "killed themselves" to persuade him to join. This early direct involvement of the wives reflects their more active role in their husbands' association than that of the wives of the Majeños.[12] When he finally joined in the second year of the Qollas performance, he became the main, or the only (as the Caporal, the leader of the comparsa admitted), innovator of the danza, creating personages, acts, and stanzas that according to him and the rest of comparsa members reveal the true, genuine personality of the *Qollavino*.[13] Emphasizing in acts, games, and verses this genuine, informal, and coarse personality of the Qollavinos, he has been able to give the Qollas of San Jerónimo that carnivalesque engaging character of the danza that has earned them local popularity. As Mr. Pinto put it, "We participate with the townspeople [*pueblo*], we play with them, we share with them, with the audience that watches us . . . that is how we have gained the esteem of San Jerónimo people."

## OF QOLLAVINO MERCHANTS IN CUSCO

The Quechua stanzas that accompany several of the stages of the Qollas performance offer extensive commentary about the characters impersonated and about the particular scenes represented. The music, in particular the organization of the text and melodic phrases, the syncopated rhythms and instrumental style, its pentatonic nature, and the high pitch and tense timbre used by the singers, are representative of a widespread pattern in the Peruvian Andes.[14]

The music for the San Jerónimo comparsa was played in the mid-1970s on kenas and tambor. This kind of flute/drum ensemble was typical of pre-Hispanic times in the Andes and in other parts of Latin

America. But because of the competition with the brass bands during the fiestas, especially with that of the Majeños, the traditional instruments have been replaced with louder ones. Today the ensembles include three trumpeters, one accordionist, and a trap-set player.[15]

The songs, the costumes, and most of the choreography that contemporary Qollas comparsas of Cusco use in their performances have been modeled after the Paucartambo *Qhapaq Qollas* version of the danza. In San Jerónimo, stanzas, personages, and "games" or "acts" have been added that emphasize the mischievous, witty, coarse, and low economic stratum characteristic of the personages. This emphasis can be appreciated in the opening stanzas of the Qollas performance of San Jerónimo, the pasacalle.

> Young ladies of San Jerónimo,
> young ladies of San Jerónimo,
> please trade with us for our blankets,
> please trade with us for our blankets.
>
> Aija![16]
>
> What would you trade with us,
> how much would you trade with us,
> with your small change of hot pepper seeds,
> with your little money of *tarwi* husks.
>
> Aija!
>
> I have brought my woman,
> I have brought my woman,
> to trade her for white corn,
> to trade her for white corn.
>
> Aija!
>
> What could we trade?
> How much could we trade?
> If we don't have enough for our dear hot peppers,
> if we don't have enough for our dear salt.
>
> Aija!
>
> Qolla, Qolla they are calling me
> Qolla, Qolla they are calling me
> but how could I be a Qolla,
> if I am the child of God? (video example 4)

The first two stanzas derive from the Paucartambo version, accommodated to fit the town of San Jerónimo.[17] The last three stanzas are unique to San Jerónimo.

In the first stanza of this pasacalle, the personality of the Qollas as traders from the puna becomes apparent.[18] The specific place of origin is not mentioned yet, but the fact that they bring blankets to exchange means that they are coming from a wool-producing area, in other words, from the puna. The second stanza is more specific in indicating that the Qollas are traditional or indigenous traders who use barter instead of money. The two elements that are mentioned as the tokens for exchange with San Jerónimo women (to whom the two first stanzas are addressed) are hot peppers and tarwi. Tarwi are the seeds of a wild, indigenous highland leguminous plant (genus *Lupinus*) consumed by the Andean population, which from the perspective of regional or national metropolitan elites is considered peasant or Indian food. In San Jerónimo most townspeople eat tarwi. It is sold mainly in the local market by poor peasants, most commonly women, who collect it from the district's mountain slopes, where it grows wild.

Hot peppers or chili peppers, as reiterated in the fourth stanza, are a highly valued seasoning in highland cuisine and in Peruvian cuisine in general. They are not produced in the high punas. *Ají, uchu* (Spanish and Quechua for "hot pepper"), and *picante* (Spanish for "hot" as derived from a chili pepper) are three commonly used words in Cusco to denominate exquisite and tasty dishes (most commonly a kind of stew served hot or cold) eaten particularly during celebrations. The finest of all is called *chiri uchu* ("cold chili" in Quechua), which is served during the fiesta and other important social events such as weddings.

The Qollas' costume and paraphernalia confirm their identity as merchants from the Altiplano and more directly their association with the llamas and other auquénidos. Most of the performers (about seventeen out of twenty) wear identical Qolla costumes. As in most "traditional" Cusco comparsas, the Qollas danza is performed only by men.[19] In the two fiestas in which I participated while living in San Jerónimo, the number of performers varied in each of the annual presentations and from moment to moment during the fiesta.[20] The core group was usually composed of twenty performers, two of whom were young boys (about eight years old). The remaining two personages were the *Imilla* and the *Rakhu*. Among the Qollas the Caporal stood out for his leading role.

The Qollas costume, as the comparsa members themselves pointed out, is a highly stylized version of how cusqueños, especially those from the valleys, perceive the "genuine" llama drivers/merchants from the Altiplano (figs. 3, 4, and 21). The Qollas wear black work boots, ankle-high with metal toe and rubber soles, known in Peru as "miner's boots." Underneath and up to their calves they wear thin white (cotton

Figure 21.   San Jerónimo Qollas coming out of the church, holding candles. San Jerónimo, Cusco, 1989. Photo by Fritz Villasante.

or polyester) socks that can be clearly seen in the space between the bot-toms of their noticeably short slacks and the tops of their boots. The Qollas' shoes show that even under stylization the Qollas costume has kept the association of the llameros with the low-stratum hardworking laborer. According to the performers they wear this kind of strong work boot because the llameros walk along rough and long routes and this kind of shoe is the most appropriate for this strenuous type of activity.

Their slacks are dark blue (wool, cotton, or synthetic) and about five inches shorter than regular-length trousers. The Qollas explained that the space between the slacks and the boots is mandatory because they had to show that they did not have any extra protection from the whipping, an activity that often breaks out during the Qollas performances. They complete their costumes with long-sleeve, button-down shirts (one day white and the other blue) and, on top, hand-knitted V-neck burgundy pullover vests. Over their vests and tied diagonally across the chest they wear a series of elements (fig. 21).

First, they wear a *phullu*, or small, rectangular wool blanket worn as a shawl, red or brown with different-colored stripes. The phullu is folded in two into an imperfect triangle and secured across the chest (over the left shoulder and under the opposite arm) with a big safety pin. This blanket-shawl, better known as *lliklla* when used as a piece of clothing, is most commonly worn by peasant women, who drape it over their shoulders and tie it under their necks. The women use the lliklla to carry their babies and/or their things. Peasant men also carry their things in llikllas when they work in the fields or travel.

Over the phullu, and also across the chest, they tie a walqa. *Walqa* ("necklace" in Quechua) is a wool rope from which the Qollas hang a stuffed baby llama or vicuña (an even more precious auquénido), colorful wool twine with pom-poms at the end, and a row of small metal bells.[21] This piece of the costume condenses a series of iconic symbols that associate the Qollas with the llamas and with their activity as llameros. The baby llama is the most obvious one.[22] The colorful twine, or *soguilla*, is a stylization of the twine and ropes that the llama drivers use to tie the cargo on the back of the llama. The pom-poms are like those that llamas have implanted in their ears when they are branded. The bells are imitations of the llama bell (equivalent to the cowbell), and when the Qollas move or run, these bells are supposed to sound like a herd of llamas.

Across the chest and tied in the opposite direction, the Qollas wear two warak'as and two *chusp'as*. The warak'a is a woolen sling that the Qolla, like the Maqt'a of the Majeños danza, carries tied around his chest or waist. Both danza personages use it often as a whip. This warak'a, or any woolen rope tied around the chest, for both the Qolla and the Maqt'a is a sign that associates these characters with the indigenous identity, specifically with the role of peon or servant that a large portion of the region's population has been subjected to. This rope or warak'a is a sign of the strenuous physical tasks that highland peons or peasants often undertake, because they often use it to strap extremely heavy cargoes to their backs. The meaning of the warak'a used as a whip is discussed below.

The chusp'as are small (approximately 4 by 6 inches), colorful, hand-woven wool bags, most often used by peasants to carry coca leaf and *lliphta,* the coca-leaf catalyst. The Qollas wear two other small bags (a little bit larger than the chusp'as) called the *pukuchus.* These llama-skin purses hang down from their belts, one on the right side and the other on the left, and are used by the Qollas to carry *q'añihua* grain. This puna grain (as confirmed by one of the song verses analyzed below) is supposed to be the main food supply for Altiplano inhabitants and in particular for llama herders. Chusp'as and pukuchus are both signs of indigenous identity and of an itinerant highland inhabitant.

The Qollas' masks, called *waq'ollos* in Quechua, resemble full-faced ski masks. This kind of hand-knit wool mask, which covers the whole head and leaves only two holes for the eyes and one for the mouth, is also known in most of Peru as *pasamontañas* (literally "to go over mountains"). This same kind of mask is worn by other Peruvian highland danza characters like the Ukukus in Cusco and the *Avelinos* in Junín departamento (Mendoza 1989), who generally impersonate subversive buffoons. Furthermore, in Cusco the waq'ollo is associated with characters that move between the boundaries of the human and the animal, as is the case of two of the most important ritual characters of the region: half human–half bear Ukuku (see below) and the Qollas. The Qollas' waq'ollo is made of white wool. The top of the head, the eyes, the eyebrows, and the thin mustaches are highlighted with blue wool. Red wool is used to delineate the lips and the tip of the nose. The waq'ollos match the blue-and-white, long, knitted woolen scarves and *mitones* (gloves that extend halfway along the fingers). The mitones have llama designs. Wool vests, scarves, and gloves protect the Altiplano people from the extremely low temperatures of the punas.

The most precious and expensive piece of the Qollas' costume is the *montera,* a highly stylized version of the conical–flat top hat worn by some Cusco peasants.[23] The montera is a clear marker of indigenous ethnic identity in Cusco and Peru. The Qollas montera is a flat rectangle (approximately 20 by 10 inches) finely embroidered with shiny beads and spangles, with colorful ribbons and silver coins hanging down (figs. 3, 4, and 25). The shiny appearance of the monteras, as a Qolla stanza explains, replicates the snowfall in the punas. The Qollas tie the montera under their chins. They take their monteras off while performing most of their choreography, games, or acts. Features of the Qolla costume such as the montera and the mustaches drawn on their masks clearly indicate that the performance is a *Qhapaq Qolla*.[24]

The Qollas take a live llama wherever they go during their performance (except inside the church). The llama is decorated with colorful wool pom-poms in its ears (showing which herd it belongs to), a metal bell hangs from its neck, and on its back a load is wrapped around with coarse wool blankets and tied down with wool ropes. On top of the cargo the Qollas tie rustic clay pots filled with grass (video example 4).

Another feature that characterizes the Qollas as llama drivers is the piece of llama wool that they simulate spinning while doing their pasacalle. Moreover, according to the performers, the basic step of the pasacalle itself, done while singing and spinning, imitates the way both llamas and llameros walk. This step is a slow trot in which the performers lift their feet slightly from the knees, veering their bodies right and left as they advance. This is one of the several features of the Qollas performance in which the characteristics of the llamas and the llameros merge.

While very stylized Paucartambo costumes portray a *Qhapaq* (wealthy) Qolla, the pasacalle stanzas of jeronimianos depict the Qollas as merchants of scarce economic resources. This becomes particularly explicit in the fourth stanza, where the Qollas lament that they probably will not have enough to trade for their two dearest seasonings, namely, hot peppers and salt. Salt, like hot chilies, is not produced in the punas. People from those high-altitude areas, for whom salt is essential to cure and dry their scarce meat, have always had to procure it from the lower regions. In the fourth stanza the Qollas fear that their puna products will not be valuable enough to trade for the valley products.

The third stanza, unique to San Jerónimo, while staying with the theme of trade or barter, introduces the mischievous, witty and at the same time "wild" or not fully socialized character of the Qolla impersonated by jeronimianos. These performers sing, "I have brought my woman, to trade her for white corn." Corn is another highly valued element of highland diet produced in well-irrigated valleys such as the one where San Jerónimo is located. In explaining this stanza the composer, Mr. Pinto, insisted that corn is the valuable San Jerónimo product that has always been the most attractive for Qollavino merchants who have come to the town. He also said that this stanza was supposed to express the mischievous *(travieso)* character of a Qolla.

The Qolla performers in San Jerónimo often described the characters that they impersonated as being *traviesos* (mischievous), *juguetones* (playful), or *jocosos* (witty). They also said that this personality of the

Qolla character was supposed to derive from the actual informality, lack of propriety, and not fully socialized identity of people from the Puno Altiplano or from the puna. According to dominant Cusco ideology, the Qollavinos epitomize the *neto* (genuine) uncivilized highlanders. The following testimony of a jeronimiano Qolla is representative of the underlying concept about the nature of the Qollao (Altiplano) people that the jeronimianos impersonate: "[Our danza] is the stylization of a Qollavino. . . . [he] is a person who does not speak well, not even Quechua, he has an accent, we try to imitate the true Qolla. Because of his nature, he is a person sort of witty, playful, and he has an informal personality, he spends his time playing." In this testimony the characteristics of social marginality or incompleteness, that is, he "does not speak well, not even Quechua, he has an accent," and of an entertaining and attractive personality, "witty" and "playful," become apparent. Marginality and wit were two characteristics that went hand in hand when performers and townspeople in general explained the personality of the Qollas to me.

In the last pasacalle stanza, again unique to San Jerónimo, there are insightful commentaries that highlight the ambivalent character of the Qolla as portrayed by jeronimianos. The Qollas first lament that people call them "Qolla," as if Qolla were a pejorative name: "Qolla, Qolla they are calling me." Then they immediately respond to that derogatory remark by asking, "[H]ow could I be a Qolla if I am the child of God?" This response implies again that to be called a Qolla means to be "wild" or outside the boundaries of humanity, because it suggests that if a man is a believer or religious, in other words, if he is "civilized" and deserving like all other "children of God," people should not call him a Qolla. A further implication of this response, supported by other stanzas sung by the Qollas, is that townspeople should consider Qollas equally deserving human beings, "children of God," because they are, after all, faithful repentant pilgrims.

It becomes apparent, then, that in portraying the Qollavino llama drivers/merchants, jeronimianos have drawn upon regional and national prejudices against the puna inhabitants in general, and their Altiplano neighbors in particular. In doing this, jeronimianos have associated the Qolla character with the concept of the coarse yet genuine indigenous inhabitant of the highlands. Through this association between the Qollao inhabitants and indigenous identity, jeronimianos have explored their own ambivalence about partially belonging to that indigenous identity and partially belonging to an urban world that marginalizes the indigenous population. On the one hand, as explained in chapter 3, the fact that people of San Jerónimo live neither a thoroughly rural nor an urban life has made it imperative for members of emergent socioeconomic groups, such as those who have formed the Qollas comparsa, to identify with urban mestizo culture and to leave behind the markers of indigenous/rural identity. On the other hand, for the members of this San Jerónimo comparsa, their performances give them an opportunity to make evident and feel proud of the markers of indigenous identity that still characterize them and many other jeronimianos (e.g., Quechua proficiency). The Qollas of San Jerónimo have explored this ambivalence through the use of grotesque images, the subversion of some elite stereotypes, and the carnivalesque dimension of the danza performed within ritual celebration.

The strong tendency for stylization of danzas deriving from the private and state institutions of folklore, particularly in Cusco because of its role as a tourist center, has affected the performance of the Qollas danza in Cusco. A tendency to reduce the grotesque dimension of the danza is clear in the efforts of some paucartambinos and in the folkloric presentations of the Centro Qosqo in Cusco city. Nevertheless, some San Jerónimo townspeople and other cusqueño inhabitants maintain the carnivalesque dimension of the danza in their ritual performances and even promote a movement toward destylization of the danza. The creation of the Rakhu personage by Mr. Pinto in San Jerónimo is an example of this effort.

## THE RAKHU AND THE IMAGE OF THE UNPOLISHED, GENUINE QOLLAVINO

The first year that Mr. Pinto performed with the Qollas in San Jerónimo, he impersonated a character similar to his role of Maqt'acha in Contradanza. He carried it out dressed as an *Inkacha*.[25] The Inkacha costume is like that of the Maqt'a: stylized, stereotypical Indian dress.[26] Very often cusqueños interchangeably use the two names *Inkacha* and *Maqt'acha* to refer to a male danza personage who, dressed in Indian costume, plays an ambivalent, clownish, and subversive role.[27] These personages often engage in a playful battle with the leader of the danza, of whom the Inkacha or the Maqt'acha is supposed to be a servant or subordinate. They also stand in contrast to the main group of dancers, from whose performance the Maqt'a and Inkacha are at the margin, sometimes clearing space in the crowd for these dancers to perform and sometimes trying to subvert that performance, joking with them. In San Jerónimo and in other mestizo towns, the Maqt'a or Maqt'acha personage, with its specific costume and mask features, has almost completely replaced the Inkachas. This seems to be a result of the popularity that the Paucartambo Maqt'a has acquired.

The role impersonated by Mr. Pinto the first year of his performance was not very successful. According to members of that first comparsa the Inkacha dress, as well as the contrasting role that he was supposed to play vis-à-vis the Caporal and the rest of the dancers, did not work for the Qollas. In their words, "*No le caía*" (it did not fall in place). It seems that the Qollas dancers as well as their Caporal, themselves impersonating mischievous, playful, and subversive "indigenous" characters, did not offer a fertile ground for the performance of a personage defined by its opposition to order and authority. Therefore, Mr. Pinto decided to go in the opposite direction, inventing a personage whose grotesque and unpolished characteristics replicated the purportedly "genuine" Qolla, the Rakhu. He did this the second year of his performance, the third of the Qollas comparsa in San Jerónimo.

*Rakhu* means "coarse" in Cusco Quechua, and that is exactly the quality that this personage is supposed to impersonate.[28] According to Mr. Pinto and to all the comparsa and noncomparsa members who explained this character to me, the Rakhu is the impersonation of the "genuine" (*neto*), unrefined, unpolished inhabitant of the punas. Most of them also explained the metonymic relationship between the personality of the Rakhu and the coarse quality of the clothing that he wore. This clothing was supposed to replicate in a nonstylized fashion how the llameros in the past "really" dressed and how the contemporary llama herders of the remote highland areas continue to dress.

Most of the Rakhu costume is made out of bulky *bayeta,* the same coarse wool material also used for some pieces of the Maqt'a's clothing. While bayeta cloth has been produced industrially for some time and is dyed different colors, the bayeta worn by the Rakhu is only of natural wool colors. He wears bayeta pants, shirt, and jacket. His pants are secured by a wool sash, and he wears very thick hand-knitted wool socks. During the days of the fiesta, he alternates shoes, from ojotas, rubber sandals made out of tires (worn by peasants to work in the fields and also worn by the Maqt'as), to calf-high rubber boots (the waterproof type often worn by peons). He wears a waq'ollo as a mask, identical to that worn by the Qollas but without the blue wool, and around his neck a long white scarf that he wraps around twice. On top he wears a beat-up old conic wool hat that replicates a poor peasant-type hat often worn while working in the fields. On his back he carries a *q'epi,* a bundle supported by the shoulders and tied across the chest, which is also made out of bayeta. He also carries two rustic handwoven blankets, often one

Figure 22. San Jerónimo Rakhu and Qolla performing an "act" during the fiesta. San Jerónimo, Cusco, 1989. Photo by Zoila S. Mendoza.

over his shoulder and the other on his extended arm. Finally, he also has a warak'a (figs. 22 and 23).

A couple of years after the first appearance of the Rakhu, Mr. Pinto created his female companion, the *Rakhu Qoya*.[29] This female character was also performed by a man. Unfortunately, the Rakhu Qoya was not part of the comparsa during the two fiestas that I witnessed. Comparsa

Figure 23. San Jerónimo Rakhu and Imilla performing during the evening of the entrada of the fiesta. San Jerónimo, Cusco, 1990. Photo by Zoila S. Mendoza.

members explained to me that the dancer had been pulled out of the comparsa by his wife, who was ashamed of the vulgar role her husband played. Nevertheless, I saw another Rakhu Qoya performed by jeronimianos, that of "little Qollas" comparsa.[30] He/she was dressed almost exactly like the Rakhu but wore a bayeta skirt on top of the pants and carried a fake baby, also made out of bayeta, on the q'epi. Townspeople recalled that the Rakhu and the Rakhu Qoya used to perform the most amusing and engaging skits of the entire comparsa.

In 1989 the Rakhu alone did his own share of playful interaction with the crowd that watched him. Most of his performance, or his *números* (skits or acts), as he and townspeople call them, were separate from the Qollas group performance. Most of the time the Qollas, like the rest of the townspeople, became part of the audience with whom the Rakhu constantly interacted. Mr. Pinto changes his acts or skits every year, and that "surprise," as he put it, is one of the factors that makes him so attractive to the public. The first year that I observed his performance, in one of his skits the Rakhu imitated a street vendor from the Amazon jungle who sold magical potions for sexual potency. A widespread belief in Peru about the Amazon people is that their thorough knowledge of the forest has provided them secrets about sex and love. It is said, for example, that Amazonian women give male victims bewitching potions to make these victims love and marry them. It is very common in Cusco city markets and public plazas to see street vendors offering these Amazonian curative and sex-stimulating herbs and potions. Most of this, as well as of other Rakhu performances, was carried out in Quechua, a language that the vast majority of jeronimianos speak. The same was true of most of the Qollas skits.

As mentioned, the Rakhu and the group Qollas performance engage the audience in direct participation. In Mr. Pinto's own words, "We play with the people." This playing with the people often consists of a vulgar joke, or an unexpected prank or blow delivered by one of these characters. The Rakhus frequently go around striking persons in the audience on the head with their blankets or with a sack full of ashes, so when a person gets hit a cloud of ashes forms in the air. Jeronimianos recalled that the Rakhu Qoya surprised people and made them laugh with a chicken foot.[31]

In the second year that I observed the fiesta, the Rakhu performance was even more important than the first year. Between the 1989 and 1990 fiestas the Qollas had been lamenting the fact that the Rakhu was too lonely in his performances, that his interaction with the Rakhu Qoya was what the townspeople used to laugh at the most. This preoccupation had two results in the 1990 fiesta. In the first place, in order to have the opportunity to perform his sexual pranks with a female personage, the Rakhu took over the place of the Caporal, the Qolla leader, in the main "act" or "game," the *chinka-chinka,* in which the Qollas make the most direct allusions to sexual relationships. Second, another male Rakhu appeared in the performance. The two put together an "act" in which they confronted each other fighting over the Imilla, the female personage of the Qollas, and where they used transgression and stereotypes as their main means to cause people's laughter. I describe here a few aspects of that performance (video example 4).

Surrounded by Qollas and more than a hundred spectators, the Rakhus confronted each other in *yawar unu*, the whipping battle described below. They did not follow the formal pattern of the battle. For example, they broke into dance and twirled each other. They did not remain stoic when receiving blows, as the Qollas usually do while doing the yawar unu, but instead exaggerated falls, rolling on the ground. The crowd and other Qollas cheered them on and encouraged them to fight. It was clear that the Rakhus sought to gain immediate reactions from the crowd, especially laughter. When they stopped the whipping, they faked a reconciliation with a big hug. While embracing, they moved their pelvises in a humping motion, momentarily alluding to homosexual behavior. At this point, the Imilla jumped in to separate them, hitting their heads together as punishment. Faking a new reconciliation, they joined hands and began to dance a qhaswa, an indigenous carnival piece that has sexual connotations.[32] They performed the qhaswa with exaggerated stompings and hops typical of staged folkloric presentations that purportedly replicate "Indian" style.

While dancing the qhaswa one Rakhu pointed to the crowd and, when the other looked away, kicked him in the rear, knocking him to the ground. The crowd roared in delight at this slapstick. When they faced each other, the music switched to a very popular cumbia. This Colombian Afro-Caribbean music/dance style is associated in the Andes with coastal culture. The Rakhus referred to the perceived sensuality of this music by wiggling their rears, gyrating their pelvises, and shaking their shoulders in feminine fashion, thereby mimicking coastal "Latin" dances (see chapter 6). Between dances they continued the slapstick, using karatelike kicks and rolling on the ground. When one dancer sneaked in a kick to the testicles, the victim writhed around in exaggerated pain, to the delight of the audience. The melody then switched back to the yawar unu, and instead of using their warak'as, they used their blankets as whips. Throughout the performance, they had been taking off and throwing to the ground their q'epis, blankets, and layers of top clothing, implying sloppiness. The performance ended with the purported death of one of the Rakhus when the other choked him with his blanket and then sat on top of him. The music changed to the funeral march, and the Qollas surrounded him and mourned his "death" with a loud wail. They pretended to carry him to the cemetery.

The group of Qollas also engaged in direct interaction with the public, presenting new skits every year along with their known choreographic sections. In 1989, for example, in the main plaza of the town the Caporal stood between the two lines that the Qollas had formed and gave militarylike orders, "right, left, halt," and so forth. The Qollas did everything wrong, pretending not to understand the directions given in Spanish and even attempting to confuse the Caporal himself. The crowd laughed heartily at their military ineptitude. Subsequently, the Caporal had all the Qollas line up and, going down the one line, he gave them consecutive numbers, one, two, three, and so forth. When he returned and asked them their number, they acted confused and gave him the wrong answer. The crowd roared in laughter at their mistakes, which were, like the first example, based on their confusion with Spanish and on their lack of formal education. The Caporal pulled the Qollas out of the line as a sign of punishment as they made the mistakes.

As the performances just described exemplify, the Rakhu and the Qollas attempt to engage the crowd in communal participation and laughter. In these efforts, they emphasize their unpolished and coarse nature. This incomplete or not fully socialized personality of both the Qolla and the Rakhu is often associated with their "indigenous" or "genuine" identity (i.e., lack of knowledge of Spanish or formal education, coarse clothing, "Indian"-style dancing). In making this association with the socially marginal, whose behavior is portrayed as uncontrolled and informal, both personages, the Rakhu and the Qolla (which in different degrees are one and the same), engage in transgression and profanation focusing on the lower parts of the body and in particular sexuality. While doing this they also subvert some stereotypes promoted by the instituciones culturales about the "Indian" dancing style (e.g., when the Rakhus exaggerated the qhaswa style) and his "aggressive" nature (e.g., when the Rakhus turned the yawar unu into sexual activity). This was more clearly shown in the Rakhu performance, but the Qollas, in their more patterned group performance, also highlighted the sense of transformation and renewal that the enactment of the human life cycle such as sex, birth, and death, bring to the fiesta performance.

## SEX, BIRTH, AND REGENERATION IN THE QOLLAS PERFORMANCE

The core choreographic parts of the Qollas danza that have been modeled after the Paucartambo *Qhapaq Qollas* and that are repeated with some local modifications bring together many images that exalt

Figure 24.   San Jerónimo Qollas performing one of their games or skits during the fiesta. San Jerónimo, Cusco, 1989. Photo by Fritz Villasante.

the ever-changing, unfinished character of human life. Images of sex, reproduction, and death are central in much of the Qollas performance, in which the subject is, in Bakhtin's words (1984, 20), brought "down to earth" and turned "into flesh." Moreover, several of these performances blur the boundaries between the human and the llama worlds, presenting ambivalent, grotesque images that fuse both.

The choreography of the Qollas does not necessarily follow a fixed sequence. Some sections are often connected with each other, and stanzas are sung at a particular moment of the celebration. However, of all the Cusco danzas, and certainly of the San Jerónimo ones, it is the one whose performance takes the most unexpected turns according to the rapport that is established with the crowd. In San Jerónimo the Qollas wander around the town during the fiesta more than any other comparsa, trying to capture the most appropriate moments in which to attract the most attention from the townspeople with their números or juegos (fig. 24). The Imilla has a central role in several of these acts or games.

The Imilla is the female character who, along with the Caporal, has a leading role in the danza. Performed by a man, this character impersonates the wife of the Caporal and the mother of all the Qollas. All the comparsa members agree that she represents the number-two authority in the danza. Contrasting with the role of the Dama of the Majeños, the Imilla has an active role in the performance and is the central actor of several parts of the performance.[33] Many contrasts stand out between the female roles in both danzas. The main ones derive from the fact that one is impersonated by a man and the other by a woman. The Imilla has the characteristic risqué and grotesque character of carnivalesque role reversal, the very aspect of the performance that the Majeños have tried to eliminate as improper. The contrasts can also be established at the level of the social sector that each one represents. The passive, "decent" beautiful Dama ("lady" in Spanish), with her clothes and performance, impersonates wealth and leisure. The Imilla, on the other hand, impersonates a hardworking, authoritative, and fecund woman who, if not spinning, stacking up or untying the cargo, or directing an activity, is punishing her children (the Qollas) when they misbehave or giving birth to a new one.

The explanations that the Qollas gave me when I inquired as to the reasons for having a man play the role of a woman combined two related aspects. First, the very obvious one was that, if a woman were performing the role, the vulgarity and grotesque dimensions deriving from the role reversal would not work. In other words, only a man performing the role can allow for the all too open female sexuality displayed by the Imilla and the transgression in the recurrent Qollas sexual games.[34] Second, because the Qollas performance required physical strength and male courage, a real woman could never fulfill the role.[35] Below I analyze some aspects of the definition of virility by Qollas comparsa members, which highlights physical strength as the main element that defines their male courage.

The Imilla's costume, while stylized like that of the Qollas (with the exception of the hat), resembles much more the clothes of an Andean town mestiza (or chola) than the costume worn by the Dama.[36] The Imilla wears a long, calf-length pollera skirt, made of thick wool, with an embroidered strip in the middle. Underneath, she wears four thick petticoats that make her skirt extremely flared. She wears a padded bra and a long-sleeve blouse typical of the Altiplano mestiza. Over the shoulder she has a phullu similar to that of the Qollas but draped over her shoulders. Her face is covered with a piece of thin black cloth, which, wrapped around the head, still allows the performer to breathe. The Imilla has the same kind of montera as the Qollas and carries a warak'a. Her spinning material and implements are more sophisticated than those of the Qollas. She carries a distaff and a ball of yarn with which she skillfully pretends to spin while doing the pasacalle. Finally, the Imilla covers her legs with long, white wool socks and wears white tennis shoes to give her agility (fig. 23).

The chinka-chinka, a favorite part of the Qolla performance in which the Imilla plays a central role, is often performed as one of their main juegos in climactic moments of the fiesta, such as that after the main procession of the central day. *Chinkay* in Quechua means "to get lost" or "to disappear." In the context of this particular performance it refers to sneaking off for sexual intimacy. This part of the choreography has two subsections, each having a set melody and a particular stanza sung by the Qollas during the performance.[37] While in the 1990 San Jerónimo performance the Rakhu took the place of the Caporal to perform the chinka-chinka, it is usually performed by the latter.

When the chinka-chinka melody begins, the Qollas take off their monteras, join hands, and form a circle. As the circle forms, the Caporal starts chasing the Imilla. Following the music, the dancers move to the side as well as forward and backward. The circle rotates, closing and opening up. During the chase, the Qollas try to protect the Imilla from the Caporal, tripping and blocking him. He gestures to her obscenely, threatening to capture and "have" her. The crowd laughs at the chase and the sexual innuendo. Meanwhile, the Qollas sing the following stanza repeatedly:

> For what you told me, we will sneak off
> ay, sneak off, sneak off [chinka-chinka]
> why would I sneak off
> ay, sneak off, sneak off
> with a mestiza with disheveled hair?
> ay, sneak off, sneak off
> with a mestiza with matted hair?
> ay, sneak off, sneak off.

Following a common pattern of Qolla stanzas, in the chinka-chinka the Qolla makes a statement, in this case a proposal to a woman to sneak off with him, and immediately comments on that statement. Sometimes the comment takes an unexpected turn to convert the stanza into a prankish one and sometimes it clarifies or confirms the initial statement. The chinka-chinka is an example of the former. After having made the romantic proposal, the Qolla makes fun of, or rather insults, that woman who, according to the comment, does not deserve the Qolla's love. *T'ampa uma* (matted hair) or *isanga uma* (disheveled hair) are two insults used against women to indicate their sloppiness or lack of the domestic skills that define a proper woman. A proper woman, as a sign of her feminine skills, would always have her hair perfectly braided.

When the Caporal captures the Imilla in the middle of the circle, they embrace and the music changes. He twirls her to the music, and they dance with their arms locked. The Qollas change their dance, breaking the circle by letting go of the other dancers. They bring their arms up and down, palms inward, their hands meeting in a quick clap. They move their legs in the same motion, lifting their knees in a high hop. This movement is supposed to celebrate the capture and, as the lyrics indicate, sexual pleasure in general. The Qollas sing,

> Doing this gives me pleasure
> doing this gives me pleasure
> climbing to a rock peak
> climbing over a bridge.

After the capture the performers make allusions to sexual intercourse. In the 1990 performance the Rakhu fell to the ground and the Imilla sat on top of him, covering his face with her skirt and bouncing on him. When she got off him, he waved his hand in front of his nose, indicating that her intimate parts stank. In the lyrics the dancers, in an allusion to sexual climax, refer to the pleasure provided by climbing to a high point. The sexual allusions of the chinka-chinka were confirmed by all the Qollas performers, who often explained it to me, saying that the Qollas, as children of the Caporal and the Imilla, first protected their mother from their father's sexual aggression and that when they finally made love, they were very happy for them (video example 4).

Romance and sex are common themes in the Qollas performance, as is also exemplified when they sing the wayno *Chask'aschay* (my little star).[38] They sometimes sing this wayno in a group while flirting with the women in the audience. They also do it in small groups while drinking during the fiesta. *Chask'a* (star) is a common image that Quechua-speaking men use to enamor or compliment women. They call them *chask'a ñawi* (starlike eyes) or simply *chask'aschay*. Jeronimianos have added verses to this well-known wayno, once again emphasizing the prankish, mischievous character of their performance. I indicate below which are the stanzas invented by jeronimianos.

> If there is a star in the sky
> my little star
> let your heart be in me
> my little star
>
> [unique to San Jerónimo]
> Whether or not you give me your love
> my little star

someone will be there to love me
my little star

Let's go to my Qolla land
my little star
we will just eat the q'añihua grain
my little star

[unique to San Jerónimo]
Every night we will go to bed
my little star
your stomach will not swell
my little star

[unique to San Jerónimo]
Whether it swells or not
my little star
it doesn't matter to me
my little star

Birth or reproduction, implied in Chask'aschay by the swelling of the stomach, is also enacted in a part of the Qollas choreography called the *inini*. In this scene of reproduction, llamas and humans come together in the same act. When the Qollas commented on the inini, they said that it was both an imitation of how the llamas give birth and an enactment of how the Imilla delivers a new Qolla. *Inini* is an onomatopoeic term that refers to the sound of pain (in-in) that the llama purportedly makes when giving birth.

The inini is not accompanied by any particular melody that announces to the public that this performance is approaching. In fact, in order to capture the attention of the fiesta participants, the Qollas often perform the *puka cinta* right before the inini. In the *puka cinta* (red ribbon), which is accompanied by a characteristic melody, the Qollas line up, holding the person in front either by the waist or by one hand, and they run in a serpentine figure.[39] The Imilla leads this movement, pulling this ribbonlike line, as the performers called it. The line goes through the crowd and, forming spirals or circles, traps people in the middle (video example 4). Once they have attracted a crowd around them they proceed to do the inini.

In the inini the Qollas form a circle surrounding the Imilla. The Imilla squats in the middle, and as the Qollas start closing the circle they start screaming shrilly. As the Qollas crouch and bend their heads over the Imilla, closing the circle completely, the noise gets more intense. Soon after the circle has closed and the Imilla has pulled out a little Qolla doll from underneath her skirt, the Qollas turn around and, giving a quick jump, spit outward, imitating the llama. Llamas are known to spit on people's faces as a self-defense act; they do this especially if these people are strangers and the llamas feel threatened by them.

There are two other parts of the Qollas' choreography in which they impersonate animal behavior: the *wala-wala* and the *khuchi taka*. In the wala-wala the Qollas line up, holding the person in front by the waist. They run in a serpentine figure, like the puka cinta. At the call of a bugle, they scream "Wala-wala," break the line, and run in one direction. They regroup and repeat this once or twice. This scene imitates the herding of llamas. *Wala-wala* is an expression used by Aymaras in order to incite the llamas or other animals to run.

The *khuchi taka* (pig fighting) is done most often as a transition from one skit or game to another. In whatever formation the Qollas are, at the beginning of the melody the group breaks down, and the dancers run around in all directions in the area where they were performing. Throwing their whole bodies, particularly their shoulders, they try to knock each other over. They try to surprise the victim, striking him when he's not looking. They do not, however, use their arms to grab one another, since, according to the Qollas' own testimony, they are imitating how pigs and almost any kind of animal fight. One dancer sometimes kneels or stoops behind another one in order to make him fall. The crowd is delighted when a Qolla is knocked to the ground.

The coarse or rude but nonetheless skillful way in which the Qollas use their bodies during performance is displayed not only when they impersonate animal behavior. As described above, the Rakhu performances as well as the chinka-chinka show much of that coarseness and vulgarity. But there is also another favorite performance of the Qollas in which these qualities are emphasized. In it the Qollas draw upon the metonymic relationship between the llameros and their cargo. This section is known by the performers as either the *ch'arki tawqa* or the *carga paskay*. The names refer to each of the two parts of the performance that replicate llamero commercial activities as they arrive at a town. *Ch'arki tawqa* means stacking up jerked meat (ch'arki), and it replicates the process by which these merchants arranged this product that they had brought to exchange with the valley people. In this performance the Qollas themselves become the ch'arki.

To make a ch'arki tawqa two dancers lie face down next to each other, their heads pointed in opposite directions. Two others jump on top of them from the side, forming a perpendicular second layer. Pairs of dancers join in to form three or more layers (the pile is sometimes formed by layers of four dancers rather than two). To the amusement of the crowd and the distress of those on the bottom, each dancer jumps on energetically, landing hard on his fellow dancers. At the end it becomes a boisterous pile-up as dancers stack themselves on top and the music moves into a faster tempo. Throughout the process, the Imilla directs the participants and arranges the pile. She often climbs on the top at the end to culminate this first part.

In the second part, the carga paskay, the Imilla grabs the dancers and separates them from the pile. *Carga paskay* means "untying the cargo or load," and, in doing this and in arranging the pile, the Imilla replicates the purported task of the wife of the merchant. The performance is accompanied by a militarylike melodic phrase (with duple meter) repeated over and over and played at faster tempo at culminating points. With the percussion giving the driving pulse and the repetitiveness of the melodic phrase, this music generates a sense of excitement and competition. This melody is always played when the Qollas become engaged in intense or violent physical interaction (video example 4).

In much of their prankish and disorderly behavior the Qollas resemble another popular Cusco comparsa character, the Ukuku, who, like many of the Qollas performances, impersonates the blurring of the boundaries between the animal and the human worlds.[40] The ambivalent half-bear and half-man Ukuku is a central personage in today's most important pilgrimage in Cusco, Lord of Qoyllorit'i. This figure plays an important role for the comparsas and in general for all the people who participate in that pilgrimage.[41] Ukukus, like Maqt'as and other Maqt'a-like personages, offer an ambiguous contrasting element to the main comparsa dancers, at moments serving them and guarding their orderly performance (i.e., protecting with their whips the space where the performance takes place) and at times subverting it with their clownish behavior (Poole 1990a). The Ukuku, like the Qolla, stands out as an agile, skilled, and witty dancer who transgresses rules and boundaries that separate the civilized from the wild, the animal from the human, and evil from good. It seems that precisely because of this undefined, ambivalent nature, the Ukuku has been deemed the most suitable to mediate the encounter between the pilgrims and the Lord of Qoyllorit'i. This encounter, which takes place at the top of a glacier, epitomizes the unity of the cosmos, in which boundaries between above and below, the divine and the human, blur as happened, it is told, when the Lord appeared to the shepherd child.

In San Jerónimo the Qollas seem to play a role similar to that of the Ukukus in Qoyllorit'i in terms of their position as mediators between the powerful imagen central to the ritual and the powerless devotee. While all the dancers and fiesta sponsors play this mediating role between the community and the powerful Saint Jerome, the Qollas, through their songs of repentance, their whipping battles, and their grotesque images of unpolished, ever-changing human nature, seem to embody most directly the feeling of renewal and transformation experienced by fiesta participants. Deep respect for and fear of powerful forces over them (i.e., God, Saint Jerome, death) and acknowledgment of their weak and sinful nature are clear in the Qollas songs. This is also enacted in a few nonverbalized performances and is self-consciously stated in the way in which the performers perceive the characters that they impersonate. San Jerónimo Qollas often said that both the Qolla character and comparsa members are the most faithful believers and at the same time the most sinful men of the town. They said that this ambivalent nature is made evident in their whipping battles, the yawar unu and the *callejón oscuro,* in which they purify themselves through physical suffering.[42] The Caporal of the comparsa told me, "All the sinners of San Jerónimo should come join us because we really give it to each other; in the yawar unu we really suffer."

## SINS, FEAR, AND STRENGTH IN THE QOLLAS PERFORMANCE

We have brought our souls [repeat]
knotted with our sins [repeat]

[refrain]
we are only Qollas
we are only llama drivers.[43]

Please only you my Father [Saint Jerome] can untie them
with your golden quill hand

In life or death
protect us with your shadow

Call us with your cowboy hat
we, your children with humble hearts

When your Lord gets angry
you, my patron, plea for us

[unique to San Jerónimo]
If you yourself get angry, my patron
who could we go to?

My partners from last year
are no longer here

Ay, my dear Father
Ay, my patron [44]

Some are in faraway lands
some are in the heart of the earth

Father, bless us
we, your wild Qollas

If we are alive, we will return
if we are dead, we will be with the Lord

[unique to San Jerónimo]
When death the enemy reaches us
please remember us. (audio example 11; video examples 5 and 7)

The many stanzas that the Qollas sing at the church atrium of San Jerónimo and at the cemetery are explicit about the character of the Qollas as sinful but nonetheless repentant faithful pilgrims who pay homage to their powerful patron saint. As the two stanzas unique to San Jerónimo reveal, jeronimianos seem to have a particular interest in exploring the relationship between the respect and fear that they feel for their patron saint and their uncertainty about death and the afterlife. Through portraying themselves as repentant sinners and admitting their "wild" nature, they acknowledge the powerful superiority of their patron, seek his pardon, and hope that he will intercede when "death reaches" them. Going beyond these repentance songs, the Qollas also seek this forgiveness and blessing by engaging in whipping battles and physical punishment. But this physical flagellation serves other purposes. Besides purifying the Qollas or cleansing their sins, it proves their physical strength and courageous virility. Therefore, the Qollas performance in San Jerónimo explores and enacts the various relationships between wild behavior and devotion, respect and fear, sin and repentance, life and death, and physical strength and manhood. Moreover, this performance probes the different connections between all these different fields of personal and social experience.

When Qollas comparsa members commented on the ambivalence of being an unpolished sinner and a faithful devotee, most often they tended to fuse the character they impersonated, the Qollavino, with their own personalities outside ritual performance. As exemplified by the Caporal's line quoted above, "All the sinners of San Jerónimo should join the Qollas," there is an identification between the sinful nature of the jeronimiano comparsa member and the stereotypical, "genuine" Altiplano inhabitant. This identification becomes total when the jeronimiano sinner is the one who goes through the actual purifying whipping.

While it is clear that the Qollas' perception of their patron saint as an implacable, punishing authority figure has been shaped by Catholic concepts of sin, punishment, and flagellation, there are other elements that have made this patron saint a particularly authoritative and threatening figure for these jeronimianos.[45] In this perception, they have woven together the physical characteristics of the icon of their patron saint (or imagen), evangelizing teachings that refer to the personality of Saint Jerome and his powers as intermediary between humans and the unknown (i.e., death and the afterlife), and jeronimianos' awareness of the abusive nature of powerful authority figures.

The particular physical representation of Saint Jerome worshipped in San Jerónimo highlights his prestige and majesty. Townspeople call him "doctor," an allusion to his scholarly accomplishments. But while the Majeños sought to imitate his prestige, the Qollas see themselves as his subordinates. The Qollas' fear and feeling of subordination to the saint's powers are explicitly acknowledged, as exemplified by the commonly heard phrase, "We are slaves of the patron."[46] The Qollas often referred to the "formal" and stern looks of the imagen of their patron saint. One Qolla said, "He is not any saint, look at his face," and then went on to describe it as a "formal" face. Another Qolla described this imagen as having a grouchy look on his face. In the description of this formal and serious-looking imagen of their patron, the Qollas emphasized that these characteristics derived from his superior position as doctor of the church. In their stanzas the Qollas mention his "golden quill hand" and his "cowboy hat" as signs of this imagen's appeal to power and superiority.[47]

The stories about the punishments that this patron saint has inflicted on people who have refused to serve him (i.e., by dancing in the comparsa or assuming a cargo) are much more common than any that point out the benefits that he has brought. Even the stories about the good that he has done for them are phrased to point out the dangerous nature of their patron. Based on the widespread belief repeated in many punishment stories, jeronimianos say that when this saint appears in one's dreams it is a bad omen and one should be particularly careful because death might be hovering.

Sudden death is one of the main worries or fears of jeronimianos who spend most of their time on the road. The Qollas know from experience that any of them, young or old, can die at any moment in a road accident. Since the Qollas comparsa formed in San Jerónimo, several members have had tragic deaths, and, interestingly enough, the stories told about these deaths point out a punishment from the patron as the cause. When the Qollas sing their stanzas about death in the cemetery and in the church atrium, they do it with lamenting voices, expressing sadness, many times openly crying. The audience also often bursts into tears, remembering their own loved ones who have died. One of the saddest moments, besides when they sing in the cemetery at the tombs of their fellow comparsa members, is when, on the last day of the celebration in front of the church, they say farewell to each other, to Saint Jerome, and to the townspeople. In their sad songs they express their fear that it might be the last time they are all together in their fiesta because, like some former fellow comparsa members, by the next fiesta they could be in the "heart of the earth" (video example 7).

The Qollas, however, feel relieved after the fiesta because they have accomplished their tasks and expiated their sins. As one of the stanzas goes: "Fortified with your blessing, to our town we begin to walk, ay my dear Father, ay my patron." This purification, which will be in their favor if death surprises them, has been attained mostly by going through the yawar unu and the callejón oscuro, two parts of their ritual performance from which they keep long-lasting scars.

The *yawar unu* ("bloody water" in Quechua), sometimes also called *yawar mayu* (river of blood), usually begins with the Qollas' forming two parallel lines, although sometimes it is done in a circle.[48] The Caporal and the Imilla move freely in the space left in the middle, checking the formation and giving the initial instructions. The rest of the Qollas stand straight, arms folded, and in the same slow trot in which they did the pasacalle, they lift their feet slightly from the knees, rotating in a semicircle. Their upper bodies remain rigid. While dancing, they start singing:

> Don't cry my dear brother
> don't cry my dear brother
> if you find yourself in bloody water
> if you find yourself in a river of blood
>
> [unique to San Jerónimo]
> I will not cry
> I will not cry
> even if I find myself in bloody water
> even if I find myself in a river of blood (audio example 10)

They untie their warak'as (wool slings) from their chests and put them around their necks, ready for use. The Caporal places himself in the front of the two lines. Two dancers—one from each side—meet in the middle. Standing side by side, each puts one arm around the other's

Figure 25.   San Jerónimo Qolla wearing walqanchis during the fiesta cachar-pari. San Jerónimo, Cusco, 1990. Photo by Zoila S. Mendoza.

shoulders. With their arms around each other, they move with their trotlike step toward the Caporal, bow, and return. They do this three times.

Still between the two columns, they separate and, while maintaining their trotlike movement and moving in semicircles, eye each other as if in confrontation. One dancer extends the warak'a in his hands and makes slow threatening movements. He suddenly whips the other with his warak'a, striking below the knee, usually between the ankle and the calf. The other dancer, the recipient, bravely remains in his dance position with his arms locked. He frequently hops to try to dodge the sling. They then rotate positions and change roles. They each take about five turns (video example 4).

At this point, a new melody is played at a much faster tempo, the same melody played when they perform the carga paskay and the callejón oscuro. The dancers grab and thus neutralize each other's left arms and simultaneously whip with the right. After five or six frenzied blows, either the Caporal, or more often the Imilla, breaks in to stop the struggle. The two dancers return to the column while the others meet their partner in the middle in a hug. The next couple remains in the middle and repeats the process. Throughout all of this, the Qollas in the lines continue to dance in their semicircular fashion. After all the dancers have performed the yawar unu, the melody changes again, leading to a new section, often the khuchi taka.

The main yawar unu performance the central day of the festivity is often initiated by the battle between the Imilla and the Caporal. This particular competitive interaction between the two leaders was one of the most eagerly awaited parts of the Qollas performance until 1990, when the Caporal who had performed in this role for about fifteen years retired. The comparsa member who continues to perform the Imilla started to perform that role the same year the Caporal did. One ingenious prank that jeronimianos often pointed out to me was that one year, at the precise moment in which the Caporal was striking the Imilla, she pulled out the little Qolla doll from underneath her skirts, as in the inini, pretending to have given birth to a new Qolla. They all remembered that the whole audience burst into laughter.

The *callejón oscuro* (dark alley), like the yawar unu, is an extremely popular performance frequently repeated by the Qollas during the fiesta.[49] The dancers form two parallel lines and whip each dancer when one, sometimes two, run through the middle. Dancers use different strategies to avoid the blows: some run fast, others hop up and down, while others attempt to distract the whippers (video example 4; fig. 26). After the callejón oscuro they often do the khuchi taka.

Another instance in which the Qollas engage in whipping is when the new members of the comparsa are initiated. This act is performed at the church atrium on the central day of the celebration. In this *bautizo* (baptism) the new Qolla kneels and quietly, with arms folded, has to stand the fierce blows that the Caporal gives him. Most Qollas of

Figure 26.   San Jerónimo Qollas performing callejón oscuro during the fiesta.
San Jerónimo, Cusco, 1990. Photo by Zoila S. Mendoza.

San Jerónimo, when explaining that this danza is only for courageous, "real" men, pointed out the bautizo as the main initiation ritual in which they proved their virility. They said that many jeronimianos love the danza and would like to join it but they get scared away by the pain that they have to endure when initiated. Others, they claimed, are just as scared of the frequent yawar unus and "dark alleys" that they have to go through if they become Qollas.

The Qollas often referred to the yawar unu and the callejón oscuro as opportunities to pay for their faults, mistakes, or sins while proving their "machismo." Many Qollas used the word *machismo*, emphasizing the positive aspects of exalting one's masculinity. Anthropologists who have studied whipping battles in Cusco, including those in which Ukukus participate, have found them associated with acts of renewal and displays of masculinity (Allen 1983; Orlove 1994). They have also found that this demonstration of manliness is often associated with indigenous identity. One of the most recent analyses has pointed out that "male violence" displayed in the so-called ritual battles seems to be associated with the identity of the people of the *provincias altas* (the high-altitude provinces, perceived by Cusco dominant ideology as the wild lands), which is "expressed through perceived continuities with the past of an ethnic group called the *Kanchis*" (Orlove 1994, 157).

As shown in chapter 2, Cusco city intellectuals have constructed much of the notion of the "authentic" Cusco indigenous identity by associating the pre-Hispanic past with the distant highland rural areas. Their idea of the remoteness of these highland areas was itself constructed in relation to the emergent centralism of the capital city. One of the characteristics that was emphasized in this construction of the "authentic Indian" was his warriorlike and aggressive spirit often displayed in violent whipping battles. Folkloric on-stage presentations since the 1920s therefore emphasized this particular feature of the Indian "ethos." Among the various other meanings that San Jerónimo Qollas have associated with their whipping battles, the idea that this activity is representative of an "Indian" ethnic/racial identity is clearly present. It is present in their perception that this whipping is directly related to their Qolla personage and to comparsa members' sinful, coarse, and unpolished personalities, which they best explain in contrast to the Majeños comparsa.

## THE ABUSIVE, ORGANIZED MAJEÑO AND THE PLAYFUL, INFORMAL QOLLA

The contrast that San Jerónimo people have established between the powerful Majeños and the "low-level" Qollas goes beyond the ritual performance of these two comparsas. The members of the Qollas comparsa perceive themselves and are perceived by the rest of the townspeople as belonging to a lower stratum and having a less polished and less fully socialized personality than the Majeños comparsa members. While acknowledging this, however, the Qollas take pride in the fact that their mischievous, prankish, and vulgar ritual performances have awarded them jeronimianos' love and recognition.

For the Qollas and for many townspeople, the Majeños are the living example, inside and outside performance, of the abusive nature of wealthy elites. While the Majeños' haughtiness and their power to impose their will is widely known, and even respected, it is also criticized. The Qollas comparsa members are among those who oppose and criticize the Majeños' contemptuous attitudes. For example, while the Majeños often behave as if they were the authorities of the organization of the fiesta, the Qollas have ignored the position that the Majeños have assumed in organizing the novenas and the amarre for this event (see chapter 3). The Qollas also often publicly complain that, when they are performing, the Majeños go by with their loud brass band and disturb their performance. An example of how the Qollas explained the abusive nature of the Majeños illustrates the point: "We have to respect them [the Majeños] while they humiliate us, that's how it is. Because the muleteers, that is to say, the Majeños, are our bosses [patrones]; that's how it is. . . . Well that is how it was in the past anyway, then, the Majeños had everything and we were their cholos."

A perspective in which the Majeño is considered the hacendado or the patrón and the Qolla is considered his cholo or peon, is also often alluded to by the Majeños themselves. In their interaction during the fiesta the two comparsas emphasize this asymmetrical relationship by teasing each other, the Majeños calling the Qollas "cholo" or "servant" and the Qollas calling the Majeños "hacendado" or "patrón." Assuming the role played regularly by prankish Maqt'as, the Qollas attempt to play jokes on the serious and formal Majeños.

As perceived by the performers themselves and by most townspeople, the members of the Qollas comparsa are the best suited to impersonate these characters. For example, Qollas performers have an obvious command of Quechua, they can move and dance like "indigenous" people, and they enjoy informality and prankish behavior. This implies that the everyday social and cultural identity of the performer has also become identified, in contrast to that of the Majeños, as belonging to a lower social stratum and to a more indigenous background. For example, it is acknowledged by Qollas comparsa members and townspeople alike that, because of their Qolla-like personality, perceived as informal and playful, the members of the Qollas comparsa cannot reach the level of organization and social prestige of the Majeños .

In fact, while I conducted my research, much of the Qollas' frustration about not being as successful or as prestigious as the Majeños derived from their failure to form as well organized a folkloric association as the one Majeños had crystallized in the mid-1980s. The following are typical opinions about their frustrated attempts to create a formal association: "We do not seem to be able to accomplish it," "We even cry a lot but we can't make it crystallize," "We have been trying for some time now, and look, the Majeños did it right away." This failure was often blamed on their immature and irresponsible behavior, which, as they acknowledged, is typical of their informal character. They often said that they are too irresponsible for these kinds of formal affairs, in that they often start talking about them yet end up getting drunk.

Some older members thought that the possibility of constituting a serious and prestigious organization was doomed when they started to accept too many young, immature members and men of lower socio-economic status such as butchers and masons. These older members, who support the idea of becoming a strict and organized folkloric association, are currently promoting a Majeños-like control of the membership and trying to attract transportistas rather than any other kinds of members. They are also trying to give the performance a more "orderly" and coordinated character by attempting to eliminate some of the carnivalesque aspects of the performance. Nevertheless, there are still enough members of the comparsa, like Mr. Pinto, who continue to fight for keeping the unfinished, unpolished character of the danza that has awarded them their local recognition. As he put it, "My only consolation is that everybody loves us and that our children are imitating us"; with this statement he was expressing his hope that there will always be enough jeronimianos who love to get engaged in carnivalesque performance and his belief that not everything has to be perfectly planned and controlled.

Cusqueños who perform the Qollas dance-drama make evident and rework Andean historical and cultural contradictions. For this group of San Jerónimo transportistas, the effects of this performance in their everyday lives has been Janus-faced. On the one hand, like the prestigious Majeños comparsa, the Qollas comparsa members have achieved local recognition as promoters of local "traditions" and have marked their social identity as transportistas. On the other, by choosing a dance that emphasizes "indigenous" identity they have experienced a crucial paradox at the heart of Cusco regionalism and Peruvian nationalism. The Qollas dance-drama, like a large percentage of Cusco and Peruvian "traditions," has its ultimate source of authenticity and validation in a marginalized and oppressed "indigenous" culture. This "indigenous" identity simultaneously is a source of pride and a pejorative marker of marginality. San Jerónimo Qollas have dealt with this paradox and their own ambiguity about partially belonging to this "indigenous" identity by emphasizing the carnivalesque dimension of the danza.

Like the Maqt'as, Ukukus, and similar fiesta characters throughout the Andes and like the "changing, playful, undefined forms" of medieval Carnival, the Qollas of San Jerónimo give fiesta participants a sense of renewal and transformation (Bakhtin 1984, 11). Their unfinished, undefined character and their constant repetition of the themes that allude to purification and regeneration (i.e., whipping battles for cleansing, representation of death and birth), have earned them the love and appreciation of their fellow townspeople. The Qollas have centered

their carnivalesque performance on exploring and enacting the ambiguities and potentialities of marginalized ethnic/racial and social groups
in regional and national society: Indians, peasants, and cholos, the
vast majority of the population. They have done it mainly by showing the two sides of a "genuine" highlander, who at times behaves like
a mischievous sinner, making people laugh, and at others like a repentant faithful pilgrim who fears death, making people cry.

The San Jerónimo Qollas have also emphasized and develop further
the carnivalesque dimension of the *Qhapaq Qollas* danza as an strategy
to compete with the Majeños. In doing this they have counteracted the
strong pressure for the stylization of "traditional" danzas deriving from
Cusco city artists and intellectuals' promotion of folklore. However, because of the strong association of the Qollas danza with the "genuine"
but lower social strata of the society, jeronimiano members of this comparsa have been identified by their fellow townspeople as belonging to
a low social stratum and an indigenous background. For all jeronimianos the performance of the Qollas danza during the patron-saint fiesta
is what makes the principles or values associated with "indigenous"
identity audible and tangible and at the same time part of the performer's personality.

In order for us to understand more fully the significance of the Qollas
performances in Cusco, we need to analyze them in their own logic (cf.
Fabian 1990; Erlmann 1991, 1996). Instead of trying to find a single
core principle underlying those performances, we need to "accept the
challenge" embodied in the discrepancies and disjunctures that we find
in those performances (Erlmann 1991, 689). Cusco audiences love the
Qollas performances because they laugh at the characters' ingenious
sexual pranks, cry in sadness, and vibrate with religious fervor with their
songs, and because they identify with much of the social inadequacies
and the subversion of elite stereotypes about indigenous identity the
dancers portray. At the same time, Cusco people are aware that most of
the values the Qollas incarnate in their ritual performances are representative of the marginal population in contemporary local, regional,
and national society. Nevertheless, as long as the Qollas can make the
fiesta a realm for the exploration of paradoxes that emerge out of the situation of a dominated but skillful and resourceful indigenous population, they will continue to shape the social and cultural experience of
their fellow Cusco people.

But the young generation of cusqueño comparsa performers have
found different ways of exploring the paradoxes and contradictions surrounding Cusco, highland, and Peruvian identities. Two comparsas of

young jeronimianos, the Tuntuna and the Mollos, like many others in the Cusco region, consciously draw from cultural elements outside of Cusco in order to contest the gender and ethnic/racial stereotypes promoted by regional and local elites. As I explain in the next chapter, this has created controversy.

# Contesting Identities
# through Altiplano Danzas
## *Gender and Generational Conflicts*
## *in the Cusco Region*

As the time for the main mass and procession of the third day of the fiesta approaches, an upbeat, repetitive tune played loudly by a brass band attracts the attention of townspeople toward one of the main streets of the town. Recognizing the tune, children and young people in particular run toward that street to greet the members of what seems to be their favorite comparsa, the Tuntuna. The young members of this comparsa, half of whom are women, are wearing bright, shiny, synthetic costumes, and they are not wearing masks. The men and women alike are wearing long sleeves with white ruffles, which are highlighted as they vigorously use their arms while dancing. In two lines, first comes the group of women with a female leader who guides their movements with a whistle. They are wearing white shirts and short turquoise flared skirts, several petticoats underneath the skirt, and white knee-high high-heel boots. As the women advance, they swing their hips energetically, twirling their skirts and showing their petticoats while stretching one arm forward at the same time that they put the opposite foot well in front of the other. Behind come the men, also in two lines, with a male leader guiding them with a whistle. Their shirts and tapered pants are shiny purple, both heavily embroidered, as are their wide black belts. They wear black ankle-high boots with heels a little lower than those worn by the women. They move forward as they leap side to side, stamping twice on each foot and stretching their arms to the side. While leaping they stay stiffer, more upright, than the women. As the whole group reaches the main plaza, they move toward a wide flat space next to the church where they will demonstrate the choreography that they have prepared for that year.

Only a few months after I had begun my field research in Cusco, an event in the capital city reverberated throughout the entire region. This incident, which became known as the "events of Corpus," generated a series of open antagonisms that pitted young members of cusqueño comparsas who performed danzas from the "Altiplano" (such as the Tuntuna described above) against a coalition of civil, religious, and "cultural" authorities (i.e., members of instituciones culturales) who opposed that performance. These confrontations, which have contin-ued into the 1990s, demonstrated the relevance of comparsa perfor-mance and of state and private instituciones culturales in the definition and redefinition of local and regional identity among cusqueños. In par-ticular, they made evident that these danzas were being used by young cusqueños, especially women, to construct a new public identity that contested the gender and ethnic/racial stereotypes promoted by the instituciones. Here I will discuss in some detail the confrontations that emerged in the town of San Jerónimo, demonstrating how a "folkloric" institution such as the comparsa can become a site for transformation rather than conservation of cultural values and roles. Moreover, I will show how danza performance can be the focus of struggle over identity and social relations, an arena where tension is always present and con-frontations and contestation can sometimes take place. The choice of danzas from outside Cusco made by the two comparsas of young jero-nimianos, the Tuntuna and the Mollos, tells us important things about the generational gap between this generation of dancers and that of the Qollas and the Majeños and about changing views on ethnic/racial and gender identities.

## THE "EVENTS OF CORPUS"

The events, or rather event, of Corpus refers to the 1989 celebration of the festival of Corpus Christi in Cusco city—since colonial times one of the main Cusco city rituals (see chapter 1)—in which "Altiplano" danzas outnumbered those considered "traditional" for Cusco. These danzas are known in Cusco as Altiplano danzas because they have reached Cusco primarily through the southern Peruvian Altiplano (high plateau) in the neighboring Puno departamento. The Peruvian and Bolivian Altiplano form a geographical and cultural unit viewed as dis-tinct from Cusco.[1] The immediate reaction of Cusco city authorities and "cultural" experts (i.e., members of instituciones culturales), widely publicized by the media, was to explain this event as a consequence of what they called the "invasion from Puno" and to start a campaign to prohibit the performance of those danzas in Cusco. While most of the danzas performed at that event were originally from Bolivia and belonged to a common repertoire of the transborder culture shared by the people of the Peruvian Altiplano and much of Bolivia, cusqueños called the danzas as well as the "invasion" *puneñas,* referring, often pejoratively, to their Puno neighbors.

As noted in chapters 4 and 5, if one were to make a regional hierarchy according to cusqueño dominant ideology about the relative prestige of southern Andean Peruvian departamentos, Arequipa would be at the top, Cusco next, and Puno at the bottom. Racism as well as economic and political power play a central role in this classification. Cusqueños consider people from Arequipa to be the "whitest" and most "aristocratic" of the area, while they see people from Puno as more "indigenous" or "lower status" than themselves. This view of people from Puno, especially of the llama drivers from that departamento, as being the most "genuine" or "indigenous" people of the Andes is clear in the Cusco Qollas danza (see chapter 5). Interestingly enough, young comparsa performers seem to discard this racist discrimination against their neighbors not only by not looking down upon the cultural practices of puneños but, on the contrary, looking up to them as an alternative model for their own public performances.

Although most of the performers at the 1989 Corpus celebration were actually cusqueños or *puneños* brought from Puno by cusqueños who frequently traveled to the area, the opponents of the performance of Altiplano danzas blamed migrants from Puno in the city of Cusco for "invading" their neighborhoods and their most important ritual. Nevertheless, as I inquired into the motivations of these opponents, it became apparent that their strong reaction to the event of Corpus was based on their realization that these danzas had become so popular among young cusqueños that their spread was virtually unstoppable.

I was able to explore the motivations of both the opponents of Altiplano danzas and of the performers of these danzas because, as explained in chapter 1, thanks to my ongoing research on comparsas, both groups sought my opinion as an "expert" on the subject. My reputation as an expert was established at the regional level, and I was interviewed on regional radio programs, invited to give public talks, and asked to write for local magazines and journals on the issue of the so-called puneño invasion. This privileged position at the regional level increased even more my status as a respectable researcher in San Jerónimo. As a consequence, not only was I invited to participate in discussions at the town hall among local comparsas and fiesta sponsors about the popularity and "propriety" of Altiplano danzas, but I also noticed that townspeople, comparsa and non–comparsa members, often felt that they needed to give me their opinion about these issues.

In San Jerónimo the public and private debates about the "correctness" of the young townspeople's performance of Altiplano danzas in the town's main religious festivity—the patron-saint celebration—centered on two issues, on which performers and opponents held, although not always openly, different views.

The first was the role of women in public ritual performance, more specifically ritual danza performance. The second was the frames of reference under which local identity was to be defined. In the discussion about both issues it was clear that the changing social experience of jeronimianos, especially of women, had led them to explore these two issues through adopting Altiplano danzas. They had used the wider national and international repertoire at hand, leaving behind regionalist, male-centered models of cusqueño folklore by adding cosmopolitan and transnational elements to the negotiation of local identity and to their definition of "folklore." I was able to closely explore motivations that young jeronimianas had for performing Altiplano danzas and to inquire about their frustrations about the conservatism of many of their fellow townspeople and Cusco city "cultural" authorities, because they saw me as a young woman with a modern and cosmopolitan view.

Numerous factors must be considered to understand the popularity of Altiplano danzas among young cusqueños. These include migration within Cusco departamento and between Cusco and Puno, smuggling across the Peru-Bolivia border, urban growth in the Cusco region, expansion of the national educational and communication systems, and the role of the international media in promoting certain musical styles as representative of "Andeans" and others as representative of a "Latin" identity. The "Andean" musical styles have mainly come from the Bolivian urban tradition of "folkloric" music internationally popularized by groups such as Inti Illimani, Savia Andina, Kjarkas, and Proyección Kjarkas. The "Latin" styles are the very popular Afro-Caribbean styles of cumbia and salsa.

## THE TUNTUNA, THE MODERN, URBAN "FOLKLORE" OF THE SOUTHERN ANDES

The most popular of the Altiplano danzas in the whole Cusco region is the Tuntuna. It is usually performed by about thirty dancers between twelve and twenty years old, half of whom are women. Unlike the Majeños and the Qollas dancers, most of these young cusqueño performers do not attribute any specific meaning to their danza. They do not wear masks or say that they represent any particular personages; they only assert that it is a danza whose vitality and happiness is extremely contagious ("danza alegre y contagiante").

Nevertheless, some of the performers, often the leaders, have traveled to Puno and have learned from their neighbor Tuntuna performers that their danza imitates the way in which black slaves in Bolivia used to dance. This meaning is similar to the one given to their danza by the performers of the *Caporales,* a Bolivian danza from which the Tuntuna derives.[2] *Caporal* was the colonial name given to the overseers of indigenous workers or black slaves in the haciendas, and, as we have seen in previous chapters, it is the contemporary name given to the leaders of the comparsas. In Bolivia some of the paraphernalia used in the *Caporales* danza links the meaning of the danza with the theme of black slavery, that is, the leaders carry whips with which they hit the ground and guide the troupe as if they were guiding slaves.

Even though it is not explicitly recognized by the Tuntuna performers in Cusco, another direct link of their danza to the experience of blacks in Bolivia is the musical style to which both the Tuntuna and the *Caporales* dance. This is a style known as *saya,* which is very upbeat and has a fast tempo, a predominant duple meter, and a limited number of phrases of different lengths, which are repeated many times. This saya style is a modified version of the one that is currently performed by Afro-Bolivians and which has acquired a central role in the black movement in that country (Templeman 1996).

The favorite melodies danced to by the Cusco Tuntuna comparsas are those popularized by the Bolivian group Proyección Kjarkas. During my field research this group performed in Cusco twice, and most young jeronimianos, certainly all the Tuntuna performers, went to these concerts.[3] Proyección Kjarkas performs several of its most popular melodies in saya style. Nevertheless, for the Tuntuna performance during the fiesta even those melodies that were not originally composed or performed as sayas by this and other internationally popular "Andean" music groups, are turned into sayas by the brass band that accompanies the performance. This band is like that of the Majeños (with tubas, trumpets, trombones, drums, and cymbals), only larger, and determines the texture of the music. The antiphony and the call-and-response structure with the high and the low brass are clear (audio example 13).[4]

The history of the development and popularization of what is today considered the "Andean" or "pan-Andean" musical style, to my knowledge, remains to be written. Nevertheless, some aspects of it have started to be elucidated (cf. Wara Céspedes 1984; Leichtman 1989). As mentioned above, this style emerged from the Bolivian urban tradition of "folkloric" music during the 1960s and 1970s. In the mid-1960s the Bolivian upper classes displayed for the first time an interest in "folk" music, going to the first *peña folklórica* in the capital city, the Peña Naira, "where musicians from both the city and the provinces could be heard" (Wara Céspedes 1984, 225).[5] This interest by the upper classes seems to have been stimulated by the fact that Andean music and instruments had started to become popular abroad, particularly in Europe.

The Bolivian urban music that developed as representative of Andeans and that became popular in Europe was not only popularized by Bolivian groups but also in an important way by Chilean groups such as Inti Illimani, whose members had gone to Europe in exile after the fall of President Salvador Allende (1973). Several musicians going into exile went through Bolivia and participated in peñas (Wara Céspedes 1984, 228). Therefore, the style that has been popularized by North American and European media as "Andean" has a clear Bolivian imprint. This fact is resented by members of Cusco instituciones culturales who argue that because of the media influence all that young local people and tourists want to hear is that kind of generic "Andean" music. These Cusco traditionalists particularly resent the fact that this "pan-Andean" style, with its profuse use of bamboo panpipes and *bombos* (large bass drums), resembles the music of Puno much more than that of Cusco.

Saya style is for young cusqueños something that unites them with the rest of the urban "modern" youth of the southern Andes. At the same time, this music is a link between what they consider their own— "Andean" or "southern Andean"—and what comes from the outside, such as the popular Afro-Caribbean styles of cumbia and salsa, which they dance at their parties.[6] It is also a link between what is considered "folkloric," that is, their performance of the Tuntuna, and the Afro-Caribbean styles that are identified with an international, cosmopolitan urban identity. Therefore saya, the kind of music played for the Tuntuna, is experienced by the performers as something that bridges their "folkloric" danza practices and their nonritual modern bailes.

One of the most obvious connections between saya, cumbia, and salsa is that shoulder shaking for both men and women and hip swinging for women are central to dancing all three. These motions, which are not typical of highland traditional danza or baile, are perceived by cusqueños as being sensual. This perceived sensuality of international "Latin" music and dance is no doubt also stimulated by the media marketing of these forms, as can be appreciated in salsa album covers and videos that show scantily clad women in provocative poses.

As mentioned in chapter 1, the Tuntuna performers, especially women, were interested in learning shoulder shaking from me since I had quite a bit of experience dancing cumbia and salsa while growing up in Lima. In their rehearsals it was obvious that they had not mastered this motion and that they were trying hard to incorporate it into their danza, particularly in coordination with their hip swinging.

Cumbia, an originally Afro-Colombian style, became very popular in Lima in the 1960s. Already in that decade this style and other international Latin American ones "had become an index of urbanism particularly for migrants from the highlands" (Turino 1990, 19). This was when highland migrants in Lima and in other large cities of the country combined elements from wayno, a typical highland genre (see chapter 4), cumbia, and the electronic instrumentation of rock music to create what is known as *cumbia andina* (Andean cumbia) or chicha music (Turino 1988, 1990). Although chicha had become one of the most popular urban forms in Peru by the 1980s, its importance, at least in the mass media, had declined toward the 1990s (Bolaños 1995). During my research young jeronimianos danced (baile) some chicha at their parties and bailes sociales (see chapter 3).

Salsa, another international Afro-Caribbean style, became very popular in Lima during the 1970s and 1980s, and its popularity expanded quickly into the provinces. In the early 1990s it was still a popular style among young cusqueños. All three, cumbia, chicha, and salsa, are associated by cusqueños and highlanders not only with an urban, cosmopolitan, transnational culture but also with the culture of the coastal metropolis, Lima.

The Tuntuna costumes vary from town to town, but they have some common features. These include the bright, shiny, synthetic materials that the costumes are made of; long sleeves with prominent waves of white ruffles, worn by men and women alike; and the use of ankle-high and knee-high high-heel leather boots for men and women respectively (figs. 27–30; video example 8). The women wear blouses and flared skirts, decorated by rows of tucks and ending a few inches above their knees. The several petticoats worn underneath the skirt are clearly seen while the women dance, because of their constant hip movement. These skirts are considered short by most cusqueños, compared to the longer ones worn by older cusqueñas. The men wear heavily embroidered shirts, tapered pants, and wide belts. In San Jerónimo the men wore thin scarves tucked into their shirts and small, flat-top, brimmed hats

Figure 27.  A young San Jerónimo woman performing the Tuntuna during the fiesta. San Jerónimo, Cusco, 1990. Photo by Fritz Villasante.

hanging down their backs. San Jerónimo female performers had similar hats hanging down their backs. The members of this group make their own costumes, the men and the youngest women with some help from their mothers.

The Tuntuna does not have a set choreography. Some basic steps are kept year after year, and from these steps the performers create new combinations of movements. The danza is performed in two groups, one of men and the other of women, with both groups in parallel lines (generally between two and four) and the group of women usually performing in front (video example 8). Each group has a separate leader who guides the movements of the dancers with a whistle. They come together only on a couple of occasions during the fiesta, making what

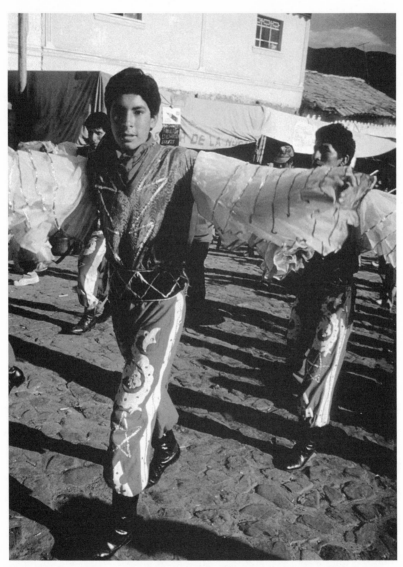

Figure 28.   Young San Jerónimo men displaying their bright, shiny, synthetic Tuntuna costumes. San Jerónimo, Cusco, 1989. Photo by Fritz Villasante.

Figure 29.   San Jerónimo Tuntuna dancers performing acrobatic and athletic movements. San Jerónimo, Cusco, 1989. Photo by Fritz Villasante.

they call a *figura* (figure or shape), which they choose every year. One that I saw being rehearsed and performed during the fiesta was the shape of a butterfly. Only for rehearsing this shape do the Tuntuna members come together, for most of the time each group decides on its movements and practices them independently.

In general one can say that the Tuntuna choreographies are much more of a parade type than for example those of the Majeños or the Qollas. The Tuntuna seems designed for going down the streets performing drills, while danzas like the Majeños and Qollas are much more danza-dramas, with sections and skits. This could be linked to the fact that the Tuntuna, like many other Bolivian danzas, was developed for Carnival celebrations in that country where parading is an important part of the celebration.

For both men and women the Tuntuna danza is full of athletic movements. This is more obvious for the men, whose movements such as high jumps and turns in the air are acrobatic (fig. 29; video example 8). The basic dance step for women is a short jump or hop side to side while shaking their shoulders (fig. 30; video example 8). While advancing or moving from one point to another, they change this basic step into a less physically demanding one where they swing their hips energetically, twirling their skirts and showing their petticoats, stretching one arm forward while they put the opposite foot well in front of the other.

The basic step for the men is the same while dancing and while advancing along the streets. They leap side to side, stamping twice on each

Figure 30.   San Jerónimo Tuntuna dancers swinging their hips vigorously and shaking their shoulders. San Jerónimo, Cusco, 1989. Photo by Fritz Villasante.

foot and stretching their arms to the side. While leaping they keep a stiffer, more upright position of the torso than the women, even though they also shake their shoulders while dancing (video example 8).

Most of the danza movements are complex and require physical co-ordination: for example, while doing their basic step, the leader signals to the women, who side-step twice while circling their arms in the air and then do the same to the opposite side. Another complex move is a turn all the way around on one foot, in which the women stretch their arms in the air, and a turn in the opposite direction. The men have a similar motion to this one, but before doing it they kick high. These high kicks are common in the men's performance. In another athletic move-ment the men kick high, crouch down on all fours, extend their legs into a pushup position, quickly go back into the crouch, and rise up.

During rehearsals, and even during the performances, I could see that the women, especially the older ones, had a harder time than the men in doing both the basic steps and the more complex coordinated move-ments. The ability to make the movements required for the Tuntuna seems associated with the practice of sports and in general to exposure to physical education. Men of the town have taken part in these kinds of bodily practices for much longer and more intensely than women have, though one can see that athletic movements have also been part of the lives of the younger women from an earlier age than the older women. This I believe has had to do with the more limited opportuni-ties of formal education that women had before the 1970s.

## URBAN CULTURE AND NEW POSSIBILITIES FOR JERONIMIANAS

During the military government of Velasco in the early 1970s the growth of public education had an important impact in San Jerónimo (see chapter 3). One of the effects during the 1970s and 1980s has been women's increased access to public education. Some of them, still not the majority, have had higher education and technical training and have started to have access to urban, skilled occupations previously unavailable to women (such as accountants, teachers, and technicians). Although in general men continue to receive more education than women (i.e., parents invest more in sending men to the university or technical schools than in sending women), in this generation, thanks to coed schools, women and men are almost equally receiving primary and high-school education.

Single women under twenty years of age, first through sports and social clubs (since the mid-1970s) and later through comparsa performance in honor of their "patron saint" (since the beginning of the 1980s), have started to participate in larger numbers and more actively in public events. They formerly were either excluded from or occupied a more passive role in these events.

It should nevertheless be clear that, while the generational gap is much more visible among women, it is also apparent among men who, like women, have adopted a much more cosmopolitan outlook than the older male generations as a result of greater access to higher education and urban skilled occupations, and the growing influence of national and international mass media. This new cosmopolitan outlook among men and women is also evident in the comparsas through which young jeronimianos are struggling to impose their views over and against the dominant regional ideology about gender and ethnic/racial identity.

## Confronting the Models of the Instituciones Culturales

Through a repertoire of cusqueño traditions and the promotion of folklore (see chapter 2), the members of both private and state-sponsored instituciones culturales have without a doubt shaped the practices of contemporary adult comparsas inside and outside the city of Cusco. The danzas promoted by the instituciones generally exclude or give passive roles to women, present idyllic images of hardworking and at times lustful or aggressive indigenous peasants, and/or evoke romanticized images of the past. Therefore danzas such as the Majeños and the Qollas are encouraged by the members of instituciones culturales because they fit their model of tradition.

Danzas like the Majeños do not seem to contest the models of ethnic/racial and gender roles promoted by state and private instituciones. On the contrary these models, in particular the ever-present dichotomy patrón or hacendado/Indian servant and the passive role of women, have been used by these comparsa members to establish their local power. The Majeños comparsa is without a doubt the most powerful and prestigious of San Jerónimo and the only one in the town that has officially constituted itself a folkloric institution.

In towns like San Jerónimo where high-school education has become widespread only in the last decade and where women, still in small numbers, have started to have access to higher education and to urban, skilled occupations, the performance of Altiplano danzas seems to provide young jeronimianas with the medium through which they take action in redefining their local identity. For women comparsa performance is a principal avenue toward participating more actively and in greater numbers in public events. This participation started in the late 1970s through sports and social clubs and crystallized in the mid-1980s with the formation of two comparsas, dancing Altiplano danzas, for the patron-saint festivity of the town.

For both men and women, however, the performance of Altiplano danzas has become an effective way to become part of an emerging urban culture involving young mestizos. Like previous generations of comparsa performers, these young jeronimianos face ambiguities in defining their identity. First, they still accept that cusqueño regional identity is best represented by the type of "traditional" danzas that the instituciones culturales promote. These young jeronimianos often perform these danzas típicas or regional folklore in their high schools or institutions of higher education. But these young jeronimianos rejected the gender and ethnic/racial stereotypes promoted by those danzas and, instead, chose the Altiplano danzas when it came time to decide their own local identity through ritual performance. In contrast to traditional Cusco danzas, Altiplano danzas feature women in large numbers and leading roles, and discard the bucolic and romantic image of the Andean past and present. Without masks, dancing to the tunes of their favorite internationally acclaimed Bolivian groups, displaying athletic skills, shaking their shoulders, and wearing shiny, bright, synthetic costumes, these young performers show that they are part of a transnational culture, urban and cosmopolitan, shared by the young population of other Andean countries, and to a certain extent by other Latin American countries.

But a second ambiguity emerges when these young cusqueños perform Altiplano danzas. While they seem to overcome some dichotomies ever present in the cusqueño traditional danzas, such as white/Indian, patron/servant, urban/rural, these dances still address wider national and transnational dichotomies that are based on a relationship between center and periphery. Because these dances are considered folkloric and representative of the Andes or highland region, for local performers and their audiences they continue to be cultural forms that differentiate the highland periphery, to which cusqueños belong, from the coastal metropolis, or the Third World from Europe and North America. Nevertheless, as I explain below, thanks to the fact that they could define their danzas as "folkloric," the performers of Altiplano danzas were able to defend them as proper practice.

Jeronimianos started to dance the Tuntuna in 1983, and their comparsa was promoted and supported from the very beginning by the parents of these youngsters who had an urban economic activity: they were the owners and drivers of a bus line that connected San Jerónimo to Cusco city. The group, made of equal numbers of men and women, had been organized for educational and athletic activities. After five years, when the organization had matured, the members decided to make a public presentation in the most important ritual of the town as a way of taking an active part in such a central social event. In order to do that, they needed a danza that featured men and women in equal numbers, but they realized that most traditional mestizo cusqueño danzas do not include women, or give them a marginal or passive role. This fact was frequently recalled by young cusqueños in the confrontations with their opponents. On the other hand, the youngsters argued, all the Altiplano danzas allowed women in large numbers. Therefore this comparsa as well as the other one of young jeronimianos that emerged a few years after the Tuntuna, the Mollos, chose an Altiplano danza.

At the moment of the emergence of these two comparsas, it was clear that the repertoire available to the young cusqueños was no longer limited to Cusco music and danzas. When the comparsas arose, "Andean" music from Bolivia was played constantly on the radio and had gained great popularity among young mestizos in Cusco. At the same time cumbia, salsa, and chicha were genres that they danced (baile) at their parties. From the perspective of young cusqueños, their Tuntuna danza incorporates both those popular trends, the "Andean" and the "Latin," making their performance close both to their "folkloric" culture and to their festive practices outside of the public ritual contexts.

Young cusqueños seem to have found in danzas like the Tuntuna the vitality of renewal and change while keeping within the boundaries of the "folkloric." In the Tuntuna, for example, the sense of dynamism comes not only from the fact that the danza is full of acrobatic and athletic movements, but also from the absence of a set choreography. The fact that the dancers can create new choreography every year was another argument that the young cusqueños used to defend their danzas against their opponents. In San Jerónimo the members of the two young comparsas practice several times a week for over a month before the annual patron-saint festivity.

These young jeronimianos declared that it was too boring to repeat the same choreography every year like those who perform traditional cusqueño danzas and expressed their rejection of the regionalist ideology propagated by the members of instituciones culturales and of the adult comparsas of the town. Responding to those who criticize their performance, one said: "We always reply to them: 'why in all the public activities and religious festivals of Cusco do we always see the same

Cusco danzas? And why not bring in danzas from different parts of our country, for example, from Puno since we do not see much of that around here?' . . . I think this can be done because Peru is integrated, we have to take it as a whole, right? . . . this is a way to innovate, to make new things known here."[7]

Not surprisingly, after the "events of Corpus" the Majeños, as "the" folkloric/cultural institution of the town, led the opposition to the performance of Altiplano danzas by the two comparsas of young jeronimianos. Temporarily suspending their competition with the Majeños, the Qollas, the other main adult comparsa of the town, supported the Majeños' efforts in the name of strengthening local traditions. In public debates at the town hall, members of both adult comparsas seemed to dismiss offhandedly the argument of the young women that mestizo traditional danzas gave them almost no opportunity to perform. Nevertheless, when I interviewed some of these fervent opponents, not only did they acknowledge that most traditional cusqueño mestizo danzas were male dances, but they also manifested their prejudices against the participation of women in this kind of ritual performance. The president of the Majeños comparsa commented on the subject (1990): "You see, the young people of San Jerónimo who perform Altiplano danzas say, 'There are no other danzas besides the Altiplano ones that we can all perform, there are none.' . . . it is true, in Altiplano danzas there are a lot of women; in our danza [the Majeños] there is only one, one woman against nineteen men [laughter] she has to be open minded right? she has to know how to defend herself against all the piranhas."

This Majeño dancer said that most adult jeronimianos share his prejudice against the participation of women in this kind of public performance. They consider that it is "dangerous" for women to spend so much time without the close supervision of parents and/or partners in rehearsals and during the days of the patron-saint festivity.[8] The danger, according to this ideology, comes from the assumption that women are fragile and can be easy targets for seduction; they may be attacked by "piranhas." This danger is purportedly higher during religious festivals due to the amount of drinking and social freedom. Until very recently only single women performed in comparsas. Nevertheless, the oldest female performers of the Altiplano danzas in San Jerónimo who are no longer single have been pioneers in continuing to perform in their comparsas. They have not escaped criticism.

While during my research the prejudice against women participating in large numbers and actively in comparsas, and against married women participating in any way, was not always obvious, it was nevertheless ever present in comments such as that of the Majeño. The opponents of

Altiplano danzas had an even more hidden reason for disapproval of this kind of women's public performance. This has to do with the public display of women's bodies. In particular with respect to the Tuntuna the conservative groups were very critical of what they considered too short skirts, which, despite several petticoats, allowed most of the women's legs to show when the hips swung energetically. Another criticism was directed toward what was considered the open sensuality of the hip movement and shoulder shaking of the Tuntuna. The opponents argued that those costumes and movements were not "proper" behavior during a religious fiesta.

When this kind of moralistic argument was launched against the Tuntuna, the members of this comparsa validated their performance by appealing to the concept of folklore. They replied that their danzas were proper because they are after all "folkloric." They might not be part of Cusco folklore, they replied, but they are from Puno, and therefore these danzas were "proper" Peruvian folklore. The fact that their practices can be considered folkloric has provided the performers with a powerful tool to validate their efforts and to gain new spaces and recognition for their performances.

However, the most open criticism by the adult comparsas and members of instituciones culturales was based on cusqueño regionalist ideology. According to these critics, nothing tied those danzas to Cusco's local and regional history and sociocultural reality, referring to the rural and indigenous aspects of that reality. When this kind of argument was launched, the young comparsa performers moved the argument back to the realm of ritual performance, arguing that all townspeople have the right to pay homage to the saint in the best way they can, no matter where the danza came from.

But beyond the oral arguments made, the most powerful tool for this young generation to carry through changes in the society and oppose dominant views has been the actual performance of the danzas during rehearsals and the fiesta. Through this practice they have been able to engage more and more performers and larger audiences. Despite continuing opposition and criticism, the young comparsas of San Jerónimo have continued to perform their Altiplano danzas in the patron-saint fiesta.

## THE MOLLOS OF SAN JERÓNIMO

The afternoon of the third day of the fiesta is almost coming to an end, and several comparsas have already performed in the main square. The crowd is still large around the opening designated for such performances when a group of young people, about fourteen men and fourteen women, quickly take their place there. They form four lines, two lines of men on the outside. As a large brass band starts playing a repetitive tune, the male leader of the whole group blows his whistle, and the performance of this comparsa, the Mollos, begins. The women are wearing colorful, embroidered, calf-length flared skirts, long-sleeve shirts, shawls draped over their shoulders, and plain flat sandals. The men are wearing long white pants, which are embroidered from the knee down, and they wear long-sleeve shirts and flat sandals as well. These male dancers wear vests whose heavy embroidery matches that of their pants. Neither the men nor the women wear masks, but they wear hats typical of the Altiplano region. Following signals from the male leader, men and women coordinate their movements, which are based on a very similar basic step: barely lifting one foot after the other and sliding to one side and then to the other. They also make many slow turns made in hunched-over posture.

The Mollos is not a representative Altiplano danza in the Cusco region. During my research San Jerónimo was the only town in Cusco that had a Mollos comparsa. Nevertheless the choice of this Altiplano danza by a group of young jeronimianos tells us something interesting about the relationship between the choice of danza and the social and economic resources and cultural preferences of the performers.

The members of the Mollos comparsa all belong to families with lower economic resources than the families of the Tuntuna performers, and their lives are more linked to the peasant or rural lifestyle of the town. Like the members of the Tuntuna some Mollos performers have attempted to pursue higher education at institutes and universities. Unlike the Tuntuna members, whose studies are supported by their parents, most of the Mollos comparsa members had to abandon their studies because they had to work to support themselves or their family. Those few who have continued to study have had to work at the same time, thus prolonging their studies indefinitely. Most of the members of this comparsa, unlike those of the Tuntuna, fully participate in the agricultural activities of their families. A large percentage of the women of this group sell meat and other products in the local Sunday market. Finally, as distinct from the Tuntuna members, the young members of this comparsa often switch to Quechua in their conversations, especially for joking.

Through a series of personal interviews with the members of the Mollos and observation of their interactions during rehearsals and the fiesta, I concluded that in general these performers held more conservative views about gender roles and public use of the female body than did the members of the Tuntuna. All of this, I believe, is reflected in their choice of Altiplano danza, which can be seen as a little bit more conservative in relation to the local traditions.

This comparsa, initiated in the mid-1980s, a few years after the Tuntuna, had also originally been a youth club dedicated to sports and shared studies. One of the current leaders of the Mollos comparsa told me that the members of the club first saw their danza performed by a group from Puno in a show in Cusco city. This was probably in one of the Concursos Departamentales (see chapter 2). This member said, "At the Cusco city coliseum we saw this danza from Puno. It was a danza that was attractive, and at the same time the costumes were similar to the ones from Cusco region. . . . We liked it and said, 'Why couldn't we perform that danza?' and then we started to prepare everything."[9]

Another leader of the club and later main leader of the comparsa, a butcher, traveled to Puno to buy cattle and inquired about the danza there. This was facilitated by the fact that several members of the Mollos comparsa in Puno city were also butchers.[10] Since that first year the members of the Mollos comparsa have rented their costumes—they do not have the economic means to buy or make their own—and hired their band from Puno. In Puno, brass bands tend to be bigger, therefore louder, than those in Cusco, and they have the reputation of being better than the Cusco bands. They are definitely better suited for the performance of Altiplano danzas, because their members know better the musical repertoire that fits those danzas (audio example 14).

Despite this strong Puno influence, as the above quote points out, the Mollos costumes, particularly the female ones, resemble the costumes worn by the characters of Cusco ritual and on-stage danzas típicas much more than do those of the Tuntuna. The Mollos female costume resembles, for example, the one worn by the female character of the Qollas, the Imilla. The women wear calf-length pollera (flared) skirts made out of thick wool material with several thick petticoats underneath. They wear long-sleeve blouses with some embroidery and a belt around their waist over the blouse. Draped over their shoulders they wear a llikIla (shawl), a stylized version of the blanket-shawl that peasant women use for carrying babies or products. Both the skirts and llikllas are embroidered. They wear flat plain sandals and a round top hat

Figure 31.    San Jerónimo Mollos performers dancing along a street. San Jerónimo, Cusco, 1990. Photo by Fritz Villasante.

typical of the ones that Altiplano women wear every day (fig. 31; video
example 9).

In general the Mollos women's costumes cover a lot more of their
bodies than do those of the Tuntuna. In particular the skirts are noticeably longer and heavier and the petticoats (which the Tuntuna constantly show along with their thighs) are hardly seen. In fact several of
the Mollos comparsa members commented to me that they would never
wear the short thin skirts of the Tuntuna danza because they would be
ashamed.

That less of their legs and petticoats is seen has also to do with the
fact that the Mollos movements are slower and less athletic than those
of the Tuntuna (video example 9). The basic step of both men and
women consists of barely lifting one foot after the other and sliding
to one side and then to the other. While doing this they swing their
arms back and forth. The men tend to turn the sliding movement into
a little bit more of a leap and to shake their shoulders more. Still, their
movements are much more controlled than those of the Tuntuna male
performers.

The male costumes are also a lot less flashy than those of the Tuntuna. Only their embroidered long-sleeve shirts, which are made of

shiny, bright material, and their embroidered vests, can be compared to the striking Tuntuna male costume. The Mollos male costumes are completed by long, generally white, pants with some embroidery from the knee down and with rubber sandals, of the kind that peasant men wear in the fields. Wool socks are worn with the sandals. They also wear round top hats similar to those worn by the women (fig. 32).

Like the Tuntuna, the Mollos features men and women in equal numbers, and it does not have a set choreography, so they can innovate every year. However, there are also some differences between the two danzas. While the Tuntuna generally perform and rehearse in two separate gender groups, independently from each other, the two Mollos groups come together and coordinate movements most of the time. Also the Mollos have only one general leader for the whole group, a male. When the Mollos go along the streets, they keep the two groups separate, in two lines with the women in front. But whenever they stop to show their danza to the public, they come together and coordinate their movements. Like the Tuntuna's, this can be considered a "parade" choreography with a series of drills, though the Mollos combine their basic step with different kinds of turns that are, again, slower and less athletic than those of the Tuntuna. Within the group configuration the

Figure 32.  San Jerónimo Mollos wearing walqanchis and performing during the fiesta cacharpari. San Jerónimo, Cusco, 1990. Photo by Fritz Villasante.

gender division is somehow kept, in that the two lines of women are inside and the two lines of men outside.

Like the Tuntuna, the Mollos dancers do not wear masks and do not have a discourse about what their danza represents. When I inquired about the subject, the answers were like those of the members of the Tuntuna: the danza represented youth and happiness. But the same Mollos leader who told me about the initial idea of performing the danza in San Jerónimo and who had inquired into the meaning of the danza in Puno added an extra element to the analysis: "We really do not know how it started, but they tell us that it is an expression of youth, of that happiness that exists among young people, of that friendship that exists not only among men but also among men and women. We could say it is an expression of the happiness in a celebration after concluding our work in the fields."

I find this quote telling in that it links this danza to peasant activities and this link, which may not be explicitly stated by the rest of the Mollos comparsa, seems in keeping with some of the peasantlike features of the costumes (e.g., the sandals of both men and women and the llikllas of the women) and some of the everyday practices of the performers. In other words this danza seems to appeal more to those whose lives are still linked to agricultural activities and, in general, to the rural lifestyle that still exists in the town. Nevertheless, for the Mollos performers the choice of an Altiplano danza means that women can participate in equal numbers with men in this kind of public display. It shows that they want to break with the barriers imposed by a regionalist ideology that wants to limit their possibilities to those sanctioned by local "traditions." In relation to the latter it is also important to note that for the Mollos, as for the Tuntuna performers, it is important to incorporate into their "folkloric" performance the kind of music that has become popular among the urban youth of the southern Peruvian Andes, that is, "Andean" music derived from the urban Bolivian tradition. Although the link is not as direct as the use of the saya rhythm by the Tuntuna, the Mollos use of Altiplano music performed by a brass band links them to the same transnational urban identity.

In San Jerónimo criticism against the Mollos was mostly directed to the fact that theirs was clearly a danza from the Altiplano. I never heard any criticisms about "improper" costumes or movements. Still local authorities and adult comparsas wanted to put an end to this performance. In defending their danzas the Mollos used the same kinds of arguments used by the Tuntuna performers. They said that they had the right to do the best job they could in honoring their patron-saint and in gaining the audience's attention. Again, like the Tuntuna the most powerful tool they had for contesting their opponents' views was their performances and the resulting attention from the local audience.

## HIGH-HEEL BOOTS OR RUBBER SANDALS: SOME DISTINCTIONS BETWEEN THE TUNTUNA AND THE MOLLOS

As insinuated above, one can argue that similar distinctions that divided the Majeños and the Qollas also separated the Tuntuna and the Mollos comparsas. This, I believe, can be explained by the fact that in several ways the members of the Tuntuna and of the Majeños had similar economic, social, and cultural capitals (Bourdieu 1987) while the members of the Mollos and of the Qollas comparsas shared many of the same characteristics. Moreover, although during my research the contrast between the Tuntuna and the Mollos did not have the "highly symbolic charge" that the contrast between the Majeños and the Qollas had in San Jerónimo, the two danzas, while both being from the Altiplano, were perceived as having important differences. Finally, dancing for the Tuntuna indicated that the young person belonged to a higher-status social group than if he or she danced for the Mollos.

As mentioned above, the first Tuntuna comparsa was promoted and supported by some members' parents who owned a bus line that connected San Jerónimo to Cusco city. These transportistas belonged to the class of vehicle owners that some members of the Majeños also belonged to. This class was still a small elite in San Jerónimo in the early 1990s and was even smaller when the Tuntuna started in 1983. In fact, I found that a few members of the Tuntuna had relatives in the Majeños comparsa. Although only a few of the leading members of the comparsa were children of bus owners, this comparsa was still known in the town as that of the children of bus owners.

The Mollos was not known as being a comparsa of "children" of anybody in particular. This can be explained partly by the fact that the members of this comparsa tended to be a little older than those of the Tuntuna comparsa. But most determinant was the fact that the members of the Mollos comparsa were much less dependent economically on their parents who, as noted above, had very limited economic resources. During my research several members of this comparsa were the main economic supporters of their families.

Like some members of the Qollas comparsa, many of the members of the Mollos were butchers, such as the leader of the first comparsa. Some other male members worked as bus conductors or had temporary jobs as janitors, in construction, or in adobe or tile making. Most women, as also noted earlier, were also butchers who sold their meat at the local Sunday market. A few others who had established little retail stores in their houses also sold different products in the Sunday market.

The members of the Tuntuna comparsa sometimes looked down upon the kind of jobs that the members of the Mollos comparsa had. Once a male member of the Tuntuna told me with some disdain that "conductors and janitors dance in the Mollos." During my research most members of the Tuntuna comparsa did not have jobs but sometimes helped with their family business. For example, a few male members sometimes helped their parents driving the buses or being conductors. These members did not support themselves with these jobs, however; they were still supported by their parents. These youngsters were still primarily students at their high school, university, or other institutions of higher education, a privileged situation in San Jerónimo.

Some male and female members of the Mollos had attempted to pursue studies in universities and institutes of higher education, but the need to dedicate most of their time to work in order to support themselves and their families had for the most part gotten in the way. Also, the members of the Mollos, as opposed to those of the Tuntuna, needed to dedicate time during the year to help their families with agricultural activities and, in the case of the women, every day with domestic tasks. Like the Qollas the members of the Mollos comparsa had lives closely linked to the peasant or rural lifestyle of the town. Also like the Qollas the members of the Mollos were fluent in Quechua and spoke it at home, rehearsals, and other social gatherings. Several of the Mollos' parents that I met were Quechua monolingual speakers who knew only some basic functional Spanish.

Interestingly enough, some of the meanings attributed to the Mollos danza link it to peasant activities or indigenous/rural identity. This identity is made evident, for example, by the rubber sandals worn by both male and female dancers, and the llikllas and the polleras worn by the women. Male and particularly female costumes resembled those of on-stage dancers of danzas típicas. Also, the women felt more comfortable wearing polleras instead of the "short" skirts of the Tuntuna. The Mollos female dancers also had a slightly more conservative view with respect to dress outside of the performance. They tended to wear more skirts and dresses than the female Tuntuna dancers, who most often wore slacks or jeans, both of which signal a more modern and urban identity.

Both the male and female Tuntuna costumes, like the everyday clothing worn by the performers, signaled urban culture and modernity. The high-heel leather boots worn by both men and women and the shiny, bright, synthetic costumes cannot be seen at all as keeping some links with the traditional Cusco danzas or signaling indigenous or rural identity. The abandonment by the members of the Tuntuna comparsa of elements of traditional or indigenous culture of San Jerónimo can also be exemplified by the almost complete absence of Quechua in the interaction among these comparsa members. While I knew that several of the members of the Tuntuna spoke Quechua, I rarely heard them use that language at any rehearsal, meeting, or other kind of social gathering where they interacted with their fellow comparsa members. Finally, the more urban, therefore less indigenous or rural, identity of the members of Tuntuna was marked by the fact that these young people spent a lot more time than the members of the Mollos comparsa in Cusco city. Some of them went to private high schools in that city, something that members of the Mollos could not afford; they went to the local state schools. Because of their jobs and home activities, the members of the Mollos tended to stay more in San Jerónimo.

During my research townspeople as well comparsa members saw certain contrasting characteristics between the Tuntuna and the Mollos comparsas. The members of the Mollos and their danza were seen as being closer to the traditional/rural side of San Jerónimo than were the members of the Tuntuna comparsa. The members of the Mollos comparsa were also seen as belonging to a lower-status class than the members of the Tuntuna. Nevertheless, the members of both the Tuntuna and the Mollos comparsas, as made evident by their performance of Altiplano danzas, had left behind several of the conservative views held by the members of the Majeños and Qollas comparsas and of instituciones culturales. They had developed a different view about women's public roles and a much more cosmopolitan view, leaving behind regionalist ideologies. Members of the Mollos and the Tuntuna united to challenge conservative views, having as their main weapon the performance of their repressed Altiplano danzas.

The struggle between comparsas who perform Altiplano danzas and conservative authorities and members of instituciones culturales shows how comparsa performance, considered by performers and audiences as folkloric, has become in Cusco a site for transformation. It clearly has not filled its purported conservative role. By selecting Altiplano "folkloric" danzas and performing them in the very places where they are prohibited, young cusqueños, especially women, have devoted their efforts to transforming the dominant ideology. This ideology portrays women as passive and fragile and attempts to control the public use of their bodies. Moreover, from a regionalist standpoint the adherents of this ideology also want to deny an emergent mestizo urban and cosmopolitan identity, contesting this in the name of a cusqueño "traditional" identity that must remain rural and "Indian" and that should glorify certain aspects of the past.

The selection of Altiplano danzas and the efforts to give them local meanings through ritual performances could not be understood if one saw these performances as mere reflections of changes occurring in the rest of the society. The agency of the performers themselves requires analysis. In Cusco today, through these performances, the dancers are shaping society by opposing certain dominant views of women and of ethnic/racial identity. The disputes over the performance of Altiplano danzas in Cusco demonstrate that comparsa ritual performance can be a site for performers to engage actively in the transformation of their society.

# SEVEN

# Reflections on the Relationship between Performance and Society

> The Majeño is a danza of hacendados, and the Qolla is a *peasant* who comes from the high-altitude areas. . . . There really can't be social competition between the groups, how could there be, if they [Qollas] are from a society of a *very low* economic and social level; compared to the hacendado, what competition could there be? . . . But in the group, yes, in the way of dancing, yes, because the Qolla tends to dance better. . . . Because the Qolla *dances while playing, he is not a formal dancer.* . . . But the Majeño doesn't, he doesn't have that.
>
> Testimony of a San Jerónimo Qolla dancer (my emphasis)

> Although there are all sorts of subtle degrees and gradations in a culture it is striking that the extremes of high and low have a special and often powerful symbolic charge. . . . In other words the vertical extremities frame all further discursive elaborations. If we can grasp the system of extremes which encode the body, the social order, psychic form and spatial location, we thereby lay bare a major framework of discourse within which any further "redress of balance" or judicious qualification must take place.
>
> Stallybrass and White, *The Politics and Poetics of Transgression*

## THE HIGH AND THE LOW IN SAN JERÓNIMO

During my research in San Jerónimo, most townspeople considered the Qollas and the Majeños the two "traditional" comparsas of the patron-saint fiesta, the most important public celebration of the town. Jeronimianos—both comparsa and non–comparsa members—were quick to explain how both the Qollas and the Majeños were true representatives of local folklore because they commemorated what the muleteers from Majes and the llameros from the Qollao "really" did in the past when they went through the town. But the relevance that the presence of these two danzas had taken on in San Jerónimo's main ritual was based not only on the connection that members of both comparsas had successfully established between their danzas and the local past or on

233

the recognition that these two danzas had achieved at the regional level as prestigious mestizo "folklore." Their performance was also essential because the muleteer from Majes and the llamero from the Qollao had acquired, as Stallybrass and White put it, a "powerful symbolic charge," the Majeño epitomizing the high and the Qolla the low extremes of regional and San Jerónimo society.

Jeronimianos' association of the Majeño and the Qolla with the high and the low extremes of society did not remain at the level of the danza character but extended to the everyday social identity of the comparsa member. To be a Majeño or a Qolla in San Jerónimo meant much more than just to be a performer of that character in the fiesta. It meant that because of his ritual performance and his membership in that particular comparsa, a jeronimiano was associated either with the high social stratum, if Majeño, or with the low, if Qolla. At first the way in which this differentiation worked outside ritual seemed to me hard to grasp. It could not be established merely at the level of their social, economic, or cultural resources (Bourdieu 1987) or by an obvious ethnic/racial background (i.e., white, Indian, mestizo, or cholo). In time I learned that it was the result of a subtle combination of elements from all of these fields of sociocultural identity, whose hierarchies, extremes, and specific referents were made visible and constantly redefined in the fiesta performances of these two comparsas. For all jeronimianos the performance of the Majeños and the Qollas danzas during the patron-saint fiesta is what makes the principles or values associated with these two danzas audible and tangible and at the same time part of the performers' personality.

The members of both the Majeños and the Qollas comparsas in San Jerónimo have drawn upon the particular qualities of ritual performance to give form locally to and generate new meanings for their danzas. By putting together a series of iconic symbols (e.g., leather jackets and brass-band music, stuffed baby llamas and Quechua songs) and through metonymic and metaphoric associations (i.e., with the muleteers and the hacendados, the llameros and the inhabitants of the punas), the Majeños and the Qollas of San Jerónimo have creatively brought together different domains (ethnicity, race, class, gender, and generation) and specific situational contexts (i.e., the emergence of transportation as a central economic activity, the demise of the hacienda system, and the promotion of folklore). Through this performance Majeños and Qollas have mediated between the ideological aspects and the practical embodiment of those domains and specific situational contexts, shaping local categories that establish the basis of social distinctions.

The Majeños have associated local concepts of decency, elegance, maturity, masculinity, and modernity with bodily stiffness, swaying movements, long noses, "white" features, wide-brimmed hats, horseback riding, bottled beer, and brass-band marching music. The Qollas, at the other end, have explored the concepts of Indianness, genuineness, wit, mischief, sin, and male courage by playing sexual pranks, imitating and carrying llamas, singing Quechua songs, engaging in whipping battles, and dancing to the tunes of highland music.

Making body adornment (costuming and masking) and dance (individual and group movement accompanied by music) the focus of their actions, the Majeños and the Qollas have made danza performance a particularly transforming and creative experience within ritual. This kind of elaborated bodily praxis or bodily techniques within ritual has transported jeronimianos from their everyday world into a world where experience is redefined through exploring its ambiguities and through experimenting with its potentialities. Festive performance—in particular, danza performance, in which the human body becomes a central focus—has a pragmatic efficacy, a capacity for creating and giving expression to human and social experience.

The creative and transformative power of danza performance has helped the Majeños constitute themselves as a distinct local elite. Placing the performance of the Majeños danza at the center of their group activities, members of an emerging petite bourgeoisie in San Jerónimo have used their cultural, economic, and social resources to establish a superior position in local power relations, thereby replacing the old elites. These truck and car owners and professionals have made their association and their danza a highly condensed symbol of economic power, social prestige, and masculinity. Establishing a connection between the features that the Majeños characters impersonated and those of the performer allowed comparsa members to assimilate desirable aspects of their performance into their own daily identities.

The Qollas performance shows how ritual danza also becomes a privileged realm for the exploration of ambiguities and paradoxes of people's everyday lives. The performance of this danza has served cusqueños as a vehicle for exploring "indigenous" identity, which appeals to cultural belonging and legitimacy but also implies low status and social marginality. For a group of San Jerónimo truck drivers the effects of this performance in their everyday lives has been Janus-faced. On the one hand, like the prestigious Majeños, the Qollas have achieved local recognition as promoters of local and regional "folklore" and have marked their social identity as transportistas. On the other, by choosing a dance that emphasizes "indigenous" identity they have experienced a crucial paradox at the heart of Cusco regionalism and Peruvian nationalism. That is, the Qollas danza, like many other Cusco and Peruvian "traditions," has its ultimate source of authenticity and validation in a marginalized and oppressed "indigenous" culture.

Because of the strong association of the Qollas danza with the "genuine" but lower social strata of society, jeronimiano members of this comparsa have been identified by their fellow townspeople as belonging to a low social stratum and an indigenous background. Nevertheless, in their ritual performances, and by exaggerating the carnivalesque aspects of their danza, the Qollas criticize petit bourgeois order and stiffness and sometimes subvert stereotypes about indigenous identity fostered by regional and national elites' promotion of folklore. Through this subversion the Qollas reflect upon, rework, and make visible ambiguities and contradictions of Andean history and sociocultural reality.

The performances of the Majeños and the Qollas therefore illustrate very clearly the continuities between ritual symbolic action and everyday life. They also demonstrate how through performance ethnic/racial markers can be appropriated and redefined. Finally, they show that danza performance embodies key discourses of social order and notions of personhood.

The members of comparsas have created a field of meaningful activity that connects the fiesta and the danzas with their everyday lives. In my study I have privileged the perspective of the actors, their intentions, and their experiences—that is, their agency—analyzing them within the wider sociocultural field from which these performances emerge and which they actively shape. The full significance of the bodily techniques used by comparsa members, masking, costuming, and dance, can be understood only by analyzing how the performers see themselves and how their audiences regard them, as promoters of "tradition" and "folklore," as embodiments of particular ethnic/racial, class, gender, or generational identities, or as sponsors of the main ritual of their town.

In order to fully understand how danza and fiesta performances so deeply affect the life of cusqueños, how they have become powerful forms of social action in their own right, we should study them as part of history, of the transforming social universe. The fiesta and the danzas are important realms in which central concerns of the changing everyday experience are focused, intensified, reworked, and given new meaning. The categories manipulated and reworked by comparsas in ritual are also re-created and maintained in everyday life through a set of relationships established among cusqueños and between them and their surrounding world. But in the fiesta jeronimiano comparsa members use the superior formal power of rites to speak authoritatively to contingent social reality.

A historical perspective in the study of ritual danza performance in the Andes allows us to understand the dynamics that have made this performance such a privileged and powerful realm where identities are defined and reworked and where Andeans explore and make visible the ambiguities and unrealized potentialities of their sociocultural experience. Since the beginnings of the Andean colonial period this kind of performance has been part of a dialectic that emerged from ruling-elite efforts to curb and control the innovative, sometimes subversive, expressive forms of subordinated groups. In the twentieth century the process of "folklorization" of Andean performative practices added a new and powerful dimension to this dialectic for cusqueños.

## RITUAL AND FOLKLORE: NEW PERSPECTIVES OFFERED BY THE YOUNG GENERATION OF CUSCO PERFORMERS

In Peru, as elsewhere in Latin America and Europe, the use of the concept of folklore has had a high political charge and has encouraged a subtle form of racism on the part of those who categorize certain cultural practices as folkloric. This concept was readily applied by Cusco city artists and intellectuals to the conflictual arena of public expressive forms in order to reinterpret and curb the potential threat posed by these cultural elements. The process of folklorization permitted these artists and intellectuals to shape the idea of an anonymous "authentic indigenous" identity from which they tried to differentiate themselves. One of their main strategies was to define their own practices as "mestizo" and to reinforce this distinction between their cultural practices and those of the "Indians" through contests and festivals.

Before starting my research in Cusco I was aware that a large portion of highland public expressive forms had undergone a process of folklorization. That is, many danzas, musics, and ritual practices had been taken out of their original contexts, stylized, stripped of many of their original meanings, and converted into emblems of regional and national identity by certain elites. In my understanding of the process, I had emphasized the negative or controlling aspects of it. I had stressed that in this process some important, many times rebellious, meanings of these forms were erased (Mendoza 1989) and that this folklorization was used by national and regional elites to foster stereotypes about subjugated social groups. However, I overlooked that, as part of this process, the performers of Andean expressive forms had gained new spaces and

CHAPTER SEVEN / 238

recognition for their creative efforts. In a seeming contradiction the folklorization had provided them the means to rework and contest social values and stereotypes promoted by such elites.

My first reaction when the comparsa members of San Jerónimo exalted the key role of their performances and of their religious fiestas by calling them "folklore" was to think that they insisted on that term because it would simplify the picture for me. The term bothered me because in Peru it was used pejoratively to refer to the culture of the highlands and because through staged folkloric performances many negative stereotypes about these cultures were promoted. I thought, therefore, that by calling or considering their performances "folkloric," comparsa members were taking away value and force from them. But I learned that, for them, it had been just the opposite.

I learned about the value of folklorization as a result of having to mediate the series of open antagonisms that emerged in the late 1980s between the young members of Cusco comparsas who performed danzas from the Altiplano and a coalition of civil, religious, and "cultural" authorities who opposed such performance. In this mediation I realized the importance of taking seriously the perspectives and arguments made by the actors about their performances. The young generation of comparsa members who were leading changes in the danza forms and, with their performance, opposing conservative views about gender roles and Cusco ethnic/racial identities, were the ones validating their performances through the concept of folklore. To the moralist and regionalist arguments about the inappropriateness of their performance in the main ritual of the town, young jeronimianos validated their performances by defending them as Peruvian or Andean "folklore."

These confrontations revealed how a young and increasingly urban population, especially women who had been largely excluded from ritual dancing, use Altiplano danzas to construct a new "modern" public identity. Through folkloric Altiplano danzas, especially the Tuntuna, which feature women in large numbers and leading roles wearing shiny synthetic costumes without masks and moving athletically and sensually to transnationally popular Andean and Latin tunes and rhythms, young Cusco women contest gender and ethnic/racial stereotypes promoted by regional and local male elites. These controversies not only highlighted clashing views of gender roles, Cusco and Andean identities, and notions of tradition and modernity, but showed the power of these "folkloric" ritual performances in shaping these views.

Understanding how important it had become for the young generation to define their performances as "folkloric" led me to inquire to what extent this had also been important for the previous generation of dancers. I discovered, for example, that during the 1940s it had helped the Majeños comparsa to gain recognition and subsequently to become a new local elite. They, like the young generation of dancers today, had broken stereotypes about proper ritual behavior and local "traditions" supported by the ongoing process of folklorization. Beyond any oral arguments made, the most powerful tool for both generations of dancers to carry through changes in the society and oppose dominant views has been the actual performance of the danzas during rehearsals and rituals. Through this practice they have been able to engage more and more dancers and larger audiences. Considering their practices "folkloric" has provided the comparsa members with a powerful tool to validate their efforts and to gain new spaces and recognition for their performances.

## FINAL THOUGHTS

While some ethnographies continue to emphasize the key role that performance has in creating and expressing sociocultural reality, they are also calling our attention to the need to analyze these performances in their own logic (Fabian 1990; Erlmann 1992, 1996). According to this view, our analysis should not be geared toward finding a core principle underlying a performance but rather in "accepting the challenge" embodied in the discrepancies and disjunctures that are the very stuff of which many performances are made (Erlmann 1992, 689).

By studying the relationship between performance and society we learn that this relationship is often ambiguous and contradictory and that it is difficult to determine exactly how they shape and influence each other. Nevertheless, understanding this relationship can be easier if we privilege the agency of the performers—their perspectives, their intentions, and their experiences while performing—analyzing this agency within the wider sociocultural field from which these performances emerge and which they actively shape.

Selection of Altiplano danzas by the young Cusco performers and the efforts to give them local meanings through ritual performances, as well as use of the Majeños danza by a group of transportistas as a main vehicle for constituting a new local elite, could not be understood if one saw these performances as mere reflections of changes occurring in the rest of society. The agency of the performers themselves requires analysis.

Moreover, the disputes over the performance of Altiplano danzas in Cusco and the process by which Majeños and Qollas have become the extremes that frame jeronimianos' exploration and redefinition of identity demonstrates that such ritual performance is "the site and the means" of "creative" "experimental practice," where tension is always present (Comaroff and Comaroff 1993, xxix) and where overt confrontation and contestation sometimes take place. It also shows that these ritual practices, fiestas and danzas, draw on the increasingly broad and diverse social experience of the participants, and that these forms of bodily practices are central elements in shaping that changing experience. Danza performance in the Andes has become powerful because of its special place at the crossroads of folklore and ritual, mass media and local aesthetic preferences, tradition and modernity, and regional and national identity. Comparsa members in Cusco have converted their danzas and their associations' activities into powerful action that defies any easy characterization, stretching and questioning the boundaries of these and other historically defined polarities. Through this action they continue shaping their society.

# NOTES

1. Below I explain the specific meaning of the concept of saint in the Andes.

2. My understanding of this dialectic has been inspired by Dick Hebdige's analysis (1985) of a similar "action reaction," which accounts for the powerful meaning that some of the expressive forms of twentieth-century British sub-cultures have acquired.

3. The meaning of *patron saint* in the Andes is explained below.

4. Peru is divided into twenty-four departamentos, each departamento has a number of provinces, and every province is organized into districts. Within the districts, especially in rural settings, are smaller administrative units dependent on the administration of the districts; these are *comunidades campesinas,* or *anexos.* As of 1991 the regional government has replaced the Hispanicized name of the department, *Cusco* or *Cuzco,* with the Quechua form, *Qosqo.*

5. Pierre van den Berghe and George Primov (1977, 11–14) provide a com-plete summary of Cusco's geography and ecology. A series of studies have ana-lyzed the determinant role of geography and ecology in the development of An-dean societies; some of the already classic works are Murra 1975, Brush 1977, and Dollfus 1981. For a more recent collection of articles that review some of the classic studies on the subject, see Masuda, Shimada, and Morris 1985.

6. In the last three censuses, 1972, 1981, and 1993, an urban area was defined as a populated center that has a minimum of one hundred houses grouped together or that is the capital of a district. In 1972, 59.5 percent of the country and 36.8 percent of the department of Cusco was considered urban. In 1981, 65.2 percent of the population of the country was considered urban, 41.8 percent in Cusco (Instituto Geográfico Nacional 1989, 94). By 1993, 70.1 percent of the country was considered urban (INEI 1994b).

7. For a recent complete analysis of the contemporary situation of violence in Peru, see Poole and Rénique 1992. The bibliography in Spanish about the strong process of migration to the cities, in particular to the capital of the na-tion, is extensive. Cf. Matos Mar 1984; Degregori 1986.

8. For a concise study of the development of Cusco's regional economy in

relationship to urban growth, see Ruiz Bravo and Monge 1983. Among the most important industries of the region are those of food, textiles, and chemicals and fertilizers.

9. According to the last national census, 37 percent of the working population is occupied in agriculture (INEI 1994b, 755).

10. Regionalization and decentralization has been a long-desired process, particularly in the southern Peruvian Andes. Cf. Rénique 1988, 1991; Deustua and Rénique 1984; Tamayo Herrera 1981, 1988. However, the actual implementation of the system has brought about a series of political and economic disputes between and within the newly created regions. Because of this and the generalized economic and political crisis of the country, this process is likely to be ineffective or completely dissolved. The current president of the nation took legal measures against regionalization even before the temporary suspension of the regional governments as part of the drastic suspension of democratic institutions in the country since April 5, 1992.

11. The territory of the district includes high mountains like Machu Picol, Wayna Picol, and Ccumu, whose peaks reach over 3,600 meters above sea level.

12. For their discussion of the concepts of ideology and hegemony Comaroff and Comaroff (1991) draw strongly from Marx and Engels 1970, Gramsci 1971, Williams 1977, and Bourdieu 1977, all cited in their book.

13. For a brief discussion of the studies about ethnicity in the Andes until the end of the 1970s, see Salomon 1982.

14. For an insightful discussion of how power presents and/or "hides" itself in everyday life, see Comaroff and Comaroff 1991, 22.

15. See van den Berghe and Primov 1977 for a concise summary of the history of the racial and casta categories. While here we use van den Berghe and Primov's and other authors' summary discussion of the casta and racial classification in Peru and Latin America, those interested in the subject should see the classical works by Magnus Mörner (1967, 1970), which these authors use.

16. The peninsulares had a series of privileges over the criollos that allowed the former to obtain the most important political posts with their concomitant economic benefits such as land, Indian labor, and so forth.

17. The "noble" Indians were exempt from tribute and were given key political roles within "Indian" communities, such as the post of kurakas or caciques.

18. During the colony the "mixed blood" categories were also known as castas.

19. As various authors have argued, there was a deliberate intent to create an intermediary political elite alienated from both the conquering and conquered cultures. For that purpose the Spanish founded special schools to educate the noble offspring of Spaniards and Indians. The best known of these schools, which were run by the religious orders, was the Jesuit school for kurakas' sons in Cusco. Despite the original purpose of the Crown, some important rebellious figures who vindicated the "indigenous" society came out of these schools. In Cusco the best-known case is that of José Gabriel Condorcanqui, better known as Tupac Amaru II, who led the most important anticolonial uprising at the end of the eighteenth century.

20. The main disadvantage that "mixed blood" or castas had to face was that in claiming not to be "Indians" they had to leave their communal rights to land and the possibility of having access to political posts in such communities. As Wightman (1990, 95) explains, "Throughout the colonial period mestizos who sought leadership positions within Indian communities had to be restricted by repeated royal decrees barring castas [in the sense of 'mixed blood' explained before] from such posts."

21. The classical work on the Indian casta and fiscal interest during the colony is that of Kubler (1962), cited in Seligman 1989.

22. In Andean studies more interest, although not enough, has been paid to the construction of "Indianness" (in particular through the study of *indigenismo*) than to the construction of "whiteness." In this book I address both through the study of comparsas.

23. As Seligman (1989, 697) explains, the cholo category started to have pejorative connotations in colonial society only after miscegenation threatened to undermine the strength of the casta system.

24. For example, in most Peruvian cities, the chicha dance-music style is associated with cholo identity. This style, developed by children of highland migrants in Lima, fuses elements of highland music with elements of the Colombian Caribbean style called cumbia. This style is also known as the "Andean cumbia." See Turino 1988, 1990.

25. As Seligman (1989, 697) points out, the category of cholo has been associated with those who have casual occupations within the urban informal sector.

26. I borrow the term "de-Indianize" from De la Cadena (1991).

27. It should be noted also that all over Peru and Latin America there are a large number of "popular" saints, deceased members of local societies who have been "canonized" by the local people themselves and who are generally not acknowledged by the Catholic Church. Devotees of these "saints" do not perform dances in their honor.

28. It should be noted that throughout the Andes the imposed patron saints have been replaced by other protector images that the people have proclaimed as their real patrons (cf. Mendoza 1988, 1989).

29. In various conversations, including one in which the parish priest was present, San Jerónimo people, generally over fifty years old, mentioned names of individuals who were profiting from former cofradía lands of the patron saint. They suggested that these individuals should at least contribute something to the annual celebration. The priest even promised that he would try to recover those pieces of land for the parish so that there could be some encouragement for people who wanted to become mayordomos of the patron-saint fiesta.

30. Ares Queija (1984, 448) points out the two main currents among the orders: "The first, best exemplified by the Franciscans and, in lesser degree, by the Augustinians and Mercedarians, was characterized by the systematic destruction of all previous religious manifestations. . . . The second current, impregnated with De Las Casas's ideas, was followed by the Dominicans and, above all, by the Jesuits, and it was based on persuasion; these clergymen adopted, then, a more tolerant attitude."

31. Poole (1990a, 121) cites all the chronicles that have descriptions about sixteenth- and seventeenth-century dance in Peru. In the first decade and a half after the conquest, the chroniclers were able to observe some pre-Hispanic Inca practices such as grandiose public ceremonies, of which dances were part. In 1551, after the first church council held in Lima, some of those magnificent Inca manifestations were banned, especially, as Poole points out, those "perceived as having overt political content, such as processions of Inca royal mummies or local ancestor worship" (107).

32. As Ares Queija (1984), Poole (1990a), and Estenssoro (1992) point out, the dances that were performed outside the context of Catholic feasts were still considered idolatrous and were banned.

33. Ramos (n.d., 18) cites a document of 1768 in which the people of San Jerónimo and the local parish argue about financing the dancers for the Corpus Christi.

34. The ambiguous and subversive role of grotesque images in European Carnival has been shown by Mikhail Bakhtin (1984).

35. Cahill (1986, 48) points out that there was a particular fear of fiestas because during the eighteenth century various uprisings broke out during the celebration of local patron-saint festivities, "by coincidence or by design."

36. Even though in a general sense my focus on ritual symbolism and practices is in line with the symbolist approach of Victor Turner, I do not follow his model of ritual in seeing the fiesta and the danzas as unchanging responses to a "conflictual" but self-reproducing social order.

37. Abercrombie (1986) has questioned some aspects of the old models in his study of ritual complexes in Bolivia, arguing that through these public rituals the local sociocultural order continually emerges at the juncture of greatest potential change and conflict.

38. This "system" by which various positions of responsibility related to fiesta sponsorship are apportioned, has been interpreted in various ways. According to most studies, the "system" is supposed to characterize the "traditional" peasant community, and it will gradually disappear when these communities are "modernized" and other sources of status or prestige are incorporated into that society. Classical functionalist studies in other parts of Latin America have argued that the "system," a set of individual careers formed by a series of tightly intercalated civil offices and sponsorship positions, serves as a leveling mechanism in societies guided by the principle of the "limited good"; cf. Foster 1967. Other studies, still in the functionalist line, have shown that this "system" does not necessarily function as a leveling mechanism and that civil and religious posts form separate hierarchies; cf. Cancian 1965.

39. In her historical-anthropological analysis study of the Tswana of southern Africa, Jean Comaroff (1985) has shown that the creative and transformative qualities of ritual may be used as means for different ends. She demonstrated that, while precolonial initiation rites sought to "redress experiential paradox in conformity with established social arrangements," contemporary Zionist practice, itself a product of the dialectical interaction between indigenous social forms and elements of the culture of colonialism, "is an effort to reformulate the constitution of the everyday world [and] to deal with conflicts inadequately addressed in prevailing ideologies" (9). Comaroff has suggested

that "ritual is never merely univocal and conservative, papering over the cracks in the cause of hegemonic social order" (119).

40. Schieffelin (1976, 3) has defined a "cultural scenario" as a series of events embodying a typical sequence of phases or episodes, which between its commencement and resolution effects a certain amount of social progress or change in the situation to which it pertains. "Cultural scenarios" are, according to Schieffelin, embodied both in ritual and in everyday courses of action.

41. Drawing upon Victor Turner's incorporation of the notion of "condensation symbolism" and Talcott Parson's notion of "generalized symbolic media of interaction," Nancy Munn (1974, 580) has argued that, in ritual, iconic symbols such as acts, words, or things have the capacity to synthesize complex sociocultural meanings from many domains and specific situational contexts, becoming the vehicles through which messages are constructed and through which meanings circulate; ritual symbols convert complex sociocultural meanings into "communication currency." Along with Munn and Jean Comaroff I consider ritual constructions, such as comparsas, to "play most directly upon the signifying capacity of symbols, using them as means through which to grasp, condense, and act upon qualities otherwise diffused in the social and material world" (Comaroff 1985, 78).

42. I do not take symbols to be the basic analytic unit of my analysis of ritual performance. The dynamic change in quality brought about by ritual danza performance derives from both "the play of tropes" (Fernandez 1974, 1986) and from the manipulation of symbolic presences (Munn 1974; Comaroff 1985). It is important here to distinguish between tropologic enactment and symbolic action (Fernandez 1973).

43. This concept of cultural predicament has been developed by Clifford (1988), cited in Ness (1992). Ness (1992, 235) defines choreographic phenomena as "a range of symbolic body movements processes . . . [including] movement processes, such as ritual body movement practices, and folk dance traditions that, although they are not the work of an individual choreographer, nevertheless are composed of patterned, symbolic (whether it be latent or explicitly recognized) body movement experiences that are generally recognized as 'dance' behavior or 'dance-like' behavior."

44. This was only a one-week course on movement description and observation using effort-shape approach at the Laban-Bartenieff center for movement studies in New York City in 1988. In this course I was made aware of something that Ness (1992, 3–10) discusses in an insightful way, which is the importance of the dance ethnographer's experiencing through practice the instruction of the body for learning new kinds of movements. Through learning dance movements, through working at accomplishing a particular perfection in the performance of such dance, we can be made aware that our bodies are reservoirs of "*habitus* or lifeway."

45. Although Deborah Poole's work (1990a, 1991) shows some aspects of the creation of identity, she focuses on the dance forms and on the "structural" position of Andean dancing within Catholic rituals.

46. Erlmann (1991) explains that the Zulu term *ingoma* literally means "song."

47. During my whole stay in Cusco for field research and every time I went

back to San Jerónimo I received compliments about my performance on that occasion.

## CHAPTER 2

1. I find the Hobsbawmian concept of "invented traditions" particularly helpful to explain how members of such *instituciones culturales* have composed a "factitious" continuity between a "suitable historic past" and the repertoire of music, dances, and rituals they have created and promoted. As Hobsbawm (1983, 1–2) has defined it, " 'invented tradition' is taken to mean a set of practices, normally governed by overtly or tacitly accepted rules and of a ritual or symbolic nature, which seek to inculcate certain values and norms of behavior by repetition, which automatically implies continuity. In fact, where possible, they normally attempt to establish continuity with a suitable historic past. . . . the peculiarity of 'invented' traditions is that the continuity with it [the historic past] is largely factitious."

2. An *institución cultural* is an organization self-defined as being in charge of promoting traditions and folklore. Because the translation "cultural institution" of the Peruvian concept of instituciones culturales is problematic, due to its different implications in English and within a social-scientific discussion, I will use the Spanish term. In my discussion an *institución folklórica* (folkloric institution) is considered within the instituciones culturales and is mainly different from the latter in that it tends to have a smaller scope of activities (i.e., its audience is a particular sector within the city or the town).

3. See chapter 1 for my discussion of the compound notion of ethnic/racial identity and for some specific meanings of the ethnic/racial categories of Indian and mestizo in the context of Cusco and Peru. These categories will often appear in the following discussion, and new meanings and specific referents in the national and regional context will be added to those previously discussed. See also chapter 1 for references to studies that show the conflicts that emerged during colonial times in the realm of public expressive forms.

4. As Rowe and Schelling (1991, 5–6) explain, the impossibility of keeping the boundaries of "folklore" rigid is common in places like Peru, Bolivia, and other countries that are known for having strong "native" and "mestizo" cultures. They develop and cite some examples of these phenomena in Peru and in other countries. In chapter 6 of this book I discuss the generational conflict mentioned here.

5. For an insightful analysis of the attempts of mestizo urban groups to make themselves different from the "indigenous" population by glorifying the image of the Indian in Mexico, see Friedlander 1975.

6. This period roughly corresponds to what Tamayo Herrera (1980) calls the "second modernization of Cusco," which according to him took place between 1895 and 1945. Deustua and Rénique (1984) take the period 1897–1931 for their analysis.

7. Although access to formal education grew during this period, schooling was still limited to a small portion of the population, particularly at the high-school level. Between 1900 and 1930, 75 percent of the population still lived in the countryside, and high-school education was available only in the cities. In order to study, people had to migrate. See Deustua and Rénique 1984.

8. *Modernization* means here the introduction of new advanced agricultural techniques, development of local industries, and improvement of communication systems.

9. As mentioned in chapter 1, the glorified memory of the Incas had been used in the past for diverse purposes. In relation to expressive forms, Mannheim (1991, 73) shows that the idealization of the Incas was an important part of the resurgence of visual and literary art of the seventeenth and eighteenth centuries, when the new landed elites appropriated the memories of the Incas as a source of legitimacy.

10. Luis E. Valcárcel was born in Puno but was raised in Cusco and became one of the leading figures in Cusco's intellectual and artistic life.

11. As explained in chapter 1 the term *criollo* was originally used in the colonial period to name the people of Spanish descent born in the colonies. This term has since approximately the end of the nineteenth century applied to a repertoire of popular music and dance genres identified with coastal culture that became nationally popular. This so-called criollo repertoire was initially formed by "originally foreign genres which gradually acquired their local characteristics" (Romero 1985, 257).

12. As Rowe and Schelling (1991, 2–3) point out, however, what is different from Europe is that in Latin America industrialization and the emergence of modern culture industry have tended to coincide.

13. The concept of folklore in Cusco and Peru since the first decades of this century has been shaped by the perspective developed by William J. Thoms in 1846. This British scholar proposed the term to replace *popular antiquities*. But while the new term *folklore* continued to work as preservation of the past, "new connotations of seriousness were added since 'lore' included the meaning of teaching and scholarship and 'folk' covered both people in general and the idea of the nation" (Rowe and Schelling 1991, 4). The definition of *folklore* by Thoms is often quoted by Peruvian folklorists, artists, and intellectuals.

14. They got together in a *tetería* named La Rotonda, one of the gathering centers of the urban bohemia in those days (Oróz 1989).

15. Some of the other founders are César Valdivieso, Santiago Lechuga, Manuel Palomino, Luis Ochoa Galdo, Horacio Fortón, Avelino García, Domingo Rado, Gualberto Olivera, and Manuel Pillco.

16. This trio included Andrés Izquierdo, Justo Morales, and Luis Esquivel (*La Crónica* [Lima], June 25, 1927, cited in Vivanco 1973, 34). The yaraví is a Peruvian "slow, sad, lyrical mestizo song genre" (Turino 1997, 234). The *huayno* or *wayno* is the most widespread mestizo music-dance genre (see chapter 4).

17. *La Crónica* (Lima), June 25, 1928, cited in Vivanco 1973, 37, my emphasis. The first translation into English of most of this quote that I am aware of was by Turino (1991, 270). However, I have translated directly from Vivanco 1973, 37, and have added the last two sentences to Turino's quotation from the same source.

18. Note that in 1928 and at least for the two subsequent years there were preliminary competitions among the highlanders who had gone to Lima for El Día del Indio. One such competition was among compositions that would fall into one of three categories: "Incaic, Andean, or Criollo." Therefore Incaic was already considered a genre of national dimension (Vivanco 1973, 35).

19. I do not provide the names of my informants.

20. For example, the organization called Tradición (tradition), which had a major ethnographically and anthropologically oriented publication between 1950 and 1958. Also the Sociedad Peruana de Folklore (Peruvian folklore society). For a detailed listing of this type of more academically oriented activities in Cusco of the time, see Tamayo Herrera 1980, 299–326.

21. For an analysis of the historical emergence of the concept of popular culture, see the introduction of Rowe and Schelling 1991.

22. It was sad to see that during my visit in the summers of 1996, 1997, and 1998 the museum had to close because it couldn't pay a staff member to open the museum to the public.

23. Tamayo Herrera (1981, 279) calls this desire "neoindigenismo práctico" (practical neoindigenismo).

24. Humberto Vidal Unda, "Cusqueñismo, la filosofía de la ciudad abuela de América," Expreso, no. 5697, June 24, 1977, cited by Tamayo 1981, 172. My translation and emphasis.

25. According to the chroniclers this ceremony used to take place not there but where the central plaza of Cusco city is today.

26. In Cusco's anthem, the glory of the Inca empire and "race" and the Sun God are central symbols. See Rozas 1992 for a complete documentation of the history, lyrics, and music of this anthem.

27. Tamayo Herrera (1981) calls it "La Segunda Modernización" (the second modernization).

28. As Brisseau et al. (1978, 28–29) state, Cusco had become one of the "hottest" points on the continent because from 1947 to 1965 there was a strong peasant syndicalization, invasions of hacienda lands, and a guerrilla movement. Foreign intervention and support of the reforms needed to calm the outbursts of violence were evident during the government of Fernando Belaúnde Terry (1964–1968).

29. The Machu Picchu ruins have been known to the world of archaeologists and world travelers since their "discovery" by Hiram Bingham in 1911. In 1921 there had been an attempt by Alberto Giesecke, an American intellectual who had a strong influence in the academic development of the social sciences in Cusco, to develop tourism in Cusco, exploiting the potential of Machu Picchu and other Inca monuments.

30. Cusco city and the Huatanay and Urubamba valleys were the areas that benefited most from these projects.

31. In the late 1940s the valley of La Convención in the province of the same name emerged as a center of economic growth within Cusco departamento. As Rénique (1988, 186) explains: "Due to the boom in the export of raw materials caused by World War II and the Korean war, La Convención became the only non-coastal agrarian area directly linked to the international market. A key product of this unexpected expansion was coffee."

32. The contest was held that first year and subsequently in Garcilazo soccer stadium, where some of the previous contests had taken place. Today's equivalent of that contest, the Región Inka contest, is held in the largest sports coliseum in the city of Cusco.

33. The prohibitions were part of a larger conflict that discriminated against Puno expressive forms (see chapter 6).

34. The institute was founded in 1972 and became the umbrella organization to coordinate cultural activities and policymaking at the regional and national levels. This institución had its antecedents in the Casa de la Cultura (house of culture) created in 1962.

35. *Inkarri* is the central character of a cluster of myths collected by anthropologists in certain parts of the Peruvian Andes that for these professionals and for the state became symbolic of indigenous identity and resistance. The relevance given to these myths has been by now very much criticized as an anthropological construction of indigenous identity.

36. Thomas Turino (1991) has argued that there was an important difference between the first "cultural functionaries," that is, people who formed part of state-sponsored instituciones, and the earlier indigenistas who became interpreters of highland music. The cultural functionaries fostered the performance by rural Andeans themselves, "thus providing the possibility for somewhat greater auto-control" (272). According to Turino the position of these cultural administrators could be seen as ambiguous because, on the one hand, they fought for the national recognition and preservation of highland expressive forms and, on the other, they bowed to the greater prestige of urban institutions and Western values, acknowledging that these contexts are the final proving grounds for the highlanders' expressive forms and enhancing some stereotypes regarding this peasant population.

37. During Morales Bermúdez's regime one of the currently most important carnivalesque contests, the Festival Carnavalesco de Qoya (carnivalesque festival of Coya), was instituted. Subsequently, Alan García's regime (1985–1990) instituted in 1986 the Encuentro de Integración Nacional "Raymi Llaqta" (national integration encounter "Raymi Llaqta") and in 1987 the first Festival de Autores y Compositores Andinos (festival of Andean authors and composers).

38. During the military regime some currently important instituciones folklóricas such as Rickchariy Wayna and Filigranas Peruanas were founded.

39. See Turino 1991, 272–281, about the revalorization of Andean culture during Velasco's regime.

40. The so-called ritual battle of *Ch'iaraje,* "named for the puna (high grassland zone) site where groups of men fight with slingshots and whips, sometimes taking captives and, on occasion, killing them" (Orlove 1994, 133), has been the subject of analysis by social scientists; see bibliography in Orlove 1994, 134.

41. This definition is given in Quechua dictionaries. See Hornberger and Hornberger 1983, 196.

42. Flute and drum ensembles were typical of pre-Hispanic times in the Andes and in other parts of Latin America (Turino 1997, 232).

43. The natural resources of Paucartambo also became an attraction for tourists, since around the time of the festivity tourists could go to a place called Tres Cruces de Oro to watch a spectacular sunrise. Wealthy paucartambinos, some ex-landowning families, invested in the touristic industry, particularly promoting their town.

## CHAPTER 3

1. The Incas, however, were not the first settlers of the area. Archaeologists and ethnohistorians have shown that there had been a long history of development of pre-Inca cultures in the Cusco valley before the Incas conquered the area. Although there is no agreement on the subject, it is likely that the Incas founded the city between the eleventh and twelfth centuries; see Brisseau et al. 1978. Nevertheless, one thing that all authors agree on is that the great expansion of the empire took place in less than a century right before the Spanish invasion (cf. Mannheim 1991, 16; van den Berghe and Primov 1977, 32). In the higher parts of San Jerónimo are remains of pre-Inca settlements; the best known is the complex named Racay-racay. According to a San Jerónimo historian (and current mayor of San Jerónimo, Ccoanqui n.d.) the pre-Inca remains were located in the higher parts because at the time the lower areas were still swampy.

2. Remains of Inca-period terrace systems can still be seen in San Jerónimo in the sectors called Larapa, Kaira, and Pata Pata. Some irrigation canals from that time are still being used for agricultural purposes.

3. For example, in San Jerónimo people still have last names like Sinchi Rocca and Tupac Yupanki, widely acknowledged in Cusco and Peru as Inca names. These names appear as Inca names in school textbooks used in Peru.

4. As Karen Spalding (1984, 126) has eloquently summarized, "The structure of village and parish was basic to the Toledan plan. . . . Ideally, each village was to constitute a single parish, with a resident Catholic priest to teach and train 'these barbarians,' as Toledo dubbed them, to respect a God whose representatives on earth were chosen and deployed by the Spanish state to aid in the maintenance of its authority in this world. Juan de Matienzo, a major supporter of Toledo's programs, insisted upon the role of the Church in his argument for the necessity of the resettlement of the native population, 'because they can neither be instructed in the faith nor can they become men if they are not gathered together into towns.' Concentration also made it possible for Toledo to organize the diverse regulations sketching the vague outlines of a native political structure into an organized local political system. Village and parish were each given their native officials under the supervision of the Spanish provincial bureaucracy, the corregidor de indios and the priest."

5. As Ramos (n.d.) explains, to study the colonial church an analytical distinction should be made between the *cabildo eclesiástico,* which included the local church authorities, headed by the bishop, who administered all the economic resources ascribed to this institution (the parish priests were the local representatives of this hierarchy), and the religious orders, which had a very strong internal cohesiveness and were almost completely independent from the institutional church or *cabildo eclesiástico.*

6. The main difference between an estancia (a ranch or grazing site) and a hacienda (a sizable landed estate, normally mixing farming and ranching) was the size of the property. The estancia was smaller.

7. In 1702 a large grazing and cultivation area of San Jerónimo was sold by a Spanish *hacendado* (hacienda owner) to the Dominican order. In the 1940s

this area was bought from the order by the biggest local peasant community, Picol Orcconpuquio (Zambrano 1971; Alviz Montañez 1989).

8. These fees and services that the curas received were not registered in parish documentation. However, there exist official complaints about the abuses that the curas committed in collecting them. In 1706 the people of San Jerónimo complained, "The *cura* asked us . . . sixty pesos every year, saying that we had to invite the *corregidor* from the city of Cuzco to our patron saint festivity because there he had to elect the new *alcaldes;* this money we had to give him because he collected it with much cruelty, clubbing and whipping us. This *corregidor* never came to our parish because we always went to the city of Cuzco for the election of our alcaldes. . . . Every year for our patron saint festivity we had to give the *cura* ten mule loads of chopped wood, thirty hens, thirty chickens, and five hundred eggs, taking it by force from some Indians as it were a debt" (Ramos n.d., 21).

9. The parish priest of San Jerónimo notes in 1796, "[T]he Indians work for free in the annual retiling of the temple's roof and in all the necessary repairs. That is how I experienced it from the day I took office, because a few days after, the roof of the colateral chapel of the Anahuarq ayllu fell down and the *Cacique* (leader) and the Indians rebuilt it without charging anything to the local parish. I also find that the Indians plant, cultivate, and harvest the corn in the lands of the Church without charging anything. They also, with the production of their own plots of land, annually provide the Church with the needed candles, wafers, incense, and the oil for the lamp of the Holy Sacrament" (ibid., 8).

10. The ayllu has existed as a unit of social organization since pre-Inca times. The Incas adopted and further developed this concept as part of their sociopolitical system in order to link local populations to the state. Spanish chroniclers and early Andeanists stressed the lineage aspects of ayllu organization. This emphasis by the chroniclers came from their own preoccupation with genealogies.

11. Even when used for the purpose of kinship classification the ayllu concept has been used by Andeans in a very flexible way, shifting according to the context and to the social status, age, and identity of "ego" (Poole 1984, 140).

12. This negotiation was also true at the politico-economic level, where, as Karen Spalding (1984, 219) has shown, "Spaniards could not attempt to create their own hierarchy of authority among the Indians without risking the loss of access to and control over Indian society. . . . In the face of Indian resistance, the Spanish authorities were obliged to incorporate the traditional Andean hierarchy into the model of local government defined by colonial laws and regulations."

13. As mentioned in chapter 1 the new republican government fought the existence of cofradías as a measure to control church administration and accumulation of wealth.

14. The current organization of the country, explained in chapter 1, dates from the time of independence.

15. According to the 1940 national census, 72 percent of the population of San Jerónimo was Indian. The total population of the town at the time was 4,485. As explained in chapter 1, the category of Indian as opposed to mestizo

or white (according to the same census the remaining 28 percent of the population of the district was either *blanca* or mestiza) indicates a relative status of subordination of these members of society. The 1940 national census was the last one to consider race as a category of classification of the population (Ministerio de Hacienda y Comercio 1940).

16. While some traditional historians have portrayed this relationship as feudal (Tamayo Herrera 1981, 50), recent studies have questioned the traditional view about the *patrón*-servant relationship in the haciendas of the southern Andes, showing that peasants and landowners often had an inequitable but basically symbiotic relationship. Cf. Jacobsen 1993. Nevertheless, it cannot be denied that the image of the assymetrical relationship and the abusive nature of the hacendado have been a reality for Andeans everywhere. As will be seen in chapter 4, this is recreated in the Majeños danza.

17. The state institution that mediated in land disputes and other conflicts between landowners was the Dirección General de Asuntos Indígenas. The ayllus or parcialidades used the legal status of comunidades de indígenas in their disputes. In 1946 various ayllus, or as legally acknowledged, comunidades de indígenas, vindicated large portions of land from the Dominican hacienda Pata Pata (Zambrano 1971). In this conflict the Dirección General de Asuntos Indígenas paid the Dominican order for the land that the comunidades were to receive. The conflict had an early phase of violent confrontation between the people who ran the Pata Pata hacienda and the members of the comunidades. Since the 1940s the religious orders started to sell their properties in San Jerónimo: the Mercedarians sold their hacienda Kaira to the state, and the Dominicans started a process by which their sharecroppers could buy their land in exchange for their labor.

18. The introduction of pesticides and the subsequent improvement of health and productive conditions for the people of San Jerónimo is still remembered by people who lived there during the 1950s. In 1958 the central core of the town also obtained running water.

19. By the end of this decade formal education had become more accessible to a larger population of San Jerónimo, although this remained at the primary level; in 1963 there were two primary schools in the town. See Dirección Nacional de Estadística y Censos 1972 for the exact figures for educational level.

20. In the late 1970s San Jerónimo had its first high school, and by the mid-1980s a second one was founded.

21. The total area of the district is 93.58 square kilometers, or 9,358 hectares. The most important mountains within the territory of the district are Machu Picol, Wayna Picol, and Ccumu, whose peaks are over 3,600 meters above sea level.

22. The asentamientos that can be properly called urban are practically suburbs of Cusco city and are mostly inhabited by professionals who are from the city.

23. Since the 1970s the average population growth of this whole area has been 5.6 percent annually, which is higher than the national average of 2.5 percent and that of the fastest growing city of the country, Lima, which was 5.5 percent in the 1970s (Proyecto Ununchis n.d. a, b, c; Instituto Geográfico Nacional 1989).

24. The town and its radio urbano, which is the area where most of the people that my study focused on lived, cover approximately 67 hectares.

25. The rest of the territory of the district, which does not correspond to the town's radio urbano and to the asentamientos humanos, is divided into eight comunidades campesinas, one state agrarian cooperative, a Cusco city university experimental farm, and two anexos or smaller communities without politico-administrative independence. The four largest comunidades are Picol Orcconpuquio, Succso Aucaylle, Collana Chahuanccosqo, and Pata Pata. Although Pata Pata is legally recognized as a "farmers' association" and not as a comunidad campesina, and therefore the administration of the land and the legislation that applies to this association is different from that of the comunidades, in the district it is still known as the comunidad of Pata Pata. To become member of a comunidad one has to belong to a local family that has been in the town for several generations or to marry someone from those families. Since the agrarian reform in the 1970s, when the land was distributed among the local families and when the comunidades were favored by a new legal status, membership in these comunidades has become more regulated.

26. For example, the members of Pata Pata have the best irrigated land, and, even though the size of their plots is approximately the same as that of others, they can cultivate more profitable crops and harvest more times a year than the members of other communities.

27. Even in the comunidades the members, the *comuneros* (heads of families), own their plots of land individually. The comunidades' administrative councils organize the distribution of water, communal grazing areas or forest, and communal working parties, which are most often called to clean the irrigation ditches. The members of these councils are elected democratically every two years and are representatives to the municipal government and to other state or private administrative institutions such as banks and international aid agencies. The average size of the plots is two *topos*. The topo is a local unit of measure that is approximately one-third of a hectare.

28. According to a survey carried out in 1990, at least 60 percent of the mothers of the town were involved in commerce, but this percentage should be larger because many people in answering the survey may have not regarded commerce as an economic activity of the mother and could have just said that her main activity is to take care of the home (Mendoza 1990).

29. This number is registered by the municipality, but it is probable that there are even more estabecimientos comerciales.

30. One can see market women in the city, but their presence is limited to certain areas (such as the market and ceritain neighborhoods) and is not as predominant as in San Jerónimo.

31. According to the 1990 survey conducted in the town, in the contemporary households 40 percent of the fathers (average age 45) and 60 percent of the mothers received only primary education. In these same households 32 percent of the oldest children (average age 25) have received or are receiving higher education or technical training, and 56 percent of them have completed high school. Although men continue to receive more education than women (i.e., parents invest more in sending men to the university or technical school than in sending women), in this generation, thanks to the coed local schools, women

and men are almost equally receiving primary and high-school education (Mendoza 1990).

32. These craftsmen and unskilled workers form comparsas for the regional pilgrimage of Qoyllorit'i (which has historically been dominated by the participation of peasants and herders, although this is changing; see Poole 1988) or have a marginal participation within comparsas. If they form a whole comparsa, as in the case of the members of the comunidad Pillao Matao, their participation during the ritual is very limited and not steady throughout the years as is the case of the comparsas that are the central actors of the ritual.

33. About 25 percent of the population do not have a bathroom, and another 25 percent have only a latrine (Mendoza 1990).

34. From the beginning of his first government (1990) President Alberto Fujimori has allowed private vans to provide transportation on this route. Local owners of the bus lines and taxis are complaining about this because outsiders are taking advantage of this opportunity.

35. Since the installation of the republican state there have been presidential elections off and on. In 1968 Velasco's de facto government suspended these elections; they were reinstated by Morales Bermúdez in 1980. Only since that year can illiterate people vote in Peru.

36. Van den Berghe and Primov (1977, 210) point out how in the early 1970s the leftist university students captured the leadership of the three main comunidades of the district. Also, most townspeople vividly remember a violent confrontation between the local transportistas and radicalized local university students in 1978. These students protested against an increase in the bus fares to the city of Cusco, and the transportistas, afraid of a boycott of their bus lines, called the Cusco police, who repressed the students. No casualties were reported in that event, but the brutality of the repression, which wounded some and scared the whole town, made most local people even angrier at the transportistas than they were before the increase of fares. This confrontation originated local efforts to start a communal transportation enterprise, which failed after a few years.

37. The current mayor, now serving a second term, is a local intellectual/journalist who does not belong to a political party and calls himself an independent.

38. Even from the first round of the 1990 national elections the support for Fujimori was strong in San Jerónimo. In both rounds he received 80 percent of the vote.

39. During the colonial period this statue suffered a restoration or "operation" as local people call it (Blanco 1974, vol. 1, 224). People still comment about it, saying that the reason for the operation was that the statue was so tall that it was not easy to bring in and out of of the churches. This comment is often made with pride because tallness, as will be shown in chapter 4, is seen as a desired phenotypic characteristic. Blanco also observed that the operation was done because the statue was too big and heavy and adds that during the procedure they found "five pounds of gold in his chest." A second representation of Saint Jerome, also of colonial origin, in the church is known as the "repentant" Saint Jerome. In this statue the saint is portrayed as a pale old man kneeling and

looking up and barely clothed. This image recalls the part of the saint's life when he was undergoing penitence in the desert. While this image is placed in an individual altar on the side, townspeople do not pay too much attention to this icon, and even during the fiesta they rarely light some candles in his honor.

40. As explained in chapter 1 the evangelizing preaching, and iconography have laid the groundwork for the local elaboration of the meanings of these saints as sign-images. Evangelizing texts that circulate today describe the personality of the saint and his powers. Also, every year the main sermon of the central mass of the fiesta remarks upon the personality of Saint Jerome. In both the iconography of Saint Jerome and the preaching, his qualities as an acknowledged scholar who occupied a privileged place in the hierarchy of the church are emphasized. He is supposed to represent an ideal that jeronimianos should imitate.

41. Until the 1940s this patron-saint festivity did not have comparsas. In chapter 4 I refer to the changes in the town that led to the emergence of this festivity as the most important of the town and as the main realm for the performance of comparsas.

42. For example, the way in which commerce should be carried out during the fiesta, the taxes that vendors have to pay, the obligation to participate in the civil parade, and so forth.

43. The Qollas resisted going to those meetings.

44. The average age fluctuates between fifteen and twenty-two.

45. This participation also cost me some rough beginnings with the Qollas comparsa because, as they told me later, they had been very jealous of me dancing with the Majeños. They were relieved when I told them that I was not going to dance (danza) again with them or any other comparsa; I would just accompany and dance (baile) with all of them.

46. During the period of my fieldwork the Qollas did not organize a día familiar, and the Majeños and Tuntuna organized theirs at a different time of the year.

47. The Majeños had their día familiar only for members of their own families, and they did not intend to raise funds with this event. They had only a soccer game and then ate and drank among themselves.

48. It is very common for a couple to start living together and having children before they go through the civil and religious ceremonies. Mostly the members of local elites whose parents can afford to give a wedding before the couple is established do it that way. Weddings and baptisms are very expensive celebrations; if a person has to carry out a *cargo* (sponsorship responsibility), he or she will save money if other celebrations are also held at the same time the cargo is carried out.

49. School groups sometimes also participate in this entrada with danzas típicas.

50. The festive dish for cusqueños, which jeronimianos claim they invented, is the chiri uchu, which in Quechua means cold *ají* (*ají*, which literally means "chili" or "hot pepper," is the generic name given to any type of stew). It is a dish served at any important celebration, such as the Corpus Christi in Cusco, or at weddings or baptisms in the town. This dish has a variety of baked and

boiled meat (guinea pig, chicken, sausage, duck), a piece of cheese, a special type of fried bread, toasted corn or *cancha*, seaweed, and fish roe *huevera*. It is considered a delicacy, although the quality of the serving can vary widely.

51. San Jerónimo is known in the region for its important production of garden vegetables such as *habas* (lima beans). Their regional nickname is *phus-pus*, which in Quechua means boiled lima beans. This ponche is made of dried lima beans and cooked with herbs and sugar; at the time of serving this drink is topped with a shot of strong, sweet brandy.

52. The music for these occasions is usually played by ensembles that use electronic instruments. This music is clearly distinguishable from the music played by the bands of the fiesta. For an analysis of these bailes within the context of a fiesta, see Romero 1989.

53. To place these altars used to be an obligation of the different ayllus or parcialidades of the district until the agrarian reform. Also the main and largest altar, called *Wiracocha* (Lord) altar, used to be sponsored by one of the wealthiest and most respected local families. Today different local comunidades or associations take turns for the opportunity to be in charge of setting up this altar. A few smaller ones are still placed voluntarily by family groups of some parcialidades.

54. The first year that I witnessed the fiesta the Majeños completed their whole choreography at the atrium and the Qollas, who were supposed to go second, did not wait and started theirs in a different place in the plaza. The second year the Majeños did only a short presentation in the atrium and then went to another place, more spacious, to do their complete choreography. This second year the Qollas waited for the Majeños to finish their complete choreography and performed theirs in the same place as the Majeños.

55. This practice was originally part of the local celebration when the imagen was brought back from Cusco from the Corpus Christi. Then it was incorporated by the Majeños into the fiesta in the late 1940s. The rooster was replaced at a certain point by other items. By the early 1960s it had been replaced by flowers.

## CHAPTER 4

1. Fernandez (1986) defines this process of bringing together different domains in creative ways as "the argument of images." He explains that "metaphoric comparison is a prime form of that argument. But it is not the only one, for the predication of one domain of experience upon another is of many kinds. It is diversified by all variety in the play of tropes" (viii). Fernandez argues that one of the missions of our argumentative powers is to persuade others to recognize our performances and our place in the world. In a more recent work, Fernandez and Durham (1991) develop further the notion of the "argument of images."

2. See chapter 1 for an explanation of the differences between the concepts of danza performed by a local comparsa as ritual action, baile, and danza típica, all of which can be translated into English as "dance."

3. Paucartambo is a district capital of the province of the same name located in the southeast portion of Cusco departamento. The town of Paucartambo can be reached today from Cusco city (110 km away) on a partially asphalted road

in approximately six hours. Until the 1970s the whole province of Paucartambo was known as having very marked "ethnic" and class distinctions between a white and mestizo landowning elite and an "Indian" peasant majority. Cf. van den Berghe and Primov 1977, 212–218.

4. Hobsbawm (1983, 2) has argued that invented traditions are "responses to novel situations which take the form of reference to old situations, or which establish their own past by quasi-obligatory repetition."

5. A distinction should be made between the arrieros, who used mules as their means of transportation, and the *llameros,* who used llamas, the indigenous cargo animal, for the same end. By the seventeenth century, muleteers dominated in the important commercial routes that went through Cusco. Nevertheless, the llameros existed until the twentieth century, moving along different routes that the arrieros did not cover. These llameros were culturally different than the arrieros since they were generally members of "Indian" communities and spoke the indigenous languages (Quechua and Aymara). They also traded mostly indigenous products (see Glave 1989). I will develop this ethnic/racial difference between arrieros and llameros in chapter 5, because the Qollas comparsa impersonates the llameros.

6. See chapter 1, "Indios, Cholos, and Mestizos . . . " for the definitions of ideology and hegemony.

7. A few years after my extended period of reserach in Cusco a new all-women comparsa started in Paucartambo, the *Chunchachas.* Still the women have to be single to perform.

8. As explained in chapter 1 the rural/urban dichotomy today marks the two important poles in the definition of ethnic/racial identity. In Cusco whatever becomes identified with urban culture, such as a particular way of dressing or a music genre, becomes also an element that can make a person more mestizo and less indigenous.

9. The same mayordomo and lentraderos of the patron-saint festivity have to carry out some ritual obligations for the Octava, such as conducting a novena, hiring a band for the procession, and offering food and drink to the townspeople who accompany the imagen from Cusco. As explained in chapter 3, the traditional sponsorship posts of the fiesta such as mayordomo and lentradero have lost importance for jeronimianos and have become secondary in relation to the sponsorship of the fiesta through being the carguyoq of a comparsa. The Octava seems to have been undergoing a similar process to that of the patron-saint festivity, by which the comparsas become the main ritual sponsors and central actors of the celebration. For a detailed description of the Octava celebration in San Jerónimo in the mid-1960s, see Roca 1966.

10. During my research most of the comparsa members did not know the names of the different parts of the choreography. These names were gathered through various interviews with the different dancers in both Paucartambo and San Jerónimo.

11. As Turino explains (1993, 273), in Peru the term *wayno* must be understood according to the specific ethnographic context and in some cases, as in that of the indigenous peasants of Conima he studied, can be used as a synonym of "music" or "song" (273).

12. See Roel Pineda 1959 for a thorough description and analysis of the

wayno genre in Cusco with an emphasis on the differences in the performative aspects. Roel Pineda explains the differences between "mestizo" and "indigenous" wayno styles. He also traces the pre-Hispanic origins of the wayno.

13. I use "ideal" as deriving from "idealism," that is, as derived from the attitude of mind that lays emphasis on perfection. I do not use "ideal" in the sense of "ideal types" as defined by Max Weber, although I refer to the construction of archetypes.

14. The performance of this other danza, the *Aucca Chileno,* caused some problems and controversy among comparsa members, because some Majeños thought that this performance distracted the fiesta participants from the main performance of their danza. Therefore, this performance stopped after a couple of years.

15. In San Jerónimo, as in the rest of Cusco and Peru, transportistas always have two or three *ayudantes* (helpers) whom they order around, mistreat, and make carry out the hard work. These ayudantes are often called "cholos" or "chulillos" (servants). In addition, middle- and upper-middle-class cusqueños always have lower-status servants and sometimes *pongos* (serflike servants), whom they also call derogatory names. The mistreatment of personal servants and other people considered of lower status because of their class or ethnic/racial identity is common in Cusco and throughout Peru.

16. In Paucartambo, Maqt'as of comparsas were also in charge of serving the main performers. Nevertheless, this asymmetrical relationship remained part of the performance during the fiesta and was not a part of the relationship of the comparsa members outside ritual, as was the case with the San Jerónimo Majeños.

17. Santiago Rojas, a sculptor and mask maker originally from Paucartambo, is a famous cusqueño artist who lives in the city of Cusco. His statues and masks are found in national and international museums. The Majeños from San Jerónimo buy their masks from him because it is a symbol of prestige to be able to afford one of his expensive masks.

## CHAPTER 5

1. See chapter 2 for a discussion of the concept of tradition in Cusco.

2. My analysis of the representation of the lower body and social strata and their central symbolic roles in the definition of personal and social identity has been informed by Bakhtin's analysis (1984) of the Middle Ages and Renaissance carnival and by Stallybrass and White's discussion (1986) of Bakhtin's work and their own investigation of cultural representations of the "low other." In this chapter I use some of Bakhtin's analysis. I will use Stallybrass and White's study for my analytical conclusions in the final chapter.

3. I regard the Qollas performers as "bricoleurs" who, drawing upon their own history and sociocultural reality and working by means of signs, have constructed through their danza a new, meaningful whole. This new whole, which expresses many "forbidden contents" in "forbidden forms," is able to generate multiple meanings (Stallybrass and White 1986).

4. The buffoon/servant Maqt'a character analyzed in chapter 4 also falls into this category. In the case of the Maqt'a, his marginality is defined in ethnic/

racial terms and in terms of age, because the literal translation of the word is "adolescent boy, young man" (Hornberger and Hornberger 1983, 126).

5. In San Jerónimo a truck owner is also often a driver, but many drivers are not owners. In their commercial businesses owners establish different kinds of partnerships with their drivers. This partnership is often asymmetrical, the owner being the one who profits the most from the business. Often these partnerships are established with younger or poorer relatives. The owner/driver or the driver always has an assistant who sometimes helps him with the driving but who most often is just in charge of watching and maintaining the truck and of loading and unloading the cargo.

6. The *Saqras* comparsa has had a very erratic existence and is not considered by townspeople a traditional comparsa of San Jerónimo. After a few years the Saqras changed their danza for another, the *Sijlla;* then they did not perform for a few years; and finally, a few years ago they reactivated the danza and have had a very limited presence in the fiesta (i.e., only performing once or twice during the fiesta). Through time the socioeconomic composition of this comparsa has also changed, and it is now mostly composed of poorer bricklayers and tile makers. The *Saqras* is regionally known as one of Paucartambo's mestizo danzas.

7. For further discussion of the notion of "invented tradition" as formulated by Hobsbawm (1983), see chapter 2. Villasante (1989, 118–121) provides the different versions of the legends about the appearance of the imagen of the Virgin patron of Paucartambo, according to which the Qollas brought it to the town for the first time.

8. I keep the informants anonymous. When it is essential to refer to a particular informant, I use a pseudonym as in the cases of Mr. Martínez and (below) Mr. Pinto.

9. Three of the members of the Paucartambo comparsa, including the Caporal, went to perform in San Jerónimo.

10. A *Contradanza* comparsa continues to go every year to this important regional pilgrimage, but most of the members of this comparsa are nonjeronimiano residents of the district.

11. Mr. Pinto told me about the time his *Contradanza* comparsa performed in the city of Cusco for the Corpus Christi and the archbishop of Cusco approached him, congratulated him, and said, "This man is genuine."

12. In the Qollas' meetings, rehearsals, and ritual performances it was obvious that their wives had a more important voice in the decisions made for the fiesta than did the wives of the Majeños. The Qollas also had a special festive occasion on which they celebrate with their wives because, as the dancers said, their wives do not get to fully enjoy the patron-saint festivities because of the cooking and serving that they have to do for their husbands on that occasion. This celebration with their wives takes place annually the day of *Compadres,* two Thursdays before Sunday carnival. *Compadres* is celebrated all over Cusco and is the occasion when women play tricks on their male relatives or friends.

13. *Qollavino* is a synonym of *Qolla,* used sometimes by the San Jerónimo performers to specify the place of origin of their characters.

14. Most of the Qollas songs are structured in stanzas of four verses each.

Often the last two verses comment on the first two. When there is a refrain, it is repeated at the end of each stanza. Most of this and the following music descriptions have been written with the guidance of Philip Bohlman. Nevertheless, I am responsible for any misuse of the terms or concepts used in these descriptions. Analyzing the dance music of Paucartambo, including that of the Qollas, Turino (1997, 233) concludes that the majority "consist of between two and four short sections that are repeated in forms such as AABB or AABBCC."

15. In Paucartambo the comparsas continue to use kenas but in a widespread ensemble known as the *orquesta típica*, which in Cusco is most often composed of the kenas, a violin, a mandolin, an accordion, and sometimes a harp. Turino (1997, 233) has described the Qollas song performance as having a "densely blended timbral quality."

16. *Aija* is a vocable without a specific meaning used between song verses, according to the performers, to give encouragement to continue singing. It could be considered equivalent to the expression "Let's go!" The tone of voice in which it is pronounced changes according to the verses (i.e., when they sing the sad stanzas, they use a lamenting voice).

17. When the Qollas danza is incorporated into a town, changes have to be made because the verses address the people of the town and the local imagen.

18. As explained in chapter 4, the pasacalle is a coordinated group movement along the streets, used to travel from one point to another. In the Qollas, as in most other Cusco danzas, this is done in a two-line formation. The melody for the pasacalle song is a bass line that is repeated over and over and has a feeling of six.

19. In chapter 6 I analyze the changes that this "tradition" is undergoing with the introduction of "modern" dances from the Altiplano by young cusqueños.

20. The comparsa usually adds one or two new members every year, and an equal number retires temporarily or permanently. Also, during the fiesta some dancers separate from the group and either go home or go off to celebrate with some friends, a habit very much criticized by some formal members and by the Majeños, who believe in discipline and order during the fiesta performance. Because of this undisciplined behavior of some Qolla comparsa members, there are times during the fiesta when some of them are missing.

21. *Walqa* in this context means a hanging tied around the body. It relates to the concept of walqanchis, which are the hangings that danza performers and ritual sponsors tie across their chests at the moment of the cacharpari, or fiesta farewell.

22. Several of the performers have a fake animal because it is very expensive and difficult to get a real one.

23. Monteras were formerly worn by both sexes but are now worn mostly by women (Poole 1990a, 101).

24. The Quechua adjective *qhapaq* means "high social status." As discussed in chapters 1 and 4, "white" features, such as facial hair (mustaches or beard), indicate high social status.

25. *Cha* is a Quechua ending used as a diminutive, to show endearment, or

to emphasize lower status, as in the case of maqt'acha. The three uses overlap or emphasize each other.

26. The Inkacha wears knickers, *ojotas* (rubber sandals), a short poncho, and a montera. His mask varies but is frequently made of hand-knit wool.

27. Among Quechua-speaking cusqueños the term *maqt'a* or *maqt'acha* is also used to designate a young or not fully socialized man (i.e., unmarried); cf. Fuenzalida 1970, 57; Poole 1984, 215–216. The association with the pejorative terms *cholo* or *Indian* is made on the basis of dominant regional and national ideologies, which consider cholos and "Indians" not fully socialized members of society.

28. *Rakhu* is an adjective used to define the thick or bulky quality of objects (Cusihuaman 1976, 127). Jeronimianos have transformed it into a noun.

29. *Qoya* was the Quechua name to designate the Inca's wife.

30. The ages of the *Qollitas* (little Qollas) comparsa fluctuate between six and fourteen. This comparsa is sponsored by the parents of the dancers and has a more limited participation in the ritual than any of the adult or youth comparsas of the town (i.e., fewer public presentations and private banquets). This comparsa was initiated by the oldest son of the founder of the adult comparsa when he was ten years old in 1979. Today the kinship relationship between the adults' and the children's comparsas is not as close as in the beginning but it continues to exist; also, few of the current young dancers of the adult comparsa performed with the Qollitas. The other place within the district of San Jerónimo where this danza is performed is in the community of Huaccoto, located in the high mountain slopes of this district. It has been performed since approximately 1984, and it was taught to them by members of the comparsa of the town of San Jerónimo who worked in the quarry located in that community.

31. Pulling the tendons of the dead chicken's foot gives the effect that the foot is moving.

32. As explained in chapter 2, contemporary qhaswas, particularly in the context of folkloric presentations, make open allusions to sex and fertility. The specific piece performed was *Canas Carnival,* very often performed on stage by Centro Qosqo as representative of Cusco "indigenous" identity.

33. *Imilla* means "young woman" in Aymara, the native language of the Altiplano people.

34. Analyzing the cultural association of femininity with the negative aspects of indigenous identity in Ocongate, Cusco, Harvey (1994, 59–60) has argued that in the *Qollas* performance in that town "it appears that the combination of the male and the female that the male performance provides stops the dramas from becoming simply a representation of female—and by extension, indigenous—humiliation. It permits the expression of these sentiments without the experience of them in the enactment of the role itself. Men and women say that men have to act the parts because if women were to do so, then the male characters would have to be more restrained in their behavior. . . . Paradoxically, then, the male cannot interact with the female and create the necessary male/female combination unless the 'female' is a male."

35. As explained in chapter 3, in Cusco dominant ideology, as elsewhere, men's superiority over women is often defined in terms of physical strength.

36. People from San Jerónimo call the women who wear this characteristic kind of clothing "mestizas" and not "cholas," as these women are often called in Andean literature.

37. The meter of the melody of the first part moves back and forth between the feeling of six and the feeling of two. The second part, the fuga, has a feeling of two.

38. Wayno is the most widespread dance-song genre in the Andes.

39. The melody of the puka cinta is similar to that of the chinka-chinka, having a meter that moves back and forth between the feeling of six and the feeling of two. The puka cinta also has a stanza that alludes to the waving, ribbon-like movement of the line: "We will pull a red ribbon, and we will add a green ribbon."

40. For an analysis of the Ukuku category outside danza performance, see Allen 1983.

41. The literature about this pilgrimage is abundant. For one of the classic articles in Spanish, see Gow 1974. For one of the most thorough accounts in English, see Sallnow 1987; for a debate on the subject see Poole 1988.

42. These two are explained below.

43. The structure of the songs that the Qollas sing during the first three days of the celebration is the same as that of the first stanza, that is, each of the two verses is repeated twice and the same refrain is repeated after each stanza. There are sixteen of these stanzas, which they sing at the church atrium while in a two-line formation with arms folded. The music that accompanies these stanzas varies from a feeling of two to a feeling of three, and the timbre is more relaxed than that of the pasacalle. The stanzas are sung in a middle-range chest voice.

44. The following stanzas are examples of the songs for the day of the farewell, or fourth day of the celebration, or for the cemetery. These songs, which have fourteen stanzas, while keeping the same structure of repetition have a different refrain, indicated in the text ("Ay, my dear . . ."), and are sung with a different melody. This melody has mostly a feeling of two, and the voices of the Qollas are lamenting, expressing sadness.

45. In the two years of my research I observed that, on the evening of Maundy Thursday of Holy Week, a few men went into the sacristy, knelt in front of the priest or the económo (the person in charge of taking care of the church), and received several blows with a whip. Townspeople told me that this used to be a much more widespread practice in the past and that often wives took their husbands to receive this punishment in order for them to expiate their sins. This act of whipping replicates the flagellation of Christ before dying on the cross. This theme, the flagellation of Christ, is also represented in one of the most important imagenes and the subject of a regional pilgrimage, Sr. de Wank'a. People of San Jerónimo go every year to honor this imagen, whose chapel is close to the town. For an account of this pilgrimage see Sallnow 1987.

46. This phrase said in reference to God, "We are slaves of the Lord," derived from biblical writings, is often repeated in San Jerónimo townspeople's prayers.

47. As developed in chapter 4, the wide-brimmed hat or cowboylike hat is in Cusco a sign of high status associated with the hacendados and other mistis.

48. The melody that accompanies the yawar unu has a feeling of six.

49. Callejón oscuro is a widespread "punishing" game in Peru, commonly played in schools. Therefore the name of this section remains in the original Spanish.

## CHAPTER 6

1. The people who live in the Peruvian and Bolivian Altiplano speak the Aymara indigenous language, and especially the women dress differently than women of the Cusco region.

2. I carried out field research on Puno and Bolivian danzas in 1990 and in 1992.

3. I went to one of them with members of the San Jerónimo Tuntuna.

4. This musical description and the one above was written with the guidance of Philip Bohlman. Nevertheless, I am responsible for any misuse of the terms or concepts.

5. According to Wara Céspedes (1989, 225) "peña is defined as a circle of friends who share a common interest."

6. About the role of this kind of music in highland towns, see Romero 1989.

7. Interview with one of the leading founders of the San Jerónimo Tuntuna comparsa, 1989.

8. It is common practice in Cusco that couples live together and have children before they get married. It is also not uncommon to find single mothers, since those relationships are broken from time to time. The proper place of a woman with a partner or a child is considered to be at home.

9. Interview with male member of the Mollos, 1990.

10. I confirmed this in my research of Puno fiestas and comparsas during 1990.

# REFERENCES

Abercrombie, Thomas. 1986. "The Politics of Sacrifice: An Aymara Cosmology in Action." Ph.D. diss., University of Chicago.

———. 1992. "La fiesta del Carnaval postcolonial en Oruro: Clase, etnicidad y nacionalismo en la danza folklórica." *Revista Andina* 10, no. 2:279–325.

Allen, Catherine. 1983. "Of Bear-Men and He-Men: Bear Metaphors and Male Self-Perception in a Peruvian Community." *Latin American Indian Literatures* 7, no. 1:38–51.

Alonso, Ana. 1994. "The Politics of Space, Time, and Substance: State Formation, Nationalism, and Ethnicity." *Annual Review of Anthropology* 23:379–405.

Alviz Montañez, Reinaldo. 1989. "Copia notarial de los títulos de propiedad del convento de Santo Domingo en 1702." Archivo de la Comunidad Picol Orcconpuquio, Cusco.

Aparicio, Manuel. 1994. "Humberto Vidal Unda: Siete décadas de cusqueñismo." In *Cincuenta años de Inti Raymi,* edited by Carlos Milla, E. Miranda, and E. Velarde Pérez, pp. 125–164. Cusco: EMUFEC–Municipalidad del Qosqo.

Ares Queija, Berta. 1984. "Las danzas de los Indios: Un camino para la evangelización del virreynato del Perú." *Revista de Indias* 44, no. 174:445–463.

Arguedas, José María. 1987. *Indios, Mestizos y Señores.* 2d ed. Lima: Editorial Horizonte.

Bakhtin, Mikhail. 1984. *Rabelais and His World.* 2d ed. Bloomington: Indiana University Press.

Bateson, Gregory. 1958. *Naven.* Stanford: Stanford University Press.

Blanco, Jose María. 1974. *Diario del viaje del Presidente Orbegoso al sur del Perú.* 2 vols. Lima: Pontificia Universidad Católica del Perú, Instituto Riva-Agüero.

Bolaños, César. 1995. *La música nacional en los medios de comunicación electrónicos de Lima metropolitana.* Lima: Cicosul 18, Universidad de Lima.

Bourdieu, Pierre. 1987. "What Makes a Social Class? On the Theoretical and Practical Existence of Groups." *Berkeley Journal of Sociology* 32:1–17.

Brisseau, Jeanine. 1981. *Le Cuzco dans sa région*. Lima: Institut Français d'Études Andines.

Brisseau, Jeanine, Manuel Burga, A. Giesecke, and M. Ugarte. 1978. "El rol histórico del Cuzco como centro regional." In *Cuzco, geografía e historia: Documentos y apuntes de interpretación*, edited by Taller de Estudio Andino, Departamento de Ciencias Humanas, pp. 1–36. Lima: Universidad Nacional Agraria.

Browning, Barbara. 1995. *Samba: Resistance in Motion*. Bloomington: Indiana University Press.

Brush, Stephen. 1977. *Mountain, Field, and Family: The Economy and Human Ecology of an Andean Valley*. Philadelphia: University of Pennsylvania Press.

Cahill, David. 1986. "Etnología e historia: Los danzantes rituales del Cuzco a fines de la colonia." *Boletín del Archivo Departamental del Cusco* 2:47–54.

Cancian, Frank. 1965. *Economics and Prestige in a Maya Community: The Religious Cargo System in Zinacantan*. Stanford: Stanford University Press.

Ccoanqui, Calixto. N.d. "Reseña histórica de San Jerónimo." San Jerónimo, Cusco. Manuscript.

Celestino, Olinda, and Albert Meyers. 1981. *Las cofradías en el Perú: Region central*. Frankfurt: Editionen der Iberoamericana.

Centro Guaman Poma de Ayala. 1994. *Los retos del desarrollo agro-urbano: El caso de San Jerónimo, Cusco*. Cusco: Centro Guaman Poma de Ayala.

Centro Qosqo de Arte Nativo. 1976. "Presupuesto de 1976." Archivo Privado del Centro Qosqo, Cusco.

———. 1988. "Estatuto del Centro Qosqo de Arte Nativo." Archivo Privado del Centro Qosqo, Cusco.

Christian, William, Jr. 1981. *Apparitions in Late Medieval and Renaissance Spain*. Princeton: Princeton Unversity Press.

Comaroff, Jean. 1985. *Body of Power, Spirit of Resistance: The Culture and History of a South African People*. Chicago: University of Chicago Press.

Comaroff, Jean, and John Comaroff. 1991. *Of Revelation and Revolution: Christianity, Colonialism, and Consciousness in South Africa*. Chicago: University of Chicago Press.

———, eds. 1993. *Modernity and Its Malcontents: Ritual and Power in Post-colonial Africa*. Chicago: University of Chicago Press.

Coplan, David. 1987. "Eloquent Knowledge: Lesotho Migrants' Songs and the Anthropology of Experience." *American Ethnologist* 14, no. 3:413–433.

Cowan, Jane. 1990. *Dance and the Body Politic in Northern Greece*. Princeton: Princeton University Press.

Cusihuaman, Antonio. 1976. *Diccionario Quechua Cuzco-Collao*. Lima: Instituto de Estudios Peruanos.

Daniel, Yvonne. 1995. *Rumba: Dance and Social Change in Contemporary Cuba*. Bloomington: Indiana University Press.

Degregori, Carlos Ivan. 1986. *Los invasores de un nuevo mundo*. Lima: Instituto de Estudios Peruanos.

De la Cadena, Marisol. 1991. "'Las mujeres son más indias': Etnicidad y género en una comunidad del Cusco." *Revista Andina* 9, no. 1:7–29.

———. 1995. "Race, Ethnicity, and the Struggle for the Indigenous Self-

REFERENCES / 267

Representation: De-Indianization in Cuzco, Peru, 1919–1992." Ph.D. diss., University of Wisconsin.

Desmond, Jane, ed. 1997. *Meaning in Motion: New Cultural Studies of Dance.* Durham: Duke University Press.

Deustua, José. N.d. "Routes, Roads, and Silver Trade in Cerro de Pasco, 1820–1860: A Contribution to the Debate of the Internal Market in Nineteenth-Century Peru." Chicago. Manuscript.

Deustua, José, and Jose Luis Rénique. 1984. *Intelectuales, indigenismo y descentralismo en el Perú, 1897–1931.* Cusco: Centro Bartolomé de las Casas.

Dirección Nacional de Estadística y Censos. Departamento de Cusco. 1972. *Censos nacionales VII de población, II de vivienda.* Lima: Dirección Nacional de Estadistica y Censos.

———. 1981. *Censos nacionales VIII de población , III de vivienda.* Lima: Dirección Nacional de Estadistica y Censos.

Dollfus, Oliver. 1981. *El reto del espacio andino.* Lima: Instituto de Estudios Peruanos.

Doughty, Paul. 1968. *Huaylas.* Mexico: Instituto Indigenista Interamericano.

Duviols, Pierre. 1973. "Huari y Llacuaz, agricultores y pastores: Un dualismo prehispánico de oposición y complementareidad." *Revista del Museo Nacional* (Lima) 39:153–191.

Erlmann, Veit. 1991. *African Stars: Studies in Black South African Performance.* Chicago: University of Chicago Press.

———. 1992. "'The Past Is Far and the Future Is Far': Power and Performance among Zulu Migrant Workers." *American Ethnologist* 19, no. 4:688–709.

———. 1996. *Nightsong: Performance, Power, and Practice in South Africa.* Chicago: University of Chicago Press.

Espinoza, Carlos. 1990. "The Portrait of the Inca." Ph.D. diss., University of Chicago.

Estenssoro, Juan Carlos. 1990. "Música, discurso y poder en el regimen colonial." Master's thesis, Pontificia Universidad Católica.

———. 1992. "Los bailes de los indios y el proyecto colonial." *Revista Andina* 10, no. 2:353–389.

Fabian, Johannes. 1990. *Power and Performance: Ethnographic Explorations through Proverbial Wisdom and Theater in Shaba, Zaire.* Madison: University of Wisconsin Press.

Fernandez, James. 1973. "Analysis of Ritual: Metaphoric Correspondences as the Elementary Forms." *Science* 28, no. 182:1366–1367.

———. 1974. "The Mission of Metaphor in Expressive Culture." *Current Anthropology* 15:119–145.

———. 1975–1976. "Dance Exchange in Western Equatorial Africa." *CORD Dance Research Journal* 7:1–7.

———. 1977. "The Performance of Ritual Metaphors." In *The Social Use of Metaphors,* edited by J. D. Sapir and J. C. Crocker, pp. 100–130. Philadelphia: University of Pennsylvania Press.

———. 1986. *Persuasions and Performances.* Bloomington: Indiana University Press.

Fernandez, James, and Deborah Durham. 1991. "The Figurative Struggle over Domains of Belonging and Apartness in Africa." In *Beyond Metaphor: The Theory of Tropes in Anthropology,* edited by James Fernandez, pp. 190–210. Stanford: Stanford University Press.

Flores Galindo, Alberto. 1977. *Arequipa y el surandino.* Lima: Editorial Horizonte.

———. 1988. *Buscando un inca: Identidad y utopía en los Andes.* 3d ed. Lima: Editorial Horizonte.

Flores Ochoa, Jorge. 1979. *Pastoralists of the Andes.* Philadelphia: Ishi Press.

Foster, George. 1967. *Tzintzuntzan: Los campesinos mejicanos en un mundo de cambio.* Mexico: Fondo de Cultura Económica.

Foster, Susan L. 1991. "Dancing Culture." Review of *Dance and the Body Politic* by Jane Cowan and *Sharing the Dance: Contact Improvisation and American Culture* by Cynthia Novack. *American Ethnologist* 18, no. 3:362–366.

———. 1997. "Dancing Bodies." In *Meaning in Motion: New Cultural Studies of Dance,* edited by Jane Desmond, pp. 235–257. Durham: Duke University Press. Previously published in *Incorporations,* edited by Jonathan Crary and Sanford Kwinter, pp. 480–495. New York: Zone Books, [1992].

Friedlander, Judith. 1975. *Being Indian in Hueyepan.* New York: Saint Martin's Press.

Fuenzalida, Fernando. 1970. "Poder, raza y etnía en el Perú." In *El Indio y el poder en el Perú,* edited by Jose Matos Mar, pp. 15–87. Lima: Instituto de Estudios Peruanos.

———. 1976. "Estructura de la comunidad de indígena tradicional: Una hipótesis de trabajo." In *Hacienda, comunidad y campesinado en el Perú,* compiled by Jose Matos Mar, pp. 219–263. Lima: Instituto de Estudios Peruanos.

Glave, Luis Miguel. 1983. *Problemas para el estudio de la historia regional: El caso del Cusco.* Cusco: Centro Bartolomé de las Casas.

———. 1989. *Trajinantes: Caminos indígenas en la sociedad colonial, siglos XVI/XVII.* Lima: Instituto de Apoyo Agrario.

Gluckman, Max. 1963. *Order and Rebellion in Tribal Africa.* New York: Free Press of Glencoe.

Gootemberg, Paul. 1991. "Population and Ethnicity in Early Republican Peru: Some Revisions." *Latin American Research Review* 26, no. 3:109–157.

Gow, David. 1974. "Taytacha Qoyllur Rit'i." *Allpanchis* 7:49–100.

Hanna, Judith Lynne. 1979. *To Dance Is Human: A Theory of Nonverbal Communication.* Chicago: University of Chicago Press.

Harvey, Penelope. 1994. "The Presence and Absence of Speech in the Communication of Gender." In *Bilingual Women: Anthropological Approaches to Second Language Use,* edited by Pauline Burton, Ketaki Kushari Dyson, and Shirley Ardener, pp. 44–64. Oxford: Berg Publishers.

Hebdige, Dick. 1985. *Subculture: The Meaning of Style.* London: Methuen and Co.

Hobsbawm, Eric. 1983. "Introduction: Inventing Traditions." In *The Invention of Tradition,* edited by Eric Hobsbawm and Terence Ranger, pp. 1–14. Cambridge: Cambridge University Press.

Hornberger, Esteban, and Nancy Hornberger. 1983. *Diccionario trilingüe Quechua de Cusco: Quechua, English, Castellano.* La Paz: Qoya Raymi.

Huayhuaca, Luis A. 1988. *La festividad del Corpus Christi en el Cusco.* Lima: Consejo de Ciencia y Tecnologia.

IAA (Instituto Americano de Arte, Cusco). 1935. Cuaderno de actas no. 1. Archivo Privado del IAA, Cusco.

Ileto, Reynaldo. 1979. *Pasyon and Revolution. Popular Movements in the Philipines, 1840–1910.* Quezon City: Ateneo de Manila University Press.

INEI (Instituto Nacional de Estadística e Informática). 1994a. *Censos nacionales 1993 IX de población IV de vivienda: Resultados definitivos, Departamento de Cusco.* Lima: Dirección Nacional de Censos y Encuestas.

———. 1994b. *Censos nacionales 1993 IX de población IV de vivienda: Resultados definitivos, Peru.* Lima: Dirección Nacional de Censos y Encuestas.

Ingham, John. 1986. *Mary, Michael, and Lucifer: Folk Catholicism in Central Mexico.* Austin: University of Texas Press.

Instituto Geográfico Nacional. 1989. *Atlas del Perú.* Lima: Ministerio de Defensa.

Instituto Nacional de Cultura. 1977. "Bases para la política cultural de la revolución peruana." *Runa* 6:3–7.

Jackson, Michael. 1990. *Paths toward a Clearing: Radical Empiricism and Ethnographic Inquiry.* Bloomington: Indiana University Press.

Jacobsen, Nils. 1993. *Mirages of Transition: The Peruvian Altiplano, 1780–1930.* Berkeley and Los Angeles: University of California Press

Jiménez Borja, Arturo. 1955. "La danza en el antiguo Perú." *Revista del Museo Nacional* (Lima) 24:111–136.

Keakiinohomoku, Joann Wheeler. 1976. *Theory and Methods for an Anthropological Study of Dance.* Ann Arbor: University Microfilms.

Kelly, John, and Martha Kaplan. 1990. "History, Structure, and Ritual." *Annual Review of Anthropology* 19:119–150.

Kessel, Juan van. 1981. *Danzas y estructuras sociales de los Andes.* Cusco: Instituto de Pastoral Andina.

Klor de Alva, Jorge. 1982. "Spiritual Conflict and Accommodation in New Spain: Toward a Typology of Aztec Responses to Christianity." In *The Inca and the Aztec States, 1400–1800,* edited by George Collier, Renato Rosaldo, and John Wirth, pp. 345–366. New York: Academic Press.

Knight, Alan. 1990. "Racism, Revolution, and *Indigenismo:* Mexico, 1910–1940." In *The Idea of Race in Latin America,* edited by R. Graham, pp. 71–113. Austin: University of Texas Press.

Kristal, Efrain. 1987. *The Andes Viewed from the City: Literary and Political Discourse on the Indian in Peru, 1848–1930.* New York: Peter Lang.

Lafaye, Jacques. 1976. *Quetzalcoatl and Guadalupe: The Formation of Mexican National Consciousness, 1531–1813.* Chicago: University of Chicago Press.

Leichtman, Ellen. 1989. "Musical Interaction: A Bolivian Mestizo Perspective." *Latin American Music Review* 10, no. 1:29–52.

Lévi-Strauss, Claude. 1966. *The Savage Mind.* Chicago: University of Chicago Press.

Mannheim, Bruce. 1991. *The Language of the Inka since the European Invasion.* Austin: University of Texas Press.

Martínez, Héctor. 1959. "Vicos: Las fiestas en la integración y desintegración cultural." *Revista del Museo Nacional* (Lima) 28:235–250.

Marzal, Manuel. 1977. *Estudios sobre religion campesina.* Lima: Pontificia Universidad Católica.

———. 1983. *La transformación religiosa peruana.* Lima: Pontificia Universidad Católica.

———. 1985. *El sincretismo iberoamericano.* Lima: Pontificia Universidad Católica.

Masuda, Shozo, Tzumi Shimada, and Craig Morris. 1985. *Andean Ecology and Civilization.* Tokyo: University of Tokyo Press.

Matos Mar, Jose. 1984. *Desborde popular y crisis del estado: El nuevo rostro del Perú.* Lima: Instituto de Estudios Peruanos.

Mayer, Enrique. 1970. "Mestizo e indio: El contexto social de las relaciones interétnicas." In *El Indio y el poder en el Perú,* edited by Jose Matos Mar, pp. 87–152. Lima: Instituto de Estudios Peruanos.

Mendoza, Zoila S. 1988. "El surgimiento de un culto popular en oposición al culto de las minorías dominantes." *Kamaq Maki* 2 (June): 4–6, 16.

———. 1989. "La danza de 'los Avelinos': Sus orígenes y sus múltiples significados." *Revista Andina* 7, no. 2:501–521.

———. 1990. "Encuesta sobre aspectos socioeconómicos de San Jerónimo." Archivo Personal, Davis, Calif.

Ministerio de Hacienda y Comercio. Dirección Nacional de Estadística. 1940. *Censo nacional de población.* Vol. 8. Lima: Ministerio de Hacienda y Comercio.

Mitchell, Clyde J. 1956. *The Kalela Dance: Aspects of Social Relationships among Urban Africans in Northern Rhodesia.* Manchester: Manchester University Press.

Mörner, Magnus. 1967. *Race Mixture in the History of Latin America.* Boston: Little, Brown.

———, ed. 1970. *Race and Class in Latin America.* New York: Columbia University Press.

———. 1977. *Perfil de la sociedad rural del Cuzco a fines de la colonia.* Lima: Universidad del Pacífico.

Munn, Nancy. 1974. "Symbolism in a Ritual Context: Aspect of Symbolic Action." In *Handbook of Social and Cultural Anthropology,* edited by J. J. Honigmann, pp. 579–612. New York: Rand McNally.

Murra, John. 1975. *Formaciones económicas y políticas del mundo andino.* Lima: Instituto de Estudios Peruanos.

Ness, Sally. 1992. *Body, Movement, and Culture: Kinesthetic and Visual Symbolism in a Philippine Community.* Philadelphia: University of Pennsylvania Press.

Novack, Cynthia. 1990. *Sharing the Dance: Contact Improvisation and American Culture.* Madison: University of Wisconsin Press.

Orlove, Benjamin. 1994. "Sticks and Stones: Ritual Battles and Play in the Southern Peruvian Andes." In *Unruly Order: Violence, Power, and Cultural*

*Identity in the High Provinces of Southern Peru,* edited by Deborah Poole, pp. 133–164. Boulder: Westview Press.

———. 1998. "Down to Earth: Race and Substance in the Andes." *Bulletin of Latin American Research* 17, no. 2:207–222.

Oróz, Diómedes. 1989. "Breve reseña histórica del Centro Qosqo de Arte Nativo." Manuscript. Cusco.

Parroquia de San Jerónimo. 1935. "Libro de inventarios de la iglesia parroquial de San Jerónimo, practicado en la fecha enero 7 de 1935." Archivo parroquial de San Jerónimo, Cusco.

———. 1956. "Inventario de los arboles de eucalipto plantados en los diferentes terrenos de la iglesia, 1956." Archivo parroquial de San Jerónimo, Cusco.

Poole, Deborah. 1984. "Ritual-Economic Calendars in Paruro: The Structure of Representation in Andean Ethnography." Ph.D. diss., University of Illinois, Urbana.

———. 1988. "Landscapes of Power in a Cattle-Rustling Culture of Southern Andean Peru." *Dialectical Anthropology* 12:367–398.

———. 1990a. "Accommodation and Resistance in Andean Ritual Dance." *Drama Review* 34, no. 2:98–126.

———. 1990b. "Ciencia, peligrosidad y represión en la criminología indigenista peruana." In *Bandoleros, abigeos y montoneros: Criminalidad y violencia en el Perú, siglos XVIII–XX,* edited by Carlos Aguirre and Charles Walker, pp. 335–367. Lima: Instituto de Apoyo Agrario.

———. 1991. "Rituals of Movement, Rites of Transformation: Pilgrimage and Dance in the Highlands of Cuzco." In *Pilgrimage in Latin America,* edited by Ross Crumrine and Alan Morinis, pp. 305–338. New York: Greenwood Press.

Poole, Deborah, and Gerardo Rénique, eds. 1992. *Peru: Time of Fear.* London: Latin American Bureau.

Posta Médica de San Jerónimo. 1990. "Censo de población del pueblo de San Jerónimo." San Jerónimo, Peru: Posta Médica de San Jerónimo.

Proyecto Ununchis. N.d. a. "Datos del autocenso integral de los asentamientos humanos del eje San Sebastián–San Jerónimo." Cusco.

———. N.d. b. "Diagnóstico situacional de la zona de expansión urbana del Cusco." Cusco.

———. N.d. c. "Propuesta de estructuración urbana: Eje San Sebastián–San Jerónimo." Cusco.

Ramos, Gabriela. N.d. "Parroquias en la colonia: Sus rentas y administración." Centro Bartolomé de las Casas. Cusco. Manuscript.

Ramos Carpio, Carlos. N.d. "Paucartambo, Provincia Folklórica?" *Wayna* (Cusco) 3.

Ranger, Terence. 1975. *Dance and Society in Eastern Africa: The Beni Ngoma.* Berkeley and Los Angeles: University of California Press.

Rénique, Jose Luis. 1988. "State and Regional Movements in the Peruvian Highlands: The Case of Cusco, 1895–1985." Ph.D. diss., Columbia University.

———. 1991. *Los sueños de la sierra: Cusco en el siglo XX.* Lima: Centro de Estudios Peruanos Sociales.

Roca, Demetrio. 1966. "San Jerónimo y su participación en el Corpus Christi del Cusco." *Revista Folklore* (Cusco) 1 (July): 3–40.

Rodríguez, Junia. 1942. "Los cargos religiosos y diferentes aspectos del problema indígena." Bachelor's thesis, Universidad Nacional del Cusco.

———. 1957. "San Jerónimo a través de los años." *El Sol* (Cusco), January 1, p. 11.

Roel Pineda, Josafat. 1959. "El wayno del Cuzco." *Folklore Americano* (Lima) 6–7:129–246.

Romero, Raúl. 1985. "La música tradicional y popular." In *La música en el Perú,* edited by Patronato Popular y Porvenir pro Música Clásica, pp. 215–283. Lima: Patronato Popular y Porvenir.

———. 1989. "Música urbana en un contexto campesino, en Paccha (Junín)." *Antropológica* 7:119–133.

Rowe, William, and Vivian Schelling. 1991. *Memory and Modernity: Popular Culture in Latin America.* London and New York: Verso.

Royce, Anya Peterson. 1977. *The Anthropology of Dance.* Bloomington: Indiana University Press.

Rozas, Abel. 1992. *El himno del Cusco.* Cusco: Municipalidad del Qosqo.

Ruiz Bravo, Patricia, and Carlos Monge. 1983. *Cusco ciudad y mercado.* Cusco: Centro Bartolomé de las Casas.

Sallnow, Michael J. 1987. *Pilgrims of the Andes: Regional Cults in Cusco.* Washington, D.C.: Smithsonian Institution Press.

Salomon, Frank. 1981. "Killing the Yumbo: A Ritual Drama of Northern Quito." In *Cultural Transformations and Ethnicity in Modern Ecuador,* edited by Norman Whitten Jr., pp. 162–208. Urbana: University of Illinois Press.

———. 1982. "Andean Ethnology in the 1970s: A Retrospective." *Latin American Research Review* 17, no. 2:75–128.

Savigliano, Marta. 1995. *Tango and the Political Economy of Passion.* Boulder: Westview Press.

Schieffelin, Edward. 1976. *The Sorrow of the Lonely and the Burning of the Dancers.* New York: St. Martin's Press.

Seeger, Anthony. 1987. *Why Suyá Sing: A Musical Anthropology of an Amazonian People.* Cambridge: Cambridge University Press.

Seligman, Linda. 1989. "To Be In Between: The *Cholas* as Market Women." *Comparative Study of Society and History* 31, no. 4:694–721.

Silverblatt, Irene. 1988. "Political Memories and Colonizing Symbols: Santiago and the Mountain Gods of Colonial Peru." In *Rethinking History and Myth,* edited by Jonathan D. Hill, pp. 174–194. Urbana: University of Illinois Press.

Spalding, Karen. 1984. *Huarochirí: An Andean Society under Inca and Spanish Rule.* Stanford: Stanford University Press.

Stallybrass, Peter, and Allon White. 1986. *The Politics and Poetics of Transgression.* London: Methuen.

Stein, William. 1961. *Hualcan: Life in the Highlands of Peru.* Ithaca, N.Y.: Cornell University Press.

Tamayo Herrera, Jose. 1980. *Historia del indigenismo cuzqueño: Siglos XVI–XX.* Lima: Instituto Nacional de Cultura.

———. 1981. *Historia social del Cuzco republicano.* 2d ed. Lima: Editorial Universo.

———. 1988. *Regionalización: Mito o realidad.* Lima: Centro de Estudios País y Región.

Templeman, Robert. 1996. "Praise Singing in the Andes: Afro-Bolivian Saya and the Role of Music in the Black Movement in Bolivia." Paper presented as part of the panel "Performance, Place, Politics" at the 1996 Society for Ethnomusicology annual meeting, November.

Turino, Thomas. 1984. "The Urban-Mestizo Charango Tradition in Southern Peru: A Statement of Shifting Identity." *Ethnomusicology* 28, no. 2:253–269.

———. 1988. "The Music of Andean Migrants in Lima, Peru: Demographics, Social Power, and Style." *Latin American Music Review* 9, no. 2:127–150.

———. 1990. "Somos el Perú [We are Peru]: 'Cumbia Andina' and the Children of Andean Migrants in Lima." *Studies in Latin American Popular Culture* 9:15–37.

———. 1991. "The State and Andean Musical Production in Peru." In *Nation States and Indians in Latin America,* edited by Greg Urban and Joel Sherzer, pp. 257–285. Austin: University of Texas Press.

———. 1993. *Moving Away from Silence: Music of the Peruvian Altiplano and the Experience of Urban Migration.* Chicago: University of Chicago Press.

———. 1997. "Music in Latin America." In *Excursions in World Music,* edited by Bruno Nettl, Charles Capwell, Isabel K. F. Wong, Thomas Turino, and Philip V. Biehlman, pp. 223–250. Upper Saddle River, N.J.: Prentice Hall.

Turner, Terence. 1980. "The Social Skin." In *Not Work Alone,* edited by J. Cherfas and R. Lewin, pp. 112–140. London: Temple Smith.

Turner, Victor. 1967. *The Forest of Symbols: Aspects of Ndembu Ritual.* Ithaca, N.Y.: Cornell University Press.

———. 1969. *The Ritual Process: Structure and Anti-Structure.* Ithaca, N.Y.: Cornell University Press.

Van den Berghe, Pierre, and George Primov. 197. *Inequality in the Peruvian Andes: Class and Ethnicity in Cuzco.* Columbia: University of Missouri Press.

Varellanos, José. 1962. *El cholo y el Perú: Introducción al estudio sociológico de un hombre y un pueblo mestizos y su destino cultural.* Buenos Aires: Imprenta López.

Vidal Unda, Humberto. 1944. "Programa para la celebración del Día del Cusco." June 24. Cusco.

———. N.d. "Enviados y recibidos." Archivo personal de Humberto Vidal Unda, Cusco.y

Villasante, Segundo. 1989. *Mamacha Carmen: Paucartambo Provincia Folklórica.* Lima: Consejo de Ciencia y Tecnologia.

Vivanco, A. 1973. "El migrante de provincias come intérprete del folklore andino en Lima." B.A. thesis, Universidad Nacional Mayor de San Marcos, Lima.

Wade, Peter. 1993. *Blackness and Race Mixture: The Dynamics of Racial Identity in Colombia.* Baltimore: Johns Hopkins University Press.

Wara Céspedes, Gilka. 1984. "New Currents in *Música Folklórica* in La Paz, Bolivia." *Latin American Music Review* 5, no. 2:217–242.

Waterman, Christopher. 1990. *Jùjú: A Social History and Ethnography of an African Popular Music*. Chicago: University of Chicago Press.

Wightman, Ann. 1990. *Indigenous Migration and Social Change*. Durham: Duke University Press.

Zambrano, Oscar. 1971. "Copia notarial de la escritura de transacción y reconocimiento de Derechos . . . llevada a cabo en 1948." Archivo de la Comunidad de Picol Orcconpuquio, Cusco.

Zuidema, Tom R. 1990. *Inca Civilization in Cuzco*. Austin: University of Texas Press.

# VIDEO CONTENTS

A VHS-format video tape, order number 0-226-52010-2, is also available. To order please contact:

The University of Chicago Press
11030 South Langley Avenue
Chicago, IL 60628
U.S.A.

1. San Jerónimo Majeños Octava of the Corpus Christi in Cusco city. June 21, 1990. [3'01"]
2. San Jerónimo Majeños on horseback in the entrada of the patron-saint fiesta. September 29, 1989 and 1990. [1'09"]
3. Close-up of San Jerónimo Majeños performance, patron-saint fiesta: jaleo, taqracocha, and marinera. September 30, 1990. [9'25"]
4. San Jerónimo Qollas' pasacalle, chinka-chinka, yawar unu, rakhus, khuchi taka, carga paskay, callejón oscuro, and puka cinta. September 29 and 30, October 1, 1990. [25'09"]
5. San Jerónimo Qollas' visit to the cemetery. October 1, 1990. [3'46"]
6. San Jerónimo Qollas and Majeños meeting outside the cemetery. October 1, 1990. [1'20"]
7. San Jerónimo Qollas' songs in front of the church, including yaraví. October 1, 1990. [4'26"]
8. San Jerónimo Tuntuna performance, patron-saint fiesta. 1989 and 1990. [6'00"]
9. San Jerónimo Mollos performance, patron-saint fiesta. 1989 and 1990. [5'34"]
10. San Jerónimo fiesta cacharpari, including arranque de gallos. October 2, 1990. [7'30"]
11. Qhaswa performed by members of a peasant community of the district of Coya. 1989 Coya Festival/Contest, Urubamba Province. [3'01"]
12. *Trigu Pallay* (wheat picking), performed by urban college students

representing a peasant scene. 1995 Inca Region Festival/Contest, Cusco city. [2'45"]

13. Cusco *Carnaval Mestizo* (mestizo carnival), performed by urban school teachers. 1995 School Teachers Regional Contest, Cusco city. [1'20"]

14. *Mestiza Ccoyacha,* performed by urban school teachers. 1995 School Teachers Regional Contest, Cusco city. [1'49"]

# INDEX

African music and dance, 38–40,
244 n. 39
Afro-Caribbean rhythms, 44, 104, 186,
212, 213
Agrarian Reform Law, 9, 89, 124. *See also*
Ley de Reforma Agraria
Aguirre, Juan de Dios, 57
altares, 105
Altiplano (region and people), 47,
139, 175, 180, 224, 228, 260 n. 19;
danzas, 42, 44–45, 153, 155, 207–
10, 219–24, 225, 228, 231–32, 238,
239; mestiza, 189; music, 228;
women, 226
amarre, 100, 139, 202
Andean music, 5, 39, 72, 75, 82, 210,
211, 212, 228, 238
Andeans (people and traditions), 5, 29,
36, 39, 40, 42, 53, 58–59, 69,
73, 87, 104, 118, 142, 150, 165,
175, 210, 237, 238, 247 n. 18,
249 nn. 36–37, 251 nn. 10–12;
cofradía, 24; cosmology, 22, 168;
literature about, 87, 142,
262 n. 36; ritual, 36, 168
Andes, 3, 5, 9, 10, 11, 19, 20, 22–26,
29, 31, 36, 41, 43, 49, 55, 86, 113,
134, 155, 166, 167, 173, 186, 209,
210, 220, 237, 240, 242 n. 10,
243 n. 28, 252 n. 16
Apurímac (departamento), 69, 70
Arequipa, 21, 113, 118–19, 126, 134,
209
Ares, Queija, 243 n. 30

Arguedas, José María, 114
Argument of Images, 119, 163, 256 n. 1
arguments (concept), 31, 33, 110, 124,
138
arranque de gallos, 107
arrieraje, 112
arriero, 112, 114, 117, 118, 119, 120,
121, 124, 126, 134, 152, 154, 159,
160, 168, 257 n. 5
asentamientos humanos, 9, 92, 103,
253 n. 25
Asociación de Comparsa los Majeños,
132, 140, 152, 157, 160, 161,
163
Atahuallpa (Inca empire heir), 19, 20
Aucca Chileno, 75, 156, 258 n. 14
Avelinos, 41, 178
Awaqkuna, 59
ayllu, 86, 87, 88, 116, 120, 251 nn. 9,
11, 252 n. 17, 256 n. 53
Aymara (indigenous language), 149, 193,
257 n. 5, 261 n. 33, 263 n. 1

baile, 36, 43, 44, 100, 102, 104, 106,
107, 108, 212, 213, 221, 255 n. 45,
256 n. 2
bailes sociales, 36, 104, 213
Bakhtin, Mikhail, 188, 244 n. 34, 258 n. 2
Bakhtinian, 169
bautizo, 200, 201
Belaúnde Terry, Fernando (president), 67,
89, 248 n. 28
bendición, 107
Bohlman, Philip, 260 n. 14, 263 n. 4

Bolivia, 20, 21, 53, 113, 139, 209, 210, 211, 212, 221, 244n. 37
bombos, 212
Bourdieu, Pierre, 12, 16, 171
brass-band music, 3, 4, 6, 101, 102, 109, 110, 116, 117, 120, 121, 122, 141, 163, 174, 207, 211, 228, 234
bricolage, 166
bricoleur, 110, 258n. 3

caballero, 116, 117, 119, 130–33, 138, 154
caballerosidad, 154
cacharpari, 107, 130, 146, 150, 260n. 21
caja, 75
call-and-response, 148, 211
callejón oscuro, 195, 198, 200, 201
cambray, 145, 154
campesino (peasant), 14
capital, 16; cultural, 16, 119, 171; economic, 16, 119, 171; social, 16, 119, 171; symbolic, 16
Caporal (dance role of), 126, 141, 156, 159, 160, 173, 175, 182, 185, 187, 188, 190, 195, 198, 199, 200, 211; hat, 136; mask, 127
Caporales (danza), 148, 211
carga paskay, 193, 194, 200
cargo, 151, 255n. 48
carguyoq, 100, 103, 104, 105, 106, 108, 151, 257n. 9
carnavales, 75
carnivalesque, 154, 164–65, 169, 170, 181, 204, 205, 236, 249n. 36
Casa de la Cultura, 249n. 34
casta, 12, 13
Catholic church, 22–23, 66, 98, 197, 243n. 27, 250n. 4, 251n. 9, 255n. 40; rituals, 5, 26–29, 37, 85, 87, 100, 104, 108, 244n. 32, 245n. 45; saints, 4, 22, 23, 25, 31, 36, 87, 243n. 27
Ccoanqui, Calixto, 25
Ccumu (mountain), 102, 242n. 11, 252n. 21
Celestino, Olinda, 25, 86
Centro Científico del Cusco, 52, 55
Centro Qosqo de Arte Nativo, 50, 55, 56–64, 66, 70, 71, 75, 77, 169, 181, 261n. 32
Chambi, Martín, 57
charango, 57, 63

ch'arki, 168
ch'arki tawqa, 193
charro, 135, 141
Chask'aschay, 191, 192
Ch'iaraje (ritual battle), 75, 249n. 40
chicha (drink), 93, 133; music, 104, 213, 221, 243n. 24
chichería, 93, 94
chinka-chinka, 185, 190, 191, 193, 262n. 39
chiri uchu, 9, 104, 175, 255n. 50
choferes, 171
chola, 93, 142, 189, 262n. 36
cholo(s), 9, 10, 15, 18, 63, 90, 119, 141, 143, 154, 155–56, 162, 165, 203, 205, 234, 243nn. 23, 25, 258n. 15, 261n. 27
chullo, 143
Chunchachas, 257n. 7
chusp'a, 177, 178
cincho, 141
class (Bourdieu's concept), 16
cofradía, 22, 24–26, 86, 87, 88, 99, 243n. 29, 251n. 13
Comaroff, Jean, 10, 244–45n. 39, 245n. 41
comedia, 168
Comisión Municipal de Festejos del Cusco, 50
Comisión Municipal de la Semana del Cusco, 69
Comisión Organizadora de los Festejos del Cusco, 64
Comisión Pro-Indígena, 51
comparsa (definition of), 4, 31; characters, 15; members, 24, 99, 100, 101, 103, 106, 108, 114; performance, 5, 6, 11, 16, 20, 34, 35, 38, 44–46, 232, 255n. 41; as ritual organization, 16, 32, 48, 96, 104, 107, 124, 222, 223, 236, 245n. 41, 254n. 32
comunero, 253n. 27
comunidad de indígenas, 89, 90, 252n. 17
comunidades campesinas, 89, 90, 92, 241n. 4, 253n. 25
concurso departamental. See Concurso Folklórico Departamental
Concurso Folklórico Departamental, 69, 70, 71, 72, 73, 169, 225
Concurso Departamental de Música y Danza Andinas, 72

conducta etílica, 161, 162
Conjunto de Arte Folkórico "Kosko," 60
Conjunto Folkórico de la Corporación, 60
Contradanza, 77, 140, 172, 173, 181,
    259 nn. 10–11
Coplan, David, 40
Corporación de Reconstrucción y
    Fomento (CRYF), 66–67
Corpus. *See* Corpus Christi
Corpus Christi (celebration), 22, 24, 27–
    29, 37, 98–99, 100, 105, 121, 137,
    138, 141, 157, 208, 255 n. 50,
    256 n. 55, 259 n. 11
Cowan, Jane, 35
Coya (Inca queen), 70, 249 n. 37
criollo, 12, 53, 74, 150, 247 nn. 11, 18
cumbia, 44, 104, 186, 210, 212, 213,
    221, 243 n. 24
cumbia andina, 213
Cusco (region and city), 3, 4–5, 6, 7–9,
    10, 12, 14, 15, 16–22, 24, 26, 27–
    29, 30–31, 33–34, 36, 42, 43, 44–
    45, 46, 48–52, 54, 56–59, 60–72,
    75, 77, 81–83, 84–86, 88–89, 90–
    94, 96–97, 98, 99, 100, 102, 104,
    105, 111, 112, 113–14, 115, 116,
    119, 121–24, 125, 126, 131, 132,
    133, 134, 135, 137, 138, 139, 140,
    141, 155, 157, 164–65, 168, 169,
    171–72, 173–75, 178, 185, 206,
    207–32, 241 nn. 4–6, 242 n. 19,
    245 n. 6, 246 n. 3, 247 nn. 10, 13,
    248 nn. 20, 25–26, 28–30, 32,
    250 n. 1, 251 n. 8, 252 n. 22,
    255 n. 50, 256 nn. 3, 55, 257 nn. 7–9,
    258 nn. 12, 15, 17, 259 nn. 11–12,
    260 n. 15, 261 nn. 32–35, 262 n. 47,
    263 nn. 1, 8; comparsas, 174, 188,
    194, 238, 240; danzas, 34, 42, 45,
    181, 220, 221, 222, 231, 239,
    260 n. 18; performers, 237–40; re-
    gionalism, 49, 108, 130, 165, 204,
    236, 241 n. 8; ritual in, 117; urban
    artists, 59
cusqueña, 159, 213
cusqueñismo, 53, 56–57, 63, 64, 134
cusqueñista, 63
cusqueño (people and culture), 5, 9, 11,
    17, 18, 19, 30, 43, 48–51, 54, 55,
    57, 58, 62, 64, 65, 67, 69, 71, 72,
    73, 75, 81, 83, 91, 95, 111, 119,
    125, 137, 138, 159, 165, 169, 172,
    175, 212–13, 219, 231, 235, 236,
    258 n. 15, 261 n. 27; authenticity, 54;
    comparsas, 205, 208, 209; danzas, 46,
    55, 69, 155, 159, 162, 210–11, 220,
    221; folklore, 72, 153, 210, 223;
    identity, 232, 238
Cuzco. *See* Cusco

Dama, 109, 141, 142, 145, 147, 149,
    150, 157–58, 162, 189; mask of, 143
dance (definition of), 36, 41, 256 n. 2
dance-drama, 4, 5, 28, 36, 111, 118,
    203, 216
dance-event, 34
danza (concept), 4, 5, 24, 101, 108, 118,
    204, 244 n. 36; event, 34, 37, 48–49,
    73, 113, 119, 152, 166, 205; perfor-
    mances, 11, 26, 30, 33, 41–47, 48,
    70, 87, 99, 105, 106, 108, 110–11,
    116, 117, 120, 123, 127, 133, 145,
    151, 154, 156, 163, 208, 210, 218,
    224, 235, 239, 240, 245 n. 42
danza decente, 117, 135
danzas del valle, 9
danzas foráneas, 139
danza típica, 36, 102, 220, 225, 230,
    256 n. 2
decencia, 110, 114, 115, 116, 138, 151,
    163
decency, 4, 38, 41, 116, 166
decente, 17, 115, 117, 119, 121, 122,
    130, 131, 137, 138, 154, 155, 158
De la Cadena, Marisol, 94
departamento, 7–8, 17, 45, 50, 58, 65,
    71, 92, 124, 153
desfile cívico, 102
Desfile de Trajes Típicos (parade), 60
Deustua, 52
Día de Cusco, El, 51, 63, 65
Día del Campesino, El, 51, 72
Día del Indio, El, 51, 58, 63, 72,
    247 n. 18
Dirección General de Asuntos Indígenas,
    252 n. 17
Dominicans (religious order), 22, 28, 85–
    86, 89–90, 243 n. 30, 250 n. 7,
    251 n. 9, 252 n. 17
dueños de carro, 131, 152, 171

ecónomo, 99, 262 n. 45
elegance, 4, 6, 41, 110, 115, 134, 135,
    138, 166

elegancia, 110, 163
elegante, 154, 158
Encuentros Inkarri, 71
entrada, 3, 103, 104, 130, 136, 145, 255 n. 49
Erlmann, Veit, 33, 39–40
Esquivel, Luis, 247 n. 16
establecimiento comerciales, 93
Estampas Costumbristas, 59
estancia, 85
estandartes, 103
ethnic/racial (identity), 5, 7, 11, 12, 14–18, 33, 36, 49, 51, 126, 134, 202, 219, 236, 246 n. 3
ethnicity, 11, 13, 41, 110
Europe, 23, 54, 55, 212, 220, 237, 247 n. 12
events of Corpus, 208–9

Fabian, Johannes, 31
Farnell, Brenda, 35
Federación Departamental de Campesinos del Cusco (FDCC), 67, 72
Federación Provincial de Campesinos de La Convención, 67
Fernandez, James, 38–39, 119, 256 n. 1
Festival de Autores y Compositors Andinos, 249 n. 37
fiesta, 11, 31, 34, 35, 41, 42, 44, 46, 86, 97, 99, 102, 104, 105, 106, 108, 109, 111, 113, 117, 118, 120, 130, 131, 140, 161, 164, 166, 174, 175, 182, 183, 236, 244 n. 26; participants, 11, 151–56, 167, 195, 198, 207, 223, 238, 240; performance, 165, 187, 260 n. 20; sponsors, 194, 209, 244 n. 38, 257 n. 9
fiesta cargo system, 24, 31, 85
Filigranas Peruanas, 249 n. 38
folklore (concept), 4, 48–51, 54–55, 57, 73, 82–83, 110, 111, 113, 114, 119, 122, 124, 125, 130, 139, 151, 162, 181, 205, 223, 236–40, 246 nn. 2, 4, 247 n. 13; institution of, 29, 34, 41, 50, 58, 60, 62; promotion of, 33, 71, 234, 236; regional, 139–40, 220; urban, 210
folkloric, 36, 212, 220–21, 228, 239
folkloric institution, 11, 131, 132, 140, 219, 222, 246 n. 2, 249 n. 38
folkorization, 19, 38, 46, 48–49, 51, 54, 112, 237–39

Fortón, Horacio, 247 n. 15
Foucault, Michel, 12
Fox Incaico, 58
Fujimori, Alberto (president), 97, 254 nn. 34, 38

Galdo, Luis Ochoa, 247 n. 15
Galindo, Flores, 20
gallo capitán, 107
gamonales, 88
García, Alan, 249 n. 37
García, Avelino, 247 n. 15
García, Uriel, 62
genuineness, 4, 7, 38, 41
Giesecke, Alberto, 248 n. 29
Gootemberg, Paul, 14

habacera, 103
hacendado(s), 88, 111, 112, 113, 114, 115, 116, 117, 119, 120, 124, 125, 126, 130, 134, 135, 154, 155, 159, 160, 203, 219, 233, 234, 250 n. 7, 252 n. 16, 262 n. 47
haciendas, 5, 17, 22, 65, 68, 85, 86, 88, 89, 110, 114, 120, 124, 211, 250 n. 6, 252 n. 16; invasion of, 248 n. 28; system, 22, 30, 123, 124, 234
Hatun Acclla (Inca virgin concubine), 70, 71
Hebdige, Dick, 241 n. 2
hegemony, 10, 110, 116, 242 n. 12, 257 n. 6
Hobsbawm, Eric, 246 n. 1
Hora del Charango, 63
Huaccoto, 261 n. 30
Huatanay river, 9
Huatanay valley, 7–8, 89, 92, 248 n. 30
huayno. See wayno

iconic symbols, 6, 112, 115, 154, 167, 171, 177, 234, 245 n. 41
ideology (definition of), 10; dominant, 10, 156, 165, 166, 201, 219, 231, 261 n. 35; —, cusqueño, 94, 119, 180, 201–2; —, regional, 6
Ileto, Reynaldo, 24
imagen, 97, 98, 99, 100, 103, 104, 105, 131, 137, 138, 139, 145, 169, 197, 256 n. 55, 259 n. 7, 260 n. 17, 262 n. 45

Imilla, 175, 186, 188, 189, 190, 192, 194, 198, 200, 225, 261n. 33
Inca (empire and culture), 5, 8, 12, 18–21, 22, 27, 28, 53, 54, 55, 56–59, 62, 63, 64, 65, 66, 70, 83, 85, 244n. 31, 246nn. 3, 5, 247nn. 9, 18, 248nn. 26, 29, 250nn. 1–3; art, 53, 56–57; flag, 102; imagery, 57, 58; monuments, 71; nobility, 12; religious life, 54
Indian (racial category), 5, 11–15, 17, 18, 20, 41, 49, 53, 78, 81, 85, 86, 89, 90, 94, 111, 119, 121, 126, 143–44, 154, 155, 162, 165, 172, 175, 181, 186, 202, 205, 219, 220, 232, 234, 237, 242nn. 17, 19, 243nn. 20–21, 251nn. 8, 15, 257nn. 3, 5; casta, 13; dancing, 27, 186–86; labor, 242n. 16, 251n. 9; migration, 13; pejorative term, 14, 261n. 27; problem, 52; society, 251n. 11
Indianness, 14, 17, 53, 134, 163, 235, 243n. 22
indigenismo, 14, 19, 49, 51–56, 243n. 22
indigenista(s), 49, 50–54, 63, 73, 89, 249n. 36
indios nobles, 12
Inini, 192, 200
Inkacha, 181, 182
instituciones culturales, 49, 51, 54, 111, 112, 124, 125, 140, 143, 167, 187, 208, 212, 219–21, 223, 231, 246nn. 1–2
institución folklórica. See folkloric institution
Instituto Americano de Arte (IAA), 55, 56–57, 60, 61–63, 64, 66
Instituto Nacional de Cultura (INC), 71
Inti Illimani, 210, 212
Inti Raymi (festival of the sun), 28, 59, 63, 64, 65, 69–70, 71, 77
invention of tradition, 169, 246n. 1
Izquierda Popular (popular left), 97
Izquierda Unida (united left), 97
Izquierdo, Andrés, 247n. 16

jaleo, 133, 138, 147, 149, 150, 151
jefe, 153
Jerome, Saint, 3, 6, 22, 24, 25, 97–100, 104–5, 109, 137–38, 141, 145, 164, 194–97, 198, 254n. 39, 255n. 40
jeronimianas, 153, 218–19
jeronimianos, 6–7, 10, 16–17, 28, 30–32, 36, 41, 42, 43, 44, 48, 77, 81, 84, 89, 90, 91, 93, 95, 96, 98, 99, 102, 104–7, 108, 111, 115, 116, 118, 120, 122, 131, 132, 133, 134, 138, 139, 152–53, 158, 160, 161, 163, 166, 170, 171, 172, 179, 180, 181, 184, 185, 191, 196, 197, 200, 201, 202, 204, 205, 206, 210, 211, 218, 219–20, 221, 224, 233–34, 235, 236, 239, 255nn. 40, 50, 257n. 9, 261n. 28
Jesuits, 28, 242n. 19, 243n. 30
Jesus Christ, 23, 27, 262n. 45
jocosos, 179
juego(s), 169, 188
juguetónes, 179
Junta de Reconstrucción, 65–66. See also Corporación de Reconstrucción y Fomento
jurk'a, 101, 105, 107

K'achampa, 54, 59
Kaira (hacienda), 252n. 17
kaswa. See qhaswa
kena, 57, 75, 117, 121, 172, 173, 260n. 15
khuchi taka, 193, 200
Kjarkas, 210

La Paz, 59
Larapa, 89
Latin America, 48, 49, 54, 55, 174–75, 220, 237, 242n. 15, 243n. 27, 244n. 38, 247n. 12, 249n. 42
Lechuga, Santiago, 247n. 15
Leguía, Augusto B., 51, 58–59, 67
lentradero, 99, 100, 103, 105, 106, 131, 257n. 9
Ley de Reforma Agraria, 67, 68, 72
Lima, 5, 8, 18, 20, 26, 42, 43–44, 49, 50, 51, 58, 59, 131, 213, 243n. 24, 247n. 18, 252n. 23; church council, 28
limeña, 43
llama driver, 75, 166, 172, 175, 179, 180, 195
llamero, 167, 168, 176–77, 182, 193, 233, 234, 257n. 5

Llameros, Los (danza), 59, 169
lliklla, 177, 225, 230
lliphta, 178

Machu (danza role), 126, 141, 147, 149,
    150, 156, 157, 158–59, 162, 173
Machu-Maq'ta, 155, 156
Machu Picchu (Inca ruins), 66, 248 n. 29
Machu Picol (mountain), 242 n. 11,
    252 n. 21
Madre de Dios (departamento), 70
madurez, 110, 127, 152, 159, 163
maduro, 127, 130, 140, 152, 157
majeño (person from Majes), 113
Majeños (comparsa and danza), 4, 6–7,
    15, 16, 24, 41–42, 43, 46, 75, 77,
    80, 91, 96, 100, 101, 103, 104, 106–
    8, 109–63, 166, 167, 170–73, 189,
    197, 202–5, 208, 210, 211, 216,
    219, 222, 229, 231, 233–36,
    239, 252 n. 16, 255 nn. 45–47,
    256 nn. 54–55, 258 nn. 14, 16,
    259 n. 12, 260 n. 20; features of, 235;
    mask in, 126–27, 158, 258 n. 17
Majes (valley), 113, 115, 126, 133, 163
Mannheim, Bruce, 19, 20, 247 n. 9
Mantaro valley, 41
Maqt'a, 15, 126, 138, 141, 143–45,
    150–51, 153, 155–57, 158, 160,
    162, 177, 181–82, 194, 204,
    258 nn. 4, 16, 261 n. 27; masks, 144
Maqt'acha, 172, 181, 261 n. 27
marinera, 74, 104, 118, 122, 147, 150
Martínez, Mr. (leader of San Jerónimo
    Qollas), 170–71, 259 n. 8
masculinity, 6, 158, 201
Matienzo, Juan de, 250 n. 4
mayordomo, 25, 99, 100, 103, 105, 106,
    108, 131, 243 n. 29, 257 n. 9
Mercedarians (religious order), 22, 86,
    243 n. 30, 252 n. 17
mestiza, 93, 142, 157, 189, 190,
    262 n. 36
mestizo, 5, 6, 9–13, 14, 15, 17–18, 20,
    29, 37, 43, 44, 48, 49, 50, 57, 59,
    60, 63, 64, 77, 81–82, 84, 90, 92,
    95, 109, 111, 113, 114, 115, 117,
    118, 122, 132, 134, 138, 149, 153,
    163, 167, 168, 220, 232, 234, 237,
    246 n. 3, 251–52 n. 15, 257 n. 3,
    258 n. 12; culture, 246 n. 4; danzas,
    69–70, 73–75, 77–79, 80–84, 91,

108, 112, 125, 143, 149, 153, 162,
    169, 172, 221, 222, 247 n. 16,
    259 n. 6; regional folklore, 167, 234;
    status, 13; symbols of, 132, towns,
    181; urban male, 134, 135; wayno,
    149
metaphor, 31, 119, 126
metonym, 31, 159
Mexico, 23, 246 n. 5
Meyers, Albert, 25, 86
misa de gallo, 104, 139, 145
Misión Artística, 57, 59, 77
Misión Peruana de Arte Incaico, 53
misti, 15, 88, 262 n. 47
Mitchell, Clyde, 38, 39
modernity, 4, 38, 41
Mollos (comparsa and danza), 101–2,
    206, 208, 221, 223–28, 229–31;
    costume, 225, 226–27
montera, 178, 190
Morales Bermúdez, 71, 249 n. 37,
    254 n. 35
Morales, Justo, 247 n. 16
Mörner, Magnus, 242 n. 15
muleteer(s), 6, 75, 110, 114, 130, 163,
    167, 168, 172, 203, 233, 234,
    257 n. 5
Munn, Nancy, 245 n. 41

Ness, Sally, 34, 245 n. 43
North America, 220
Novack, Cynthia, 46
novena, 100, 101, 139, 202
número (Qollas act), 169, 170, 185, 188

Octava, 121, 138, 139, 141, 155, 157,
    257 n. 9
Odría (general and president of Peru),
    65
Ojeda, Roberto, 57
ojota(s), 143, 182
Olivera, Gualberto, 247 n. 15
Ollantay, 53, 59
orquesta típica, 260 n. 15

Palomino, Manuel, 247 n. 15
pan-Andean, 211, 212
parcialidades, 87, 252 n. 17, 256 n. 53
Pardo Durant, Luis Alberto, 57
pasacalle, 118, 133, 139, 147, 148, 149,
    150, 175, 179, 180, 189, 260 n. 18,
    262 n. 43